350

AFFORDABLE

DreamHOMESource

HOME PLANS

350 AFFORDABLE HOME PLANS

DreamHOMESource

hanley▲wood

Published by Hanley Wood
One Thomas Circle, NW, Suite 600
Washington, DC 20005

Distribution Center
PBD
Hanley Wood Consumer Group
3280 Summit Ridge Parkway
Duluth, Georgia 30096

Group Publisher, Andrew Schultz
Associate Publisher, Editorial Development, Jennifer Pearce
Managing Editor, Hannah McCann
Editor, Simon Hyoun
Assistant Editor, Kimberly Johnson
Publications Manager, Brian Haefs
Production Manager, Melissa Curry
Senior Plan Merchandiser, Nicole Phipps
Plan Merchandiser, Hillary Huff
Graphic Artist, Joong Min
Plan Data Team Leader, Susan Jasmin
Senior Marketing Manager, Holly Miller
Marketing Manager, Bridgit Kearns

National Sales Manager, Bruce Holmes

Most Hanley Wood titles are available at quantity discounts with bulk purchases for educational, business,
or sales promotional use. For information, please contact Bruce Holmes at bholmes@hanleywood.com.

VC Graphics, Inc.
Creative Director, Veronica Vannoy
Graphic Designer, Jennifer Gerstein
Graphic Designer, Denise Reiffenstein

Photo Credits
Front Cover, Main: Design HPK2300132, for details see page 147. Photo © Doug Thompson
Front Cover, Inset: Design HPK2300002, for details see page 10. Photo © Phil Bell, courtesy of Design Basics, Inc.
Back Cover, Left: Design HPK2300145, for details see page 160. Photo © Andrew Lautman, Lautman Photography.
Back Cover Top: Design HPK2300001, for details see page 6. Photo © Drummond Designs, Inc.

10 9 8 7 6 5 4 3 2 1

Printed in the United States of America

Library of Congress Control Number: 2005938828

ISBN-13: 978-1-931131-59-9
ISBN-10: 1-931131-59-7

350 DreamHOMESource
AFFORDABLE
HOME PLANS

CONTENTS

Small Spender

By choosing to build from a predrawn plan—as opposed to hiring a residential architect to create a custom home—you've already taken a big step toward building a great home at the right price. But not all predrawn plans are created equal. Designed with the cost-conscious home builder in mind, we've assembled in this book plans from the portfolios of America's top residential designers that don't sacrifice style for affordability. Every home found here offers the right mix of elegance and intimacy, rich with modern amenities, and can be built on modest budgets.

Low-cost construction is the primary consideration toward affordability. Although the simple rectangle may be the most reasonable to build, an overly wide house may not be appropriate for some sites. For instance, a 100-foot wide house may require the purchase of a large and costly lot. An equally livable arrangement with a 65-foot L-shaped house, or a 50-foot U-shaped house, will probably result in a smaller and less expensive build site.

Consider as well the energy efficiency of a square over the same size rectangle. A 20' by 80' rectangular home yields a 1,600 square-foot area with 200 linear feet of wall space, while a 40' by 40' home has an equal amount of square footage with only 160 feet of wall space. All else being equal, the square home will retain heat more efficiently than the rectangular home.

Most importantly, building an affordable home does not require settling for an unattractive design! Although added features such as bump-outs and protrusions increase building cost, the convenience and visual interest they provide will be worth the investment. For instance, a front-facing bay window or kitchen greenhouse will bring an attractive design element to an otherwise boxy plan.

Basements and attics are also budget-smart investments. They provide square footage at lower cost than primary living areas. In some areas of the country, applicable building codes may not permit the placement of a bedroom in the basement. However, full or partial basements still provide recreational space, hobby areas, laundry rooms, and storage facilities. Such inexpensive space can make a small or modest-size home significantly more livable. If a basement is not practical or possible, allocate storage and utility space in garages, attics, and large closets.

In the end, "affordable" will mean something different to each home builder, and in anticipation of this fact we've selected a portfolio of plans that embody the rules of thumb for low-cost building but don't skimp on livability. Square footage was a factor in selecting the plans, but tempered with other factors such as convenient planning, attractive details, and overall sense of style.

A SHINGLED EXTERIOR AND PLAYFUL fenestration distinguish a simple design. The balcony is modest yet practical, and adds interest to the facade.

Made to Please

A great little design makes room for creative homeowners

This highly efficient design still makes room for great entertaining spaces and an attractive second-floor overlook. The hearth-warmed great room has been placed traditionally, near the foot of the plan. Its height serves to open up the front of the home in lieu of a two-story foyer, which would be inappropriate in a home of this size: that space is better reserved for the upstairs bedrooms. Still, the brief foyer helps to introduce the interior of the home and serves the practical purpose of insulating the home from heat loss; the reach-in closet adds functionality.

The L-shaped kitchen easily accommodates a dining island and opens toward the dining area. Nearby, the washer/dryer hides conveniently behind closet doors adjacent to a full bath, whose shower could easily convert to a linen/laundry closet. Access to a rear deck allows for overflow in case of large gatherings. For even more versatility, consider customizing the plan to lessen the division between the great room and dining space. A dual-facing, see-through fireplace would separate the two rooms softly. Or remove the wall and fireplace altogether, as pictured on page 8, to create a highly cooperative casual space separated only by a wide arch.

Upstairs, the corner master bedroom enters through a walk-in closet to a bath with a corner tub and separate shower. Two other family bedrooms—each with a walk-in closet, one with an inviting window seat—share the same hall bath with the master bedroom, which is a significant way to cut building costs. A smaller family might consider converting the front bedroom into a study or office. A fine brick exterior, hipped roof, gables, and decorative windows prove that aesthetics need not suffer to accommodate a home's size or function.

① **AN ISLAND PROVIDES SPACE** for food preparation, casual eating, and even doing the dishes in this functional yet attractive kitchen.

FIRST FLOOR

SECOND FLOOR

2 **THE HOME'S ROBUST FACADE** masks a modest square footage with a broad stairway, front entry, windows, and gables. See more of this home on page 121.

2

3 **EVEN PREDRAWN PLANS** offer several options for customization. Here, the homeowners chose to extend the dining room and remove the dividing wall and fireplace from the great room, which created more open space and room-to-room flow.

4 A VANITY SINK WITH PLENTY OF DRAWERS and cabinets provides storage for a bath shared by the master bedroom and two family bedrooms. A WIDE CORNER TUB offers room for relaxation and views of the side and rear yards.

Divine Details

Artful touches like built-in plant shelves and niches let this home sit pretty in any neighborhood

1 **DRAMATIC GABLES** and stone accents give personality to this traditional design. See more of this home on page 202.

Skyward rooflines and dramatic gables greet visitors to this charming traditional home, shown here with brick and stone accents and a cobbled walkway. A small arched window lets natural light into the garage and brings an attractive focal point to the broad front gable. The two-story pedimented doorway features columns and tall sidelights, all of which brings significant height to the entry.

On the inside, the foyer is brightly lit by plenty of windows and a large transom. Other features include niches and plant shelves that help to make this space feel expansive without seeming empty and featureless. The stairs to the left of the foyer are also naturally lit. To the right of the foyer, a fireplace accompanies front- and rear-facing arched windows in the nearly 300-square-foot great room. The niche above the mantle provides a handsome frame for art pieces. With easy access to

the breakfast nook and kitchen, the great room provides an ideal space to entertain: guests can move easily from room to room without leaving anyone making last-minute kitchen preparations out of the action. Traffic to the kitchen—which has a rear-facing window and a generous amount of wrap-around counter space—can also arrive directly from the foyer. Despite the name, the nook is an ample dining area, with

② SIDE AND TRANSOM LIGHTS allow plenty of sun into the two-story foyer, while a sculpture niche brings interest to the walls.

more large windows which provide panoramic views of the rear of the home. This space can accommodate a wide range of decorating tastes, from a country cottage feel to an earth-toned Mediterranean look.

The master suite and adjoining bath reside at the left of the plan. The bedroom is characterized by tall windows at the two rear corners of the room to receive more light throughout the day and to allow views of the back yard. The placement of the windows smartly avoids obstruction by large furnishings and head boards. An ample walk-in closet is located just left of the entrance and keeps clutter out of the room. The bathroom comprises dual vanities, plenty of counter space, and a whirlpool tub. A bay window above the tub lets in natural light and views to the left of the home, conducive for long, relaxing soaks. The designers have also provided a

FIRST FLOOR

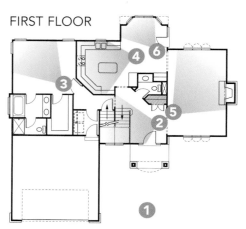

3 TALL WINDOWS at the corners of the master suite bring in natural light throughout the day.

4 RICH CABINETRY and plenty of surface space make for an attractive and functional kitchen.

SECOND FLOOR

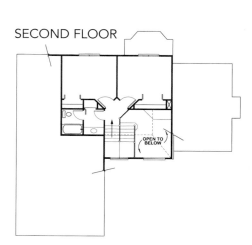

compartmented toilet—a considerate detail. Finally, a laundry room—which can easily be converted into a utility room, storage area, or mudroom—leads into the two-car garage.

The remaining bedrooms occupy the second floor. The bedrooms are identical in size and offer the owners a range of options for customization. Convert one room into an airy, stress-resistant home office, rec room, exercise room, or a library and entertainment room, and let the large closets become built-in bookcases. Of course, larger families will want to keep them as bedrooms. The shared bathroom is spacious, featuring a linen closet and compartmented toilet and tub.

5 A TRIO OF ARCHED WINDOWS at the front and rear of the great room complement the attractive fireplace at its center.

6 CASUAL DINING is bright and elegant in the bayed nook.

Big Finish—Getting It Right with Bonus Rooms

The designs collected in this section include "bonus" square footage that isn't calculated toward the total square footage count. In other words, you get more plan for your money—and because bonus space is undefined, you also get a design that can be finished to your family's needs.

When deciding how you'd like to use your bonus room—as an additional suite for a live-in parent or mature child? an office for your home business?—give thought to how else you could customize the design. A room designated as a study can become, at your request, a nursery, or a third bedroom; a den can be a media room or library; an average-sized master bath can grow into a full-fledged spa. Just consult our modification designers to add, subtract, or change rooms in the original plan. You'll be surprised to see how easily and affordably you can change a plan to your satisfaction. If you haven't done so already, read the feature "Divine Details" to find out more about what modification can do for you, or turn to page 378.

BUILDING FROM A PREDRAWN PLAN doesn't mean your options are limited. Bonus rooms and plan modification let you create the right home, easily.

Andreas Pollok, Taxi

SMALLER FAMILIES may be better served by converting a bedroom into a home office.

Ted Yarwood; Sam Gray

A BONUS SUITE with views like this will bring guests all year round.

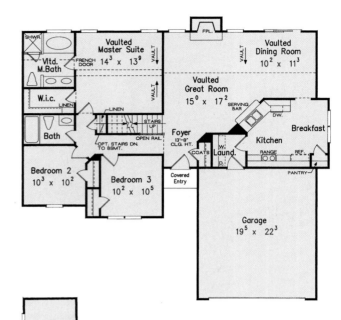

SINGLE-LEVEL LIVING IS THE HOTTEST HOUSE TREND today—as you look ahead to your future you will probably discover that you want a plan that will accommodate your changing family; this lovely ranch home is ready to do just that. A raised-ceiling foyer welcomes family and friends, leading to a vaulted great room ahead. A cozy fireplace makes this space intimate. Follow the vault to a formal dining room, serviced by an angled kitchen with a serving bar. The left wing holds the sleeping quarters, including an indulgent vaulted master suite with a private spa bath. Two additional bedrooms share a full bath. An optional bonus room is available, great for an extra bedroom, home office or studio.

HOME PLAN

HPK2300003

Style: Ranch

Square Footage: 1,354

Bonus Space: 246 sq. ft.

Bedrooms: 3

Bathrooms: 2

Width: 51' - 0"

Depth: 48' - 4"

Foundation: Unfinished Walkout Basement

eplans.com

FIRST FLOOR

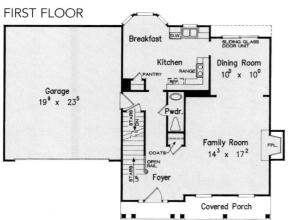

Breakfast

D.W.

SLIDING GLASS DOOR UNIT

Kitchen

PANTRY

RANGE

REF.

Dining Room
10⁰ x 10⁰

Garage
19⁹ x 23⁵

Pwdr.

STAIRS DN

STAIRS UP

COATS

OPEN RAIL

Family Room
14³ x 17²

FPL.

Foyer

Covered Porch

SECOND FLOOR

PLANT SHELF ABOVE

SHWR.

W.I.C.

Vaulted M.Bath

TRAY CLG.

Master Suite
12⁰ x 16¹⁰

LINEN

LIN.

W. D.

Opt. Bonus Room
19⁹ x 11⁵

STAIRS DN

Bath

Bedroom 2
12⁰ x 10⁰

Bedroom 3
10⁵ x 10⁰

HOME PLAN

(#) HPK2300004

Style: Traditional

First Floor: 767 sq. ft.

Second Floor: 738 sq. ft.

Total: 1,505 sq. ft.

Bedrooms: 3

Bathrooms: 2 ½

Width: 47' - 10"

Depth: 36' - 0"

Foundation: Unfinished Walkout Basement, Slab, Crawlspace

eplans.com

A CLEAR FOCUS ON FAMILY LIVING is the hallmark of this traditional two-story plan. A columned porch leads to an open foyer and family room complete with a fireplace. A dining room with a sliding glass door is thoughtfully placed between the family room and kitchen. A bayed breakfast nook works well with the roomy kitchen. On the second level a large master suite features a tray ceiling, detailed bath and a space-efficient, walk-in closet. Two family bedrooms, a hall bath and convenient laundry center round out the plan.

HOMES WITH ROOM TO GROW

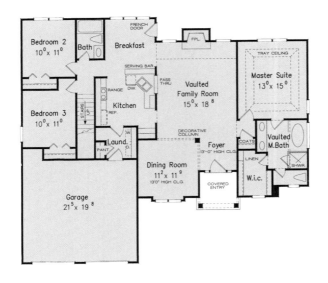

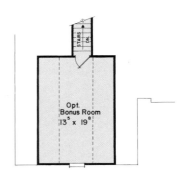

A STEEP FRONT GABLE AND A DELIGHTFUL ARCH framing the entry porch give this stately European home a distinctive look. Open design describes the spacious family room and formal dining room—tall ceilings and decorative touches like a column and fireplace set them apart. The efficient kitchen has wrap-around counters and a cozy breakfast nook. Two family bedrooms and a full bath are split from the master suite for privacy. The master suite has a vaulted master bath, tray ceiling, and a large walk-in closet.

HOME PLAN

HPK2300005

Style: New American

Square Footage: 1,544

Bonus Space: 284 sq. ft.

Bedrooms: 3

Bathrooms: 2

Width: 54' - 0"

Depth: 47' - 6"

Foundation: Crawlspace, Unfinished Walkout Basement

eplans.com

THIS HOME DEFINES CASUAL GRACE. Bold columns and a barrel-vaulted entryway create a dramatic impression; porches provide outdoor living space for relaxation. Inside, the floor plan is open and family-friendly. Custom-styled ceiling treatments enhance the elegance of the dining and great rooms and the master bedroom. The kitchen features a smart angled counter and a walk-in pantry. It also enjoys a view of the great room's fireplace. Two secondary bedrooms share a full bath, and the master suite is located in the quiet zone of the house. The master bath is complete with a double-sink vanity, separate shower, garden tub, and private toilet. A bonus room and garage storage add versatility.

 # HOME PLAN

HPK2300006

Style: Country
Square Footage: 1,547
Bonus Space: 391 sq. ft.
Bedrooms: 3
Bathrooms: 2
Width: 51' - 8"
Depth: 59' - 0"

eplans.com

HOMES WITH ROOM TO GROW

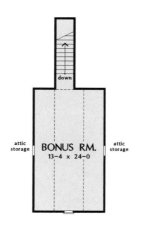

BED RM.
11-4 x 10-4

PORCH

GREAT RM.
16-0 x 16-8
fireplace
(cathedral ceiling)

BRKFST.
9-8 x 9-4

MASTER BED RM.
13-0 x 14-0
(vaulted ceiling)

walk-in closet

KIT.
9-8 x 10-0

master bath

UTIL.

FOYER
5-4 x 11-0

DINING
12-4 x 11-0

pantry

STO.

BED RM.
11-4 x 10-4

bath

PORCH

GARAGE
21-0 x 21-0

STORAGE

down

attic storage

BONUS RM.
13-4 x 24-0

attic storage

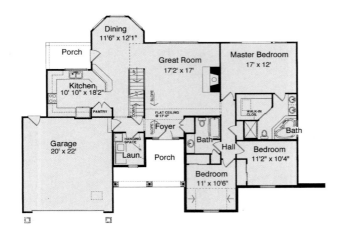

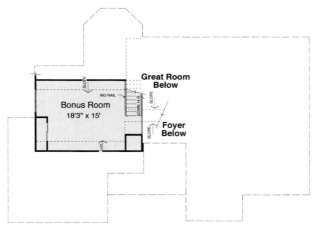

A STONE AND SIDING EXTERIOR, covered porch, and multiple gables decorate the exterior of this popular one-level home. The interior offers a spacious great room with sloped ceiling, grand view to the rear yard, and charming fireplace. The adjoining dining area expands the living space for both a casual or more formal dining experience. A large kitchen with pantry and snack bar organizes the work area. The dramatic master bath with double bowl vanity, walk-in closet, separate shower enclosure, and large walk-in closet complement the master bedroom suite. A bonus space above the garage creates an area that can be used to best fit your family's needs. Two additional bedrooms and a full basement complete this wonderful home.

HPK2300007

HOME PLAN

Style: Craftsman

Square Footage: 1,641

Bonus Space: 284 sq. ft.

Bedrooms: 3

Bathrooms: 2

Width: 62' - 4"

Depth: 46' - 4"

Foundation: Unfinished Basement

eplans.com

WITH VAULTED CEILINGS IN THE DINING ROOM and the great room, a tray ceiling in the master suite, and a sunlit two-story foyer, this inviting design offers a wealth of light and space. The counter-filled kitchen opens to a large breakfast area with backyard access. The master suite is complete with a walk-in closet and pampering bath. Upstairs, two secondary bedrooms share a hall bath and access to an optional bonus room. Note the storage space in the two-car garage.

HOME PLAN

HPK2300008

Style: Country Cottage

First Floor: 1,179 sq. ft.

Second Floor: 479 sq. ft.

Total: 1,658 sq. ft.

Bonus Space: 338 sq. ft.

Bedrooms: 3

Bathrooms: 2 ½

Width: 41' - 6"

Depth: 54' - 4"

Foundation: Slab, Unfinished Walkout Basement, Crawlspace

eplans.com

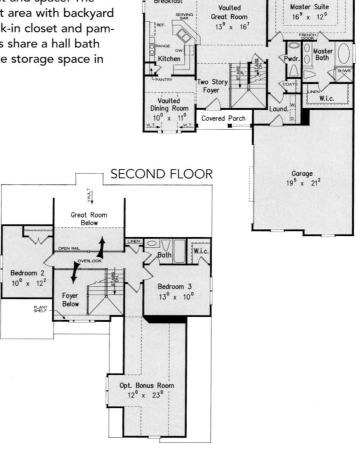

FIRST FLOOR

SECOND FLOOR

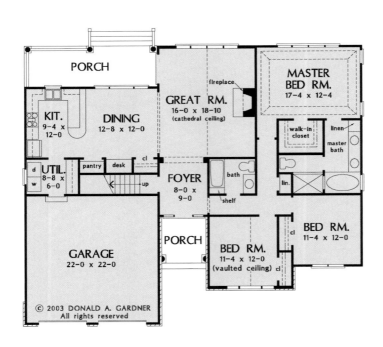

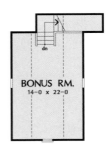

HOME PLAN

HPK2300009

Style: French Country

Square Footage: 1,676

Bonus Space: 376 sq. ft.

Bedrooms: 3

Bathrooms: 2

Width: 56' - 8"

Depth: 48' - 4"

eplans.com

THE CURVE OF THE PALLADIAN WINDOW softens the strong stone wall and gable, and a prominent dormer towers above the front entrance with its pilasters, sidelights, and arched transom that lead eyes inside. Stone creates a powerful impression on the exterior. All of the common rooms, along with the master bedroom, are positioned to take advantage of rear views through numerous windows and French doors. A cathedral ceiling and fireplace highlight the great room. The kitchen is placed to easily serve the connecting dining room, but also accesses the convenient utility room. A coat closet and pantry create storage. The bedrooms are grouped together to form the quiet zone. The master bedroom features a large walk-in closet and private bath. One of the family bedrooms features a vaulted ceiling, and they share a full hall bath.

**HPK2300010**

Style: European Cottage

Square Footage: 1,696

Bedrooms: 3

Bathrooms: 2

Width: 52' - 0"

Depth: 59' - 6"

Foundation: Crawlspace, Unfinished Walkout Basement

HOME PLAN

eplans.com

THIS THREE-BEDROOM HOME PRESENTS A FABULOUS EUROPEAN FACADE and welcomes family and visitors alike with its grand covered entrance. Inside, the foyer leads directly into the vaulted great room. Here, a warming fireplace, a serving bar from the kitchen and French-door access to the rear yard are sure to please. Mealtimes are easily handled by the large and efficient kitchen, whether they are held in the formal dining room or in the more casual breakfast room. Sleeping quarters are split for privacy, with the lavish master suite residing on the left side of the home and the two secondary bedrooms, which share a full bath, located on the right side. A two-car garage is available to accommodate the family fleet.

FIRST FLOOR

NOOK
8/8 X 8/10

DINING
9/10 X 10/4

VAULTED
MASTER
16/0 X 11/10

TWO STORY
GREAT RM.
15/10 X 19/8

GARAGE
19/4 X 21/8

UP

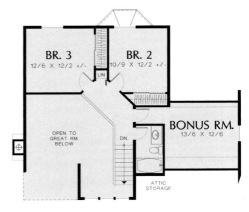

SECOND FLOOR

BR. 3
12/6 X 12/2 +/-

BR. 2
10/9 X 12/2 +/-

OPEN TO
GREAT RM.
BELOW

BONUS RM.
13/6 X 12/6

DN.

ATTIC
STORAGE

WITH SUNNY WINDOWS THROUGHOUT and a wonderful-ly open living space, this plan appears larger than its modest square footage. The great room is highlighted with a corner window, fireplace, and soaring ceiling. The dining room con-tinues the open feeling and is easily served from the kitchen. A bayed nook complements the island kitchen that also has a stylish wraparound counter. The master bedroom suite has a lofty vaulted ceiling. Upstairs, two family bedrooms share a full hall bath; a bonus room can be developed as needed.

HPK2300011

HOME PLAN

Style: Traditional
First Floor: 1,230 sq. ft.
Second Floor: 477 sq. ft.
Total: 1,707 sq. ft.
Bonus Space: 195 sq. ft.
Bedrooms: 3
Bathrooms: 2 ½
Width: 40' - 0"
Depth: 52' - 10"
Foundation: Crawlspace

eplans.com

© 2003 Donald A. Gardner, Inc.

THIS HOME OFFERS BOTH THE FLEXIBILITY OF AN OPEN FLOOR PLAN and traditionally defined rooms. A bay window and French doors invite light inside, and a front porch and screened porch extend living space outdoors. With a breakfast counter, the kitchen is the heart of the home. A fireplace, flanked by high windows, enhances the great room, but can also be enjoyed from the kitchen. Tray ceilings crown the dining room, master bedroom, and study/bedroom; double doors, leading into the study/bedroom, add sophistication. The bonus room is perfectly positioned to create an additional bedroom, home gym, or playroom for the kids.

HOME PLAN

HPK2300012

Style: Country
Square Footage: 1,727
Bonus Space: 346 sq. ft.
Bedrooms: 3
Bathrooms: 2
Width: 46' - 0"
Depth: 66' - 4"

eplans.com

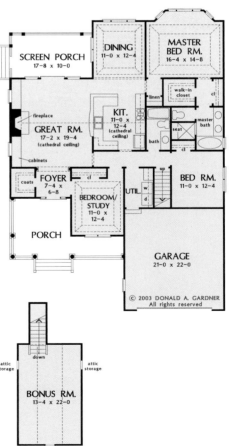

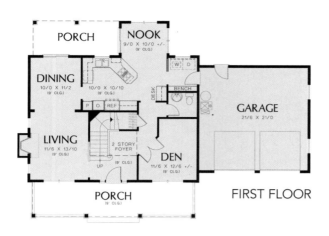

PORCH

NOOK
9/0 X 10/0 +/-
(9' CLG.)

DINING
10/0 X 11/2
(9' CLG.)

GARAGE
21/6 X 21/0

LIVING
11/6 X 13/10
(9' CLG.)

2 STORY
FOYER
(9' CLG.)

UP

DEN
11/6 X 12/6 +/-
(9' CLG.)

PORCH
(9' CLG.)

FIRST FLOOR

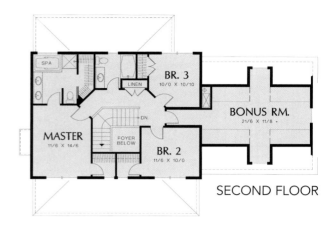

SPA

BR. 3
10/0 X 13/10

LINEN

BONUS RM.
21/6 X 11/8 +

MASTER
11/6 X 14/6

FOYER
BELOW

DN.

BR. 2
11/6 X 10/0

SECOND FLOOR

HOME PLAN

HPK2300013

Style: Farmhouse

First Floor: 954 sq. ft.

Second Floor: 783 sq. ft.

Total: 1,737 sq. ft.

Bonus Space: 327 sq. ft.

Bedrooms: 3

Bathrooms: 2 ½

Width: 56' - 0"

Depth: 40' - 0"

Foundation: Crawlspace

eplans.com

HERE'S A CHARMER FOR THE GROWING FAMILY.
Front and rear covered porches and three bedrooms,
with space for a fourth, highlight this magnificent plan.
The main living areas—dining room, living room, and
den—flow together offering great versatility in how they
are organized and used. The kitchen is joined to the rear
breakfast alcove by a counter. It opens to the garage
through the laundry room where a bench makes it easier
to take off muddy or wet foot gear before entering the
house. Upstairs, two bedrooms share a bath and a linen
closet, and the master suite enjoys many special comforts. A hallway connects to extra space over the garage
that has a dormer window.

HOME PLAN

HPK2300014

Style: Victorian

First Floor: 880 sq. ft.

Second Floor: 880 sq. ft.

Total: 1,760 sq. ft.

Bonus Space: 256 sq. ft.

Bedrooms: 3

Bathrooms: 2 ½

Width: 42' - 0"

Depth: 40' - 0"

Foundation: Unfinished Basement

eplans.com

FIRST FLOOR

SECOND FLOOR

THIS COUNTRY VICTORIAN DESIGN comes loaded with charm and amenities. The entry leads to open living space, defined by a two-sided fireplace and a large bay window. An island counter with a snack bar highlights the L-shaped kitchen. A quiet sitting area opens to the outdoors. Upstairs, the master suite allows plenty of sunlight from the turret's bay window and boasts a step-up tub, dual-sink vanity, and separate shower. Bonus space above the garage offers room for future expansion.

HOMES WITH ROOM TO GROW

THE FAMILY ROOM LOCATED IN THE TURRET OF THE FIRST FLOOR benefits from the see-through fireplace and generous fenestration. A large dining area and island kitchen with breakfast nook round out the home's common areas. Three bedrooms reside upstairs, including a spacious master suite. Dual vanities located just outside the bath provide a quaint, mid-century feel. The other two bedrooms enjoy much closet space and comfortably share a full bath. A large bonus area above the garage awaits specification.

FIRST FLOOR

HOME PLAN

HPK2300015

Style: Victorian

First Floor: 880 sq. ft.

Second Floor: 880 sq. ft.

Total: 1,760 sq. ft.

Bonus Space: 256 sq. ft.

Bedrooms: 3

Bathrooms: 2 ½

Width: 42' - 0"

Depth: 40' - 0"

Foundation: Unfinished Basement

eplans.com

SECOND FLOOR

© 1997 Donald A. Gardner Architects, Inc.

THE OPEN FLOOR PLAN OF THIS DELIGHTFUL design combines the great room, kitchen, and dining room for today's family. With light drawn through two rear dormers, the great room boasts a cathedral ceiling and a fireplace with flanking built-ins. Impress guests with this breathtaking dining room with an octagonal tray ceiling and light-filled bay windows. Tray ceilings also adorn the master bedroom and one of two secondary bedrooms. Escape to the relaxing master suite with a private bath oasis featuring a garden tub and two vanity sinks set in a bay window. An optional bonus room gives flexibility to this amazing home.

 # HPK2300016

Style: Country
Square Footage: 1,770
Bonus Space: 401 sq. ft.
Bedrooms: 3
Bathrooms: 2
Width: 54' - 0"
Depth: 57' - 8"

eplans.com

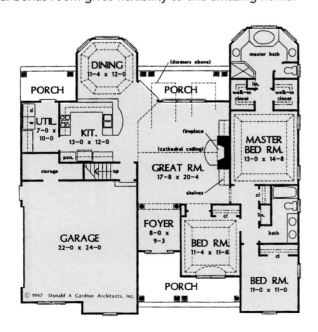

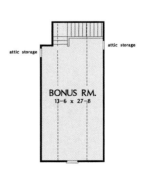

THE COUNTRY CHARM OF THIS CAPE COD-STYLE home belies the elegance inside. The beautiful foyer, accented by columns that define the formal dining room, leads to the family room. Here, the vaulted space is warm and cozy, courtesy of an extended-hearth fireplace. The kitchen is open and welcoming with angled counters that offer plenty of workspace. The laundry is conveniently located near the garage entrance. In the master suite, the star is the vaulted compartmented bath. Two additional bedrooms—both with ample closets and one with a raised ceiling—complete the plan. An optional upstairs addition includes a fourth bedroom and a full bath.

HOME PLAN

HPK2300017

Style: Country Cottage

Square Footage: 1,792

Bonus Space: 255 sq. ft.

Bedrooms: 3

Bathrooms: 2

Width: 50' - 0"

Depth: 62' - 6"

Foundation: Crawlspace, Unfinished Walkout Basement

eplans.com

HPK2300018

Style: Country Cottage

Square Footage: 1,821

Bonus Space: 191 sq. ft.

Bedrooms: 3

Bathrooms: 2

Width: 54' - 0"

Depth: 54' - 0"

Foundation: Slab

HOME PLAN

eplans.com

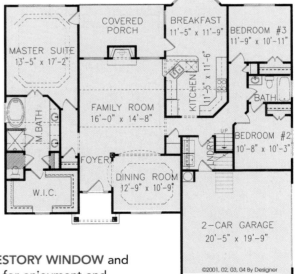

THIS EYE-PLEASING BEAUTY WITH ITS CLERESTORY WINDOW and front columns has an interior uniquely designed for enjoyment and comfort. Enter the foyer and the dining room is to the right, very elegant with its octagonal-shaped ceiling. Straight ahead, the main living room enjoys a warming fireplace and vaulted ceiling. The roomy kitchen surrounded by counter space opens to a sunlit breakfast alcove. On the left side of the plan, the dazzling master suite embraces a huge walk-in closet and sumptuous bath with a double-sink vanity. To the right, two more bedrooms share a bath and are conveniently located near the laundry. Over the two-car garage, additional space is available to be used as you want.

HOMES WITH ROOM TO GROW

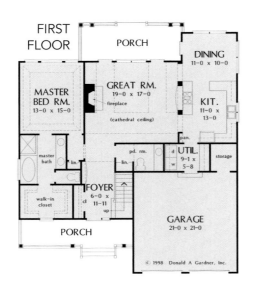

FIRST FLOOR

PORCH

DINING
11-0 x 10-0

MASTER BED RM.
13-0 x 15-0

GREAT RM.
19-0 x 17-0
fireplace

(cathedral ceiling)

KIT.
11-0 x 13-0

master bath

pan.

pd. rm.

UTIL.
9-1 x 5-8

storage

walk-in closet

FOYER
6-0 x 11-11
up

GARAGE
21-0 x 21-0

PORCH

© 1998 Donald A Gardner, Inc.

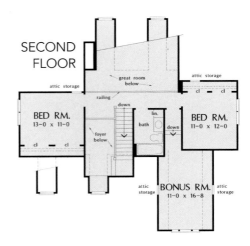

SECOND FLOOR

great room below

attic storage

attic storage

railing

BED RM.
13-0 x 11-0

down

BED RM.
11-0 x 12-0

foyer below

bath

attic storage

BONUS RM.
11-0 x 16-8

attic storage

HOME PLAN # HPK2300019

Style: Country Cottage
First Floor: 1,336 sq. ft.
Second Floor: 523 sq. ft.
Total: 1,859 sq. ft.
Bonus Space: 225 sq. ft.
Bedrooms: 3
Bathrooms: 2 ½
Width: 45' - 0"
Depth: 53' - 0"

eplans.com

GABLE TREATMENTS ALONG WITH STONE AND HORIZONTAL SIDING give a definite country flavor to this two-story home. Inside, the foyer opens to a great room, which boasts a fireplace, built-ins, and a magnificent view of the backyard beyond an inviting rear porch. The kitchen is designed for high style with a column-defined cooktop island and serving-bar access to the dining area. The master suite finishes this level and includes two walk-in closets and a private bath. Two bedrooms share a full bath and bonus space on the second floor.

©1998 Donald A. Gardner, Inc.

© 1991 Donald A. Gardner, Architects, Inc.

ARCHED WINDOWS AND TRIPLE GABLES provide a touch of elegance to this traditional home. An entrance supported by columns welcomes family and guests inside. On the main level, the dining room offers round columns at the entrance. The great room boasts a cathedral ceiling, a fireplace, and an arched window over the doors to the deck. The kitchen features an island cooktop and an adjoining breakfast nook for informal dining. The master suite offers twin walk-in closets and a lavish bath that includes a whirlpool tub and a double-basin vanity.

REAR EXTERIOR

HOME PLAN

 # HPK2300020

Style: Bungalow

First Floor: 1,416 sq. ft.

Second Floor: 445 sq. ft.

Total: 1,861 sq. ft.

Bonus Space: 284 sq. ft.

Bedrooms: 3

Bathrooms: 2 ½

Width: 58' - 3"

Depth: 68' - 6"

eplans.com

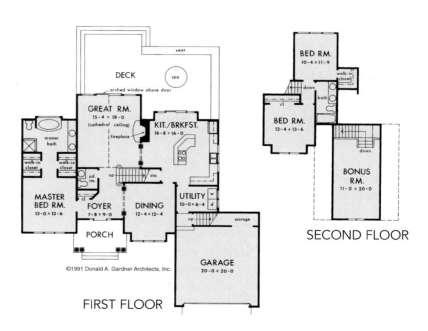

FIRST FLOOR

SECOND FLOOR

©1991 Donald A. Gardner Architects, Inc.

22'-0" X 16'-0"
6,60 X 4,80

12'-8" X 12'-8"
3,80 X 3,80

7'-8" X 11'-4"
2,30 X 3,40

12'-0" X 22'-0"
3,60 X 6,60

10'-0" X 12'-0"
3,00 X 3,60

10'-0" X 12'-0"
3,00 X 3,60

14'-0" X 14'-0"
4,20 X 4,20

12'-4" X 15'-8"
3,70 X 4,70

HOMES WITH ROOM TO GROW

ON WARM SUMMER EVENINGS, SIT AND TALK ON THE COVERED FRONT PORCH; when cold winter winds blow, curl up with your family in front of the living room fireplace. This is a two-story plan for comfort. Inside, the living room, dining area, and kitchen seamlessly fit together for maximum flexibility. An island snack bar in the kitchen makes serving quick meals a breeze. A study or home office with a nearby half-bath is a bonus that you will surely appreciate. The three upstairs bedrooms all have hallway access to the two bathrooms, another example of this home's versatility. The master bedroom with a mammoth walk-in closet is nearest the larger bath, which enjoys both a tub and shower. Additional space is available on this level for another bedroom, study, or playroom. A linen closet opens onto the hallway.

HOME PLAN

 # HPK2300021

Style: Farmhouse
First Floor: 908 sq. ft.
Second Floor: 967 sq. ft.
Total: 1,875 sq. ft.
Bonus Space: 213 sq. ft.
Bedrooms: 3
Bathrooms: 1 ½
Width: 36' - 0"
Depth: 40' - 0"
Foundation: Unfinished Basement

eplans.com

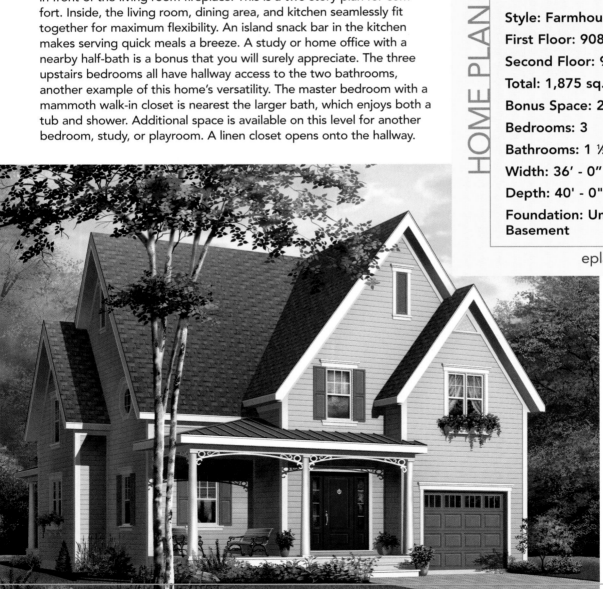

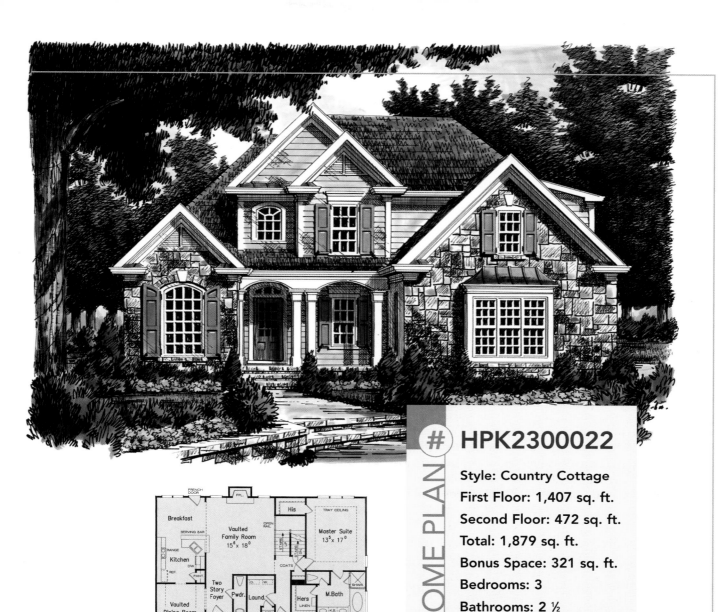

FIRST FLOOR

SECOND FLOOR

HPK2300022

HOME PLAN #

Style: Country Cottage

First Floor: 1,407 sq. ft.

Second Floor: 472 sq. ft.

Total: 1,879 sq. ft.

Bonus Space: 321 sq. ft.

Bedrooms: 3

Bathrooms: 2 ½

Width: 48' - 0"

Depth: 53' - 10"

Foundation: Crawlspace, Unfinished Walkout Basement

eplans.com

THIS CAPTIVATING THREE-BEDROOM HOME combines the rustic, earthy feel of cut stone with the crisp look of siding to create a design that will be the hallmark of your neighborhood. From the impressive two-story foyer, the vaulted family room lies straight ahead. The extended-hearth fireplace can be viewed from the kitchen via a serving bar that accesses the breakfast nook. The vaulted dining room is an elegant space for formal occasions. The first-floor master suite includes a pampering bath and dual walk-in closets, one with linen storage. Upstairs, a short hall and family-room overlook separate the bedrooms. Bonus space can serve as a home office, playroom...anything your family desires.

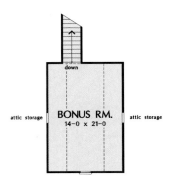

AN ARCHED WINDOW IN A CENTER FRONT-FACING GABLE lends style and beauty to the facade of this three-bedroom home. An open common area features a great room with a cathedral ceiling, a formal dining room with a tray ceiling, a functional kitchen, and an informal breakfast area that separates the master suite from the secondary bedrooms for privacy. The master suite provides a dramatic vaulted ceiling, access to the back porch, and abundant closet space. Access to a versatile bonus room is near the master bedroom.

HOME PLAN

HPK2300023

Style: Country
Square Footage: 1,882
Bonus Space: 363 sq. ft.
Bedrooms: 3
Bathrooms: 2 ½
Width: 61' - 4"
Depth: 55' - 0"

eplans.com

HOME PLAN

#HPK2300024

Style: Victorian

First Floor: 1,044 sq. ft.

Second Floor: 892 sq. ft.

Total: 1,936 sq. ft.

Bonus Space: 289 sq. ft.

Bedrooms: 3

Bathrooms: 2 ½

Width: 58' - 0"

Depth: 43' - 6"

Foundation: Unfinished Basement

eplans.com

FIRST FLOOR

SECOND FLOOR

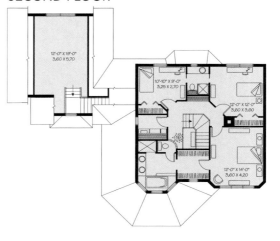

CONTEMPORARY ON THE OUTSIDE, this plan won't let you down once you're inside. A superior layout places bedrooms, a laundry room, and full baths on the second floor and living spaces on the main level. Bedrooms include the master suite with an enormous walk-in closet leading to the master bath—complete with dual-sink vanities, separate tub and shower, and a compartmented toilet. The media room brings the family together for movie night. An L-shaped kitchen has plenty of cabinet and counter space, ensuring that feeding the family around the island or in the breakfast nook will be a breeze. The dining area and adjacent family room facilitate spending cozy time with everyone.

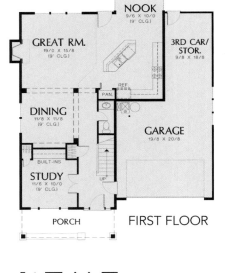

FIRST FLOOR

NOOK
9/6 X 10/0
(9' CLG.)

GREAT RM.
19/0 X 15/8
(9' CLG.)

3RD CAR/
STOR.
9/8 X 18/8

DINING
11/8 X 11/8
(9' CLG.)

GARAGE
19/8 X 20/8

BUILT-INS

STUDY
11/6 X 10/0
(9' CLG.)

PAN.

REF.

UP

PORCH

THIS HOME WOULD LOOK GREAT in any neighborhood! From the covered front porch with a bench to rest on to the trio of gables, this design has a lot of appeal. Inside, the Craftsman styling continues with built-in shelves in the study, a warming fireplace in the great room, and plenty of windows to bring in the outdoors. The L-shaped kitchen is open to the nook and great room, and offers easy access to the formal dining area. Upstairs, two family bedrooms share a full bath and access to both a laundry room and a large bonus room. A vaulted master suite rounds out this floor with class. Complete with a walk-in closet and a pampering bath, this suite will be a haven for any homeowner.

(#) HPK2300025

HOME PLAN

Style: Craftsman

First Floor: 1,082 sq. ft.

Second Floor: 864 sq. ft.

Total: 1,946 sq. ft.

Bonus Space: 358 sq. ft.

Bedrooms: 3

Bathrooms: 2 ½

Width: 40' - 0"

Depth: 52' - 0"

Foundation: Crawlspace

eplans.com

SECOND FLOOR

VAULTED
MASTER
13/8 X 12/0

BONUS
14/6 X 18/0 +
(9' CLG.)

BR. 2
11/4 X 10/0

DN

BR. 3
11/4 X 11/0

HERE IS A WONDERFUL HOME WITH A DELIGHTFUL FACADE.
Gables, dormers, a covered-porch entry, and a blending of horizontal siding and brick create interest to enhance any neighborhood. The hub of this design—the foyer, dining room, and great room—is expansive and open, lending itself well to entertaining on a grand scale. The U-shaped kitchen offers a sunny breakfast nook for less formal dining. The master bedroom suite is on the first floor for privacy, and the two family bedrooms are located on the second floor.

FIRST FLOOR

SECOND FLOOR

HOME PLAN

(#) HPK2300026

Style: Traditional

First Floor: 1,497 sq. ft.

Second Floor: 473 sq. ft.

Total: 1,970 sq. ft.

Bonus Space: 401 sq. ft.

Bedrooms: 3

Bathrooms: 2 ½

Width: 55' - 0"

Depth: 63' - 6"

Foundation: Unfinished Basement

eplans.com

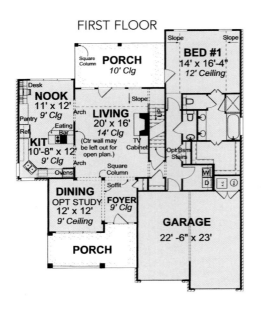

FIRST FLOOR

PORCH
10' Clg

BED #1
14' x 16'-4"
12' Ceiling

Desk
NOOK
11' x 12'
9' Clg

Pantry
Ref

Arch

LIVING
20' x 16'
14' Clg
(Ctr wall may be left out for open plan.)

KIT
10'-8" x 12'
9' Clg

Eating Bar

Ovens

Arch

TV Cabinet

Opt Bsm Stairs

Square Column

Soffit

DINING
OPT STUDY
12' x 12'
9' Ceiling

FOYER
9' Clg

Square Column

PORCH

GARAGE
22'-6" x 23'

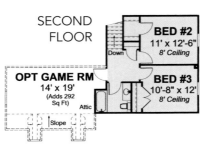

SECOND FLOOR

Down

BED #2
11' x 12'-6"
8' Ceiling

OPT GAME RM
14' x 19'
(Adds 292 Sq Ft)

Attic

BED #3
10'-8" x 12'
8' Ceiling

Slope

A CUTE VERANDA AND DUAL-ENTRY GARAGE with a brick-and-siding exterior characterize this Traditional home. Archways proliferate throughout the interior, creating an expansive effect. A dining room—convertible to a study, if one prefers—is directly to the left of the foyer, with the living room straight ahead. Through the living room to the left lies the kitchen, with breakfast nook, including an eating bar. An added feature here is a center wall that can be omitted for an open floor plan. The living room and master suite—with sloped ceilings, dual vanities and walk-in closet—let out onto the rear porch. A sloping attic, and bedrooms 2 and 3 are upstairs with a shared bath. This plan contains an option for a basement staircase behind the fireplace, and for a game room upstairs.

HPK2300027

HOME PLAN

Style: Cottage
First Floor: 1,529 sq. ft.
Second Floor: 448 sq. ft.
Total: 1,977 sq. ft.
Bonus Space: 292 sq. ft.
Bedrooms: 3
Bathrooms: 2 ½
Width: 49' - 0"
Depth: 59' - 0"

eplans.com

HOME PLAN

HPK2300028

Style: Traditional
First Floor: 1,433 sq. ft.
Second Floor: 546 sq. ft.
Total: 1,979 sq. ft.
Bonus Space: 293 sq. ft.
Bedrooms: 3
Bathrooms: 2 ½
Width: 54' - 0"
Depth: 41' - 6"
Foundation: Unfinished Walkout Basement, Crawlspace

eplans.com

BRICK ACCENTS AND A COPPER-TOPPED PEDIMENT entry will make this home a neighborhood showpiece. A two-story foyer opens to the left to a formal dining room, lit by classic multipane windows and defined by decorative columns. The vaulted great room ahead is warmed by a centered fireplace framed by windows. To the right, a spectacular master suite enjoys a tray ceiling and very private bath. Upper-level bedrooms have walk-in closets and share a full bath. Bonus space accommodates an extra bedroom, home office or recreation room.

FIRST FLOOR

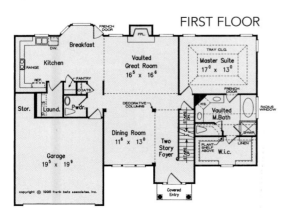

SECOND FLOOR

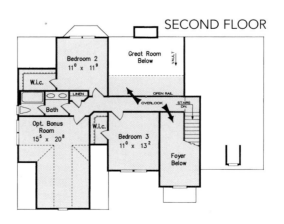

FIRST FLOOR

SECOND FLOOR

THIS TWO-STORY FARMHOUSE-STYLE PLAN is not only stunning on the outside, it is well-designed inside for the growing family. Upstairs, three bedrooms and two baths, with extra space for a fourth bedroom or playroom, highlight the possibilities offered by this home. A walk-in closet and lavish bath with a huge shower, tub, and dual-sink vanity make the master suite deluxe quality. The other bedrooms share a bath with a large double-basin vanity and access to a laundry. An open layout for the living room, dining area, and kitchen make it possible to arrange the space to best suit your family's needs. A study or home office at the front also marks this plan's versatility.

HOME PLAN

HPK2300029

Style: Farmhouse
First Floor: 971 sq. ft.
Second Floor: 1,057 sq. ft.
Total: 2,028 sq. ft.
Bonus Space: 305 sq. ft.
Bedrooms: 3
Bathrooms: 2 ½
Width: 46' - 0"
Depth: 40' - 0"
Foundation: Unfinished Basement

eplans.com

YOU CAN'T GET MORE TRADITIONAL THAN THIS! The covered front porch leads to the foyer and the living room. The massive family room enjoys a fireplace and access to the breakfast nook and kitchen with its snack bar. All four bedrooms are snuggled upstairs, including the master bedroom and its private bath. Three additional family bedrooms, a bonus room, and a full bath complete the second floor.

HOME PLAN

HPK2300030

Style: Traditional

First Floor: 1,046 sq. ft.

Second Floor: 983 sq. ft.

Total: 2,029 sq. ft.

Bedrooms: 4

Bathrooms: 2 ½

Width: 48' - 0"

Depth: 40' - 0"

eplans.com

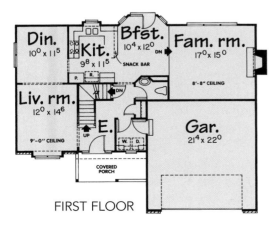

FIRST FLOOR

SECOND FLOOR

HOMES WITH ROOM TO GROW

FIRST FLOOR

SECOND FLOOR

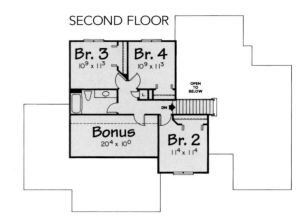

HPK2300031

Style: Traditional

First Floor: 1,411 sq. ft.

Second Floor: 618 sq. ft.

Total: 2,029 sq. ft.

Bonus Space: 214 sq. ft.

Bedrooms: 4

Bathrooms: 2 ½

Width: 63' - 8"

Depth: 48' - 4"

eplans.com

SHUTTERS, MULTIPANE GLASS WINDOWS, and a cross-hatched railing on the front porch make this a beautiful country cottage. To the left of the foyer is a roomy great room and a warming fireplace, framed by windows. To the right of the foyer, two family bedrooms feature walk-in closets and share a fully appointed bath. The efficient kitchen centers around a long island workstation and opens to the large dining/sitting room. The rear porch adds living space to view the outdoors. French doors, a fireplace, and columns complete this four-bedroom design.

HOME PLAN

(#) HPK2300032

Style: Country

Square Footage: 2,037

Bonus Space: 361 sq. ft.

Bedrooms: 3

Bathrooms: 2 ½

Width: 62' - 4"

Depth: 61' - 8"

eplans.com

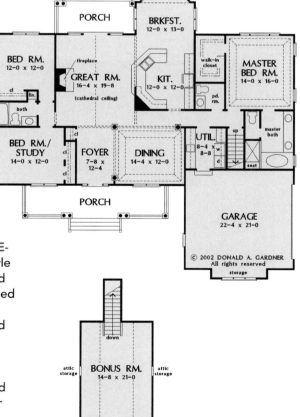

ELEGANT DETAIL BRINGS A SENSE OF FRESH REFINE-MENT to this old-fashioned farmhouse. Gingerbread-style ornamentation on the gables combines with shutters and fanlight windows on the facade. Inside, the hearth-warmed great room—which accesses the rear porch—and open kitchen will be the center of family life. Dine in the bayed breakfast nook or the tray-ceilinged formal dining room. Two bedrooms share a bath on the left of the plan. A deluxe master suite, complete with a spacious bath and walk-in closet, takes up the right wing. A utility room and half-bath are convenient to both the kitchen and two-car garage. Bonus space upstairs awaits expansion.

HOMES WITH ROOM TO GROW

FIRST FLOOR

SECOND FLOOR

CAPTURING THE HEARTLAND FEEL, this farmhouse is designed to make an impression. A welcoming front porch guides family and friends inside, where they're greeted by a two-story foyer. Columns mark the entry to the dining room. The great room features numerous windows, French doors, and a stunning fireplace. The kitchen is the hub of the home, servicing the great room through a pass-through. A cathedral ceiling visually expands the master suite, and a French door leads to the rear porch. The master bath features a double vanity, garden tub, shower with seat, and a compartmented toilet. Secondary bedrooms share a full bath with the bonus room.

HPK2300033

HOME PLAN

Style: Farmhouse

First Floor: 1,562 sq. ft.

Second Floor: 502 sq. ft.

Total: 2,064 sq. ft.

Bonus Space: 416 sq. ft.

Bedrooms: 3

Bathrooms: 2 ½

Width: 54' - 0"

Depth: 55' - 10"

eplans.com

FIRST FLOOR

MASTER BED RM.
14-8 x 14-0
(vaulted ceiling)

BRKFST.
12-0 x 11-8

PORCH

walk-in closet

cl.

KIT.
12-0 x 10-8

fireplace

GREAT RM.
17-0 x 18-0
(vaulted ceiling)

lin.

master bath

UTIL.
5-10 x 5-8

pd. rm.

sto.

up

FOYER
7-8 x 9-8
(vaulted ceiling)

DINING
11-8 x 13-8

GARAGE
22-0 x 22-0

PORCH

SECOND FLOOR

shelf

attic storage

walk-in closet

bath

great room below

BED RM.
11-0 x 12-0

down

down

lin.

cl.

shelf

foyer below

attic storage

attic storage

BONUS RM.
13-4 x 22-0
(vaulted ceiling)

BED RM.
11-8 x 11-4
(vaulted ceiling)

LOW-MAINTENANCE SIDING, A CONVENIENT FRONT-ENTRY GARAGE, and architectural details such as gables and half-circle transoms make this narrow-lot charmer perfect for beginning families and empty-nesters. An abundance of windows and an open floor plan flood this home with natural light. Custom-styled features include a fireplace, two-story great room ceiling, kitchen pass-through, and French doors leading to the rear porch. The master suite is complete with a vaulted ceiling in the bedroom, walk-in and wardrobe closets, a double vanity, garden tub, and separate shower. Two secondary bedrooms share a full bath with the bonus room.

HOME PLAN

HPK2300034

Style: Traditional

First Floor: 1,569 sq. ft.

Second Floor: 504 sq. ft.

Total: 2,073 sq. ft.

Bonus Space: 320 sq. ft.

Bedrooms: 3

Bathrooms: 2 ½

Width: 47' - 0"

Depth: 55' - 0"

eplans.com

THIS ENCHANTING FARMHOUSE LOOKS GREAT IN THE COUNTRY, on the waterfront, or on your street! Inside, the foyer is accented by a barrel arch and opens on the right to a formal dining room. An 11-foot ceiling in the living room expands the space, as a warming fireplace makes it feel cozy. The step-saving kitchen easily serves the bayed breakfast nook. In the sumptuous master suite, a sitting area is bathed in natural light, and the walk-in closet is equipped with a built-in dresser. The luxurious bath features dual vanities and a spa tub. Three upstairs bedrooms, one with a private bath, access optional future space, designed to meet your family's needs.

HPK2300035

Style: Farmhouse
First Floor: 1,383 sq. ft.
Second Floor: 703 sq. ft.
Total: 2,086 sq. ft.
Bonus Space: 342 sq. ft.
Bedrooms: 4
Bathrooms: 3 ½
Width: 49' - 0"
Depth: 50' - 0"

eplans.com

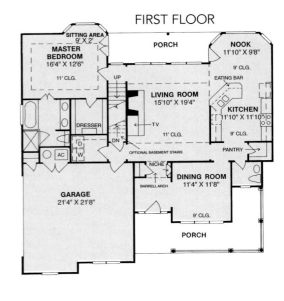

HOME PLAN

(#) HPK2300036

Style: European Cottage

First Floor: 1,488 sq. ft.

Second Floor: 602 sq. ft.

Total: 2,090 sq. ft.

Bonus Space: 1,321 sq. ft.

Bedrooms: 2

Bathrooms: 2

Width: 60' - 0"

Depth: 44' - 0"

Foundation: Finished Basement

eplans.com

A TRULY ORIGINAL ANGLE AT THE ENTRANCE of this country home belies a much more traditionally designed floor plan. There are two sets of stairs in the foyer, one leading to the second level and the other to the basement. The island kitchen and dining room enjoy the glow of the living room fireplace. The master suite with walk-in closet and bathroom are on the main level and situated next to the two-car garage. Up the short flight of stairs you'll find a convenient home office—or make it a sitting room to create a truly lavish second bedroom with a roomy closet and private bath. Finish the bonus space as a third bedroom if you wish.

FIRST FLOOR

SECOND FLOOR

BASEMENT

HOMES WITH ROOM TO GROW

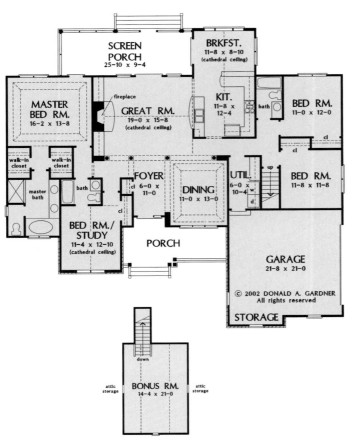

SCREEN PORCH
25-10 x 9-4

BRKFST.
11-8 x 8-10
(cathedral ceiling)

fireplace

KIT.
11-8 x
12-4

bath

MASTER BED RM.
16-2 x 13-8

GREAT RM.
19-0 x 15-8
(cathedral ceiling)

BED RM.
11-0 x 12-0

walk-in closet

walk-in closet

cl

cl

master bath

bath

FOYER
cl 6-0 x 11-0

DINING
11-0 x 13-0

UTIL.
6-0 x 10-4

up

BED RM.
11-8 x 11-8

w
d

cl

BED RM./STUDY
11-4 x 12-10
(cathedral ceiling)

PORCH

GARAGE
21-8 x 21-0

© 2002 DONALD A. GARDNER
All rights reserved

STORAGE

down

attic storage

BONUS RM.
14-4 x 21-0

attic storage

GRACEFUL ARCHES CONTRAST WITH HIGH GABLES for a stunning exterior on this Craftsman home. Windows with decorative transoms and several French doors flood the open floor plan with natural light. Tray ceilings in the dining room and master bedroom as well as cathedral ceilings in the bedroom/study, great room, kitchen, and breakfast area create architectural interest and visual space. Built-ins in the great room and additional space in the garage offer convenient storage. A screened porch allows for comfortable outdoor entertaining; a bonus room, near two additional bedrooms, offers flexibility. Positioned for privacy, the master suite features access to the screened porch, dual walk-in closets, and a well-appointed bath, including a private toilet, garden tub, double vanity, and spacious shower.

HPK2300037

HOME PLAN

Style: Craftsman

Square Footage: 2,097

Bonus Space: 352 sq. ft.

Bedrooms: 4

Bathrooms: 3

Width: 64' - 10"

Depth: 59' - 6"

eplans.com

THIS STURDY HOME WITH A BRICK EXTERIOR AND INTRIGUING GABLE LINES is well suited to make life comfortable and enjoyable for most any family. The huge island kitchen, with French-door access to the backyard, opens to a cozy dining area that will surely be a center for family socializing. A fireplace joins the dining area with the living room. A front study or home office is an especially attractive feature. The master suite with a lavish bath and a walk-in closet is also located on the first level. Above, on the second floor, two more bedrooms share a bath. Off the kitchen, a laundry and a half-bath are near the entry to the garage.

HOME PLAN # HPK2300038

Style: French
First Floor: 1,558 sq. ft.
Second Floor: 546 sq. ft.
Total: 2,104 sq. ft.
Bonus Space: 233 sq. ft.
Bedrooms: 3
Bathrooms: 2 ½
Width: 48' - 0"
Depth: 52' - 0"
Foundation: Unfinished Basement

eplans.com

FIRST FLOOR

SECOND FLOOR

FIRST FLOOR

seat
spa
DECK

walk-in closet
MASTER BED RM. 15-8 x 13-4 (cathedral ceiling)
clerestory above
BRKFST. 12-0 x 10-8 (cathedral ceiling)
lin.
master bath
UTIL. 7-8 x 7-0
fireplace
GREAT RM. 17-8 x 18-8
KITCHEN 12-0 x 13-0
d   w
bath
cl
up
cl
BED RM./STUDY 11-0 x 12-6
FOYER 6-4 x 11-6
DINING 12-0 x 13-4 (cathedral ceiling)
GARAGE 21-0 x 22-8
PORCH 19-0 x 7-0

© 1993 DONALD A. GARDNER
All rights reserved

storage

SECOND FLOOR

clerestory window with arched top

attic storage
skylight
great room below
BED RM. 12-0 x 10-4
bath
down
cl
down
attic storage
BED RM. 11-0 x 12-6 (cathedral ceiling)
attic storage
attic storage
BONUS RM. 13-0 x 22-4
skylights

THIS ATTRACTIVE FOUR-BEDROOM HOUSE offers a touch of country with its covered front porch. The foyer, flanked by the dining room and the bedroom/study, leads to the spacious great room. Here, a fireplace and window wall enhance any gathering. The U-shaped kitchen features a window over the sink and a serving counter to the breakfast room. The dining room and breakfast room have cathedral ceilings with arched windows that fill the house with natural light. The master bedroom boasts a cathedral ceiling and a bath with a whirlpool tub, shower, and double-bowl vanity. Two family bedrooms reside upstairs.

HPK2300039

HOME PLAN

Style: Traditional
First Floor: 1,694 sq. ft.
Second Floor: 436 sq. ft.
Total: 2,130 sq. ft.
Bonus Space: 345 sq. ft.
Bedrooms: 4
Bathrooms: 3
Width: 54' - 0"
Depth: 53' - 8"

eplans.com

HOME PLAN

(#) HPK2300040

Style: Traditional

Main Level: 1,382 sq. ft.

Lower Level: 766 sq. ft.

Total: 2,148 sq. ft.

Bedrooms: 3

Bathrooms: 3

Width: 40' - 4"

Depth: 52' - 0"

Foundation: Finished Walkout Basement

eplans.com

EMPTY-NESTERS WILL APPRECIATE THE SMART DESIGN and abundant amenities offered in this Traditional home. The kitchen, dining and living rooms adjoin to form a central space for eating, relaxing, and enjoying the corner fireplace. The master bedroom boasts sliding door access to the rear wood deck—adjacent to the screen porch. A second bedroom and full bath near the front door are ideal for guests or in-laws. The basement level houses a third bedroom, or a possible home office, a rec room, and copious storage space.

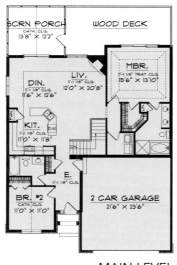

MAIN LEVEL

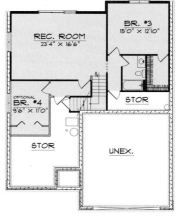

LOWER LEVEL

ENCOMPASSED IN THIS HOME ARE CUSTOM DETAILS that pair picturesque character with an exciting floor plan for graceful living. The exterior combines style, grace and a quality of details created by gabled roof lines, with stone and horizontal siding. Enter inside from a wide covered porch with a recessed door area. The foyer is flanked by the formal areas of the home. Both the living and dining room include a tray ceiling and are divided from the foyer by columns. Continuing back, the family room blends with the kitchen/breakfast area. The kitchen features an island counter, while the sink overlooks a snack bar and the outside terrace. Adjacent to the breakfast room are stairs up to the bonus room, which is located over the garage. The laundry room is a delight, with additional storage space in a walk-in closet and abundant cabinets.

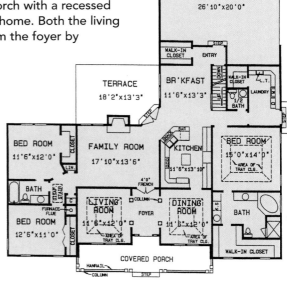

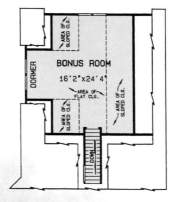

HOME PLAN

 # HPK2300041

Style: **Country**

Square Footage: **2,151**

Bonus Space: **475 sq. ft.**

Bedrooms: **3**

Bathrooms: **2 ½**

Width: **61' - 0"**

Depth: **70' - 9"**

Foundation: **Unfinished Walkout Basement**

eplans.com

FIRST FLOOR

DECK

(vaulted ceiling)

MASTER BED RM.
15-8 x 13-4

walk-in closet

lin.

master bath

bath

w d

UTIL.
7-10 x 6-8

GREAT RM.
16-8 x 17-10

fireplace

BRKFST.
11-4 x 9-0

KIT.
11-4 x 12-8

up

cl

cl

STUDY/ BED RM.
11-0 x 12-0

FOYER
5-4 x 12-0

DINING
11-4 x 12-0

GARAGE
22-4 x 21-4

PORCH

storage

SECOND FLOOR

great room below

BED RM.
11-0 x 12-0

cl

bath

cl

down

walk-in closet

BED RM.
11-0 x 13-10

(vaulted ceiling)

foyer below

BONUS RM.
15-4 x 21-4

HPK2300042

HOME PLAN

Style: Traditional
First Floor: 1,668 sq. ft.
Second Floor: 495 sq. ft.
Total: 2,163 sq. ft.
Bonus Space: 327 sq. ft.
Bedrooms: 4
Bathrooms: 3
Width: 52' - 7"
Depth: 50' - 11"

eplans.com

FOUR GABLES, A PALLADIAN WINDOW, and an admirable transom with a sunburst are eye-catching additions to this plan's exterior. On the first floor, rounded columns present the dining room, which also sports a tray ceiling. The vaulted great room accesses the rear deck and features a warming fireplace. Set at an angle, the kitchen's serving bar allows the cook to keep up with activities in both the breakfast and great rooms. The master suite includes a walk-in closet, tray ceiling, and sumptuous bath. Note the triangular shape of the tub and separate shower. Upstairs, two family bedrooms share a full bath.

HOMES WITH ROOM TO GROW

FIRST FLOOR

SECOND FLOOR

THIS HOME IS A TRUE SOUTHERN ORIGINAL. Inside, the spacious foyer leads directly to a large vaulted great room with its handsome fireplace. The dining room just off the foyer features a dramatic vaulted ceiling. The spacious kitchen offers both storage and large work areas opening up to the breakfast room. At the rear of the home you will find the master suite with its garden bath, His and Hers vanities, and an oversize closet. The second floor provides two additional bedrooms with a shared bath and a balcony overlook to the foyer below.

HOME PLAN

HPK2300043

Style: Traditional

First Floor: 1,580 sq. ft.

Second Floor: 595 sq. ft.

Total: 2,175 sq. ft.

Bedrooms: 3

Bathrooms: 2 ½

Width: 50' - 2"

Depth: 70' - 11"

Foundation: Walkout Basement

eplans.com

FEATURES THAT MAKE THIS HOUSE A SPECTACULAR HOME INCLUDE A WRAPAROUND PORCH, stone and siding exterior, and a garage that is set to the rear. Splendor continues in the interior, with a large great room that boasts a sloped ceiling, gas fireplace, and a series of windows offering a view to the rear porch. A spacious breakfast area becomes a great place to start the day, with the surround of windows and sloped ceiling. A snack bar and an abundance of counter space create a delightful kitchen. A room set to the front of the kitchen can function as a formal dining room or private study. A bath with shower is convenient to the garage entry. The master bedroom suite is designed to pamper the homeowner in encompassing comfort. Plant ledges and built-in shelves add decorative touches.

HOME PLAN

#️⃣ HPK2300044

Style: Bungalow

Square Footage: 2,183

Bonus Space: 241 sq. ft.

Bedrooms: 3

Bathrooms: 3

Width: 80' - 0"

Depth: 74' - 0"

Foundation: Unfinished Basement

eplans.com

FIRST FLOOR

SECOND FLOOR

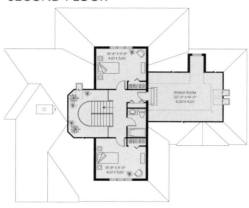

THE STONE-AND-SIDING FACADE AND ARCHED FRONT WINDOWS give this two-story home an impressive distinction matched by the charm and comfort found inside. Built-in cabinets flank the living-room fireplace; the spacious dining area is separated from the kitchen by an island counter, convenient for light meals and snacks. A double-bowl vanity, shower, and huge corner tub mark the resplendent bath in the first-floor master suite. Upstairs, two family bedrooms are separated by a bath, and additional to-be-developed space is nearby. Off the kitchen, a full laundry with a wash tub adjoins a half-bath and opens to the two-car garage. A wraparound front porch and rear deck complete this plan.

HOME PLAN

HPK2300045

Style: Farmhouse

First Floor: 1,618 sq. ft.

Second Floor: 586 sq. ft.

Total: 2,204 sq. ft.

Bonus Space: 334 sq. ft.

Bedrooms: 3

Bathrooms: 2 ½

Width: 65' - 0"

Depth: 44' - 0"

Foundation: Unfinished Basement

eplans.com

© Donald A. Gardner, Inc.

CEDAR SHAKES, SIDING, AND STONE BLEND with the Craftsman details of a custom design in this stunning home. The plan's open design and non-linear layout is refreshing and functional. The second-floor loft over-looks a centrally located and vaulted great room, and the breakfast area with a tray ceiling is virtually sur-rounded by windows to enhance the morning's light. The secluded first-floor master suite features a bay window, tray ceiling, walk-in closet, and private bath. The second-floor family bedrooms are illuminated by rear dormers.

HOME PLAN # HPK2300046

Style: Craftsman

First Floor: 1,580 sq. ft.

Second Floor: 627 sq. ft.

Total: 2,207 sq. ft.

Bonus Space: 214 sq. ft.

Bedrooms: 4

Bathrooms: 3

Width: 64' - 2"

Depth: 53' - 4"

eplans.com

FIRST FLOOR

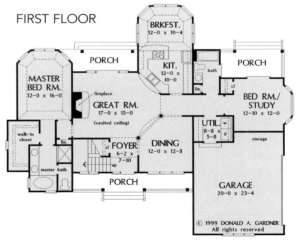

SECOND FLOOR

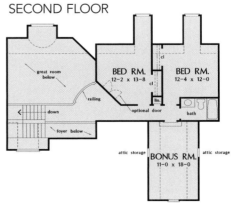

HOMES WITH ROOM TO GROW

FIRST FLOOR

SECOND FLOOR

STONE AND HORIZONTAL SIDING PAIRED WITH THE COVERED FRONT ENTRY creates a truly country flavor for this four-bedroom home. The two-story foyer opens to the dining room on the left and the great room, where a warming fireplace adds to the country atmosphere. Views are offered in the great room and the breakfast nook that adjoins the kitchen. The master suite finds privacy on the first floor; three additional bedrooms are on the second floor, along with a sizable bonus room.

(#) HPK2300047

HOME PLAN

Style: Country

First Floor: 1,476 sq. ft.

Second Floor: 735 sq. ft.

Total: 2,211 sq. ft.

Bonus Space: 374 sq. ft.

Bedrooms: 4

Bathrooms: 2 ½

Width: 48' - 4"

Depth: 51' - 4"

eplans.com

HOME PLAN

HPK2300048

Style: Craftsman

First Floor: 1,707 sq. ft.

Second Floor: 514 sq. ft.

Total: 2,221 sq. ft.

Bonus Space: 211 sq. ft.

Bedrooms: 4

Bathrooms: 2 ½

Width: 50' - 0"

Depth: 71' - 8"

eplans.com

FIRST FLOOR

SECOND FLOOR

STONE AND HORIZONTAL SIDING GIVE A DEFINITE COUNTRY FLAVOR to this two-story home. The front study makes an ideal guest room with the adjoining powder room. The formal dining room is accented with decorative columns that define its perimeter. The great room boasts a fireplace, built-ins, and a magnificent view of the backyard beyond one of two rear porches. The master suite boasts two walk-in closets and a private bath. Two bedrooms share a full bath on the second floor.

FIRST FLOOR

DECK

GREAT RM.
18-0 x 19-6
(cathedral ceiling)

BRKFST.
12-0 x 10-0

UTIL.
9-0 x 6-0

storage

master bath

walk-in closet

fireplace

balcony above

KIT.
12-0 x 12-8

GARAGE
21-0 x 20-4

MASTER BED RM.
12-0 x 16-8

walk-in closet

FOYER
7-4 x 12-4
(vaulted ceiling)

pd. rm.

DINING
12-0 x 12-0

cl

© 1998 Donald A Gardner, Inc.

PORCH

SECOND FLOOR

great room below

attic storage

attic storage

attic storage

BONUS RM.
21-0 x 13-4

down

railing

balcony

down

attic storage

BED RM.
12-0 x 13-0

bath

lin.

lin.

BED RM.
12-0 x 13-0

attic storage

walk-in closet

foyer below

walk-in closet

attic storage

attic storage

THE WIDE PORCH ACROSS THE FRONT AND THE DECK OFF THE GREAT ROOM in back allow as much outdoor living as the weather permits. The foyer opens through columns from the front porch to the dining room, with a nearby powder room, and to the great room. The breakfast room is open to the great room and the adjacent kitchen. The utility room adjoins this area and accesses the garage. On the opposite side of the plan, the master suite offers a compartmented bath and two walk-in closets. A staircase leads upstairs to two family bedrooms—one at each end of a balcony that overlooks the great room. Each bedroom contains a walk-in closet, a dormer window, and private access to the bath through a private vanity area.

HPK2300049

HOME PLAN

Style: Country Cottage
First Floor: 1,569 sq. ft.
Second Floor: 682 sq. ft.
Total: 2,251 sq. ft.
Bonus Space: 332 sq. ft.
Bedrooms: 3
Bathrooms: 2 ½
Width: 64' - 8"
Depth: 43' - 4"

eplans.com

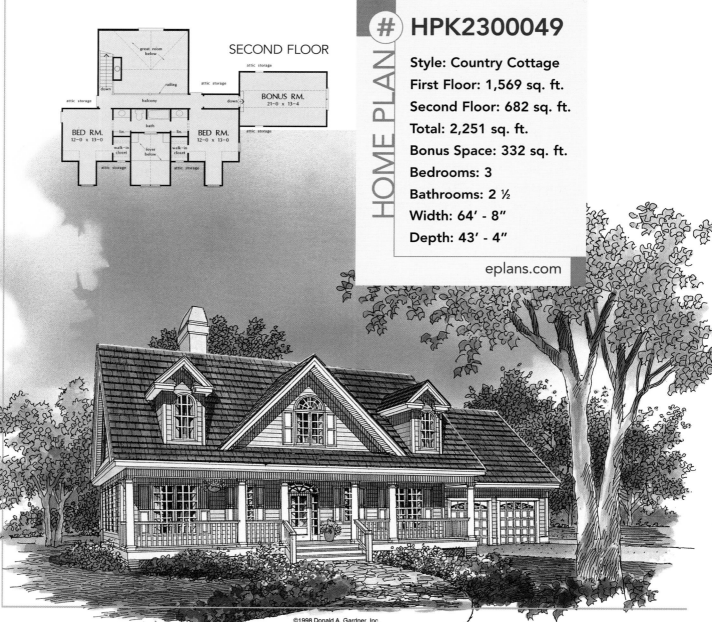

©1998 Donald A. Gardner, Inc.

THERE'S A EUROPEAN FLAVOR TO THE EXTERIOR of this bungalow, which is filled with a wide range of comforts. A graciously curved bay with arched windows encloses the formal dining room. This area conveniently opens to a fully equipped island kitchen, which also flows into a sunny family dining alcove. Sleeping quarters are divided so that the master suite on the first floor is private from the two family bedrooms on the second level. Both of these rooms open to a sitting room or den and share a bath. The master bath is full of luxuries, including an oversize oval tub and twin vanities. A large utility and laundry area is entered from the kitchen, a separate front door, or the garage.

HOME PLAN

HPK2300050

Style: European Cottage
First Floor: 1,566 sq. ft.
Second Floor: 693 sq. ft.
Total: 2,259 sq. ft.
Bonus Space: 406 sq. ft.
Bedrooms: 3
Bathrooms: 2 ½
Width: 68' - 0"
Depth: 52' - 11"
Foundation: Unfinished Basement

eplans.com

FIRST FLOOR

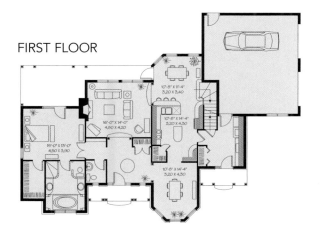

SECOND FLOOR

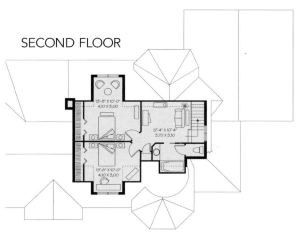

FIRST FLOOR

SECOND FLOOR

FROM THE WRAPAROUND COVERED PORCH, enter this attractive home to find the roomy master suite on the left and the formal dining room on the right. Leading through double doors from the dining area is a sunlit U-shaped kitchen with a breakfast island. This room then flows into a comfortable family room featuring a fireplace. Separate access to the garage and upstairs completes the first floor. The second floor is reserved for three family bedrooms that share a full bath.

HOME PLAN

HPK2300051

Style: Victorian

First Floor: 1,371 sq. ft.

Second Floor: 894 sq. ft.

Total: 2,265 sq. ft.

Bonus Space: 300 sq. ft.

Bedrooms: 4

Bathrooms: 3 ½

Width: 58' - 0"

Depth: 58' - 4"

Foundation: Unfinished Basement

eplans.com

© 2003 Donald A. Gardner, Inc.

HOME PLAN

HPK2300052

Style: Farmhouse

First Floor: 1,778 sq. ft.

Second Floor: 498 sq. ft.

Total: 2,276 sq. ft.

Bonus Space: 315 sq. ft.

Bedrooms: 4

Bathrooms: 3

Width: 54' - 8"

Depth: 53' - 2"

eplans.com

A METAL ROOF TOPS THE FRONT PORCH, AND COLUMNS and gables add to this classic farmhouse facade. Front and side stairs show the way to the porch, creating a warm, inviting welcome. Double doors lead into a versatile bedroom/study, and the dining room is connected to the kitchen by a butler's pantry. The great room is enhanced with a cathedral ceiling, built-in cabinetry, and a fireplace that faces the kitchen. A bay window extends the breakfast nook; French doors access the rear porch. The master suite features a cathedral ceiling, large walk-in closet, and elegant bath. Two additional bedrooms can be found on the second floor, along with a bonus room and a full bath.

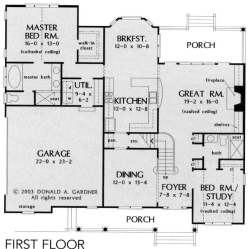

FIRST FLOOR

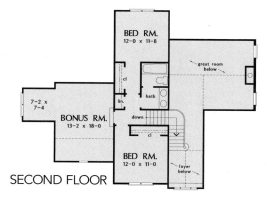

SECOND FLOOR

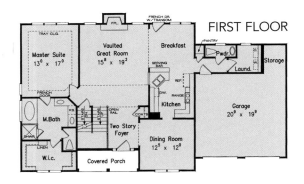

FIRST FLOOR

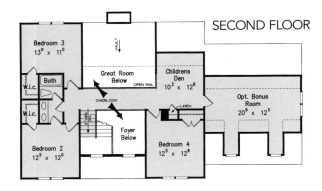

SECOND FLOOR

HOME PLAN

HPK2300053

Style: Southern Colonial

First Floor: 1,440 sq. ft.

Second Floor: 886 sq. ft.

Total: 2,326 sq. ft.

Bonus Space: 309 sq. ft.

Bedrooms: 4

Bathrooms: 2 ½

Width: 61' - 0"

Depth: 37' - 4"

Foundation: Crawlspace, Unfinished Walkout Basement

eplans.com

GRAND SOUTHERN COLONIAL STYLE GRACES THE FACADE of this fine home. Inside, an overlook from above separates the two-story foyer and vaulted great room. An angled kitchen is situated between the dining room and breakfast nook for ease in entertaining. The first-floor master suite is truly a retreat fit for royalty. Upstairs, three generous bedrooms share a children's den, a full bath and optional bonus space.

HPK2300054

HOME PLAN #

Style: Country

First Floor: 1,239 sq. ft.

Second Floor: 1,120 sq. ft.

Total: 2,359 sq. ft.

Bonus Space: 406 sq. ft.

Bedrooms: 4

Bathrooms: 2 ½

Width: 61' - 8"

Depth: 35' - 4"

Foundation: Unfinished Basement

eplans.com

FIRST FLOOR

SECOND FLOOR

THIS CLASSY HOME IS JUST RIGHT FOR A GROW-ING FAMILY looking for comfort and space to expand. The media room, informal dining nook, and kitchen are at center place and will surely be the hub of day-to-day family activity. On the far left side, the great room offers wonderful entertaining possibilities. The master suite upstairs boasts a walk-in closet and a lavish corner tub. Three other bedrooms share a bath. The space above the garage can be developed into a recreation room. A front covered porch and a rear patio offer space to extend activities outdoors; a good-sized mudroom off the garage will help keep tracked-in dirt to a minimum.

FIRST FLOOR

SECOND FLOOR

SPACIOUS, BRIGHT, AND READY FOR BUSY FAMILY LIFE, this elegant farmhouse brings a classic flavor to a modern home. Upon entry, the study is on the left and overlooks the front porch. The family room is great for casual relaxation or formal affairs. Quick snacks can be enjoyed at the kitchen's snack-bar island, and fine dining is available nearby. Utility rooms are on the right and open onto a quaint side porch. Completing this level is a two-car garage with special storage space for lawn mowers, motorcycles, or other equipment. Upstairs, the master suite delights with a unique curved-wall walk-in closet and a glamorous spa bath. Three additional bedrooms afford room for everyone, and bonus space is available to expand as your family grows.

HPK2300055

HOME PLAN

Style: Farmhouse

First Floor: 1,239 sq. ft.

Second Floor: 1,137 sq. ft.

Total: 2,376 sq. ft.

Bonus Space: 523 sq. ft.

Bedrooms: 4

Bathrooms: 2 ½

Width: 45' - 0"

Depth: 68' - 8"

Foundation: Unfinished Basement

eplans.com

REAR EXTERIOR

COVERED PORCHES IN THE FRONT AND REAR of this contemporary design serve to facilitate a smooth indoor/outdoor relationship. First-floor living spaces are wide open—you'll never miss a word of conversation if you're cooking in the kitchen and serving friends and family in hearth-warmed family room or informal dining area nearby. Also on this level are the laundry room and a full bath. Venture upstairs to find four family bedrooms, each with a spacious closet, and another full bath. Dual sinks in this bathroom help ease the chaos of morning/bedtime rituals.

HOME PLAN

HPK2300056

Style: Farmhouse
First Floor: 1,279 sq. ft.
Second Floor: 1,114 sq. ft.
Total: 2,393 sq. ft.
Bonus Space: 337 sq. ft.
Bedrooms: 4
Bathrooms: 2
Width: 68' - 0"
Depth: 36' - 0"
Foundation: Slab

eplans.com

FIRST FLOOR

SECOND FLOOR

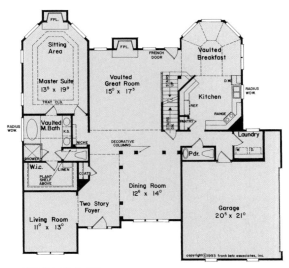

FIRST FLOOR

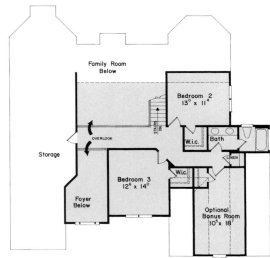

SECOND FLOOR

A CHARMING COMBINATION OF STUCCO AND STONE mixed with modern design elements gives this two-story home instant appeal. The vaulted great room continues back, culminating with a fireplace flanked by tall windows. The wraparound kitchen proves efficient with easy service to the vaulted breakfast room. The sumptuous master suite has a sitting area and a vaulted bath. Two family bedrooms are upstairs.

HOME PLAN

HPK2300057

Style: New American
First Floor: 1,796 sq. ft.
Second Floor: 629 sq. ft.
Total: 2,425 sq. ft.
Bonus Space: 208 sq. ft.
Bedrooms: 3
Bathrooms: 2 ½
Width: 54' - 0"
Depth: 53' - 10"
Foundation: Crawlspace, Slab, Unfinished Walkout Basement

eplans.com

A SOUTHERN CLASSIC, THIS LOVELY HOME WILL BECOME A TREASURED PLACE to call your own. The entry makes a grand impression; double doors open to the foyer where French doors reveal a study. To the right, the dining room is designed for entertaining, with easy access to the angled serving-bar kitchen. A bayed breakfast nook leads into the hearth-warmed family room. Tucked to the rear, a bedroom with a full bath makes an ideal guest room. The master suite is upstairs and enjoys a private vaulted spa bath. Two additional bedrooms reside on this level and join a full bath and an optional bonus room, perfect as a kid's retreat, home gym, or crafts room.

HOME PLAN

(#) HPK2300058

Style: Greek Revival

First Floor: 1,327 sq. ft.

Second Floor: 1,099 sq. ft.

Total: 2,426 sq. ft.

Bonus Space: 290 sq. ft.

Bedrooms: 4

Bathrooms: 3

Width: 54' - 4"

Depth: 42' - 10"

Foundation: Crawlspace, Unfinished Walkout Basement

eplans.com

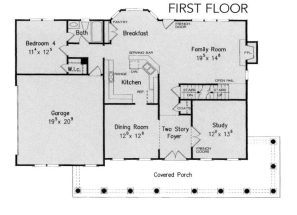

FIRST FLOOR

SECOND FLOOR

HOMES WITH ROOM TO GROW

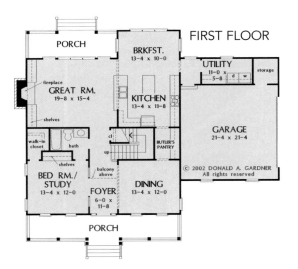

FIRST FLOOR

SECOND FLOOR

LOOKING EVERY BIT LIKE THE BIG COUNTRY HOMES OF YESTERYEAR, this plan's traditional facade belies the up-to-date floor plan inside. The two-story foyer—lit by a glorious Palladian window on top—opens to flex space on the left. This room can be a bedroom or a study, depending on your needs. On the other side of the foyer lies the dining room, which accesses the kitchen through a convenient butler's pantry. The roomy island kitchen flows into a sunny breakfast room, which in turn accesses the hearth-warmed great room. The rear porch can be accessed by the great room and the breakfast room. Upstairs, two family bedrooms share a hall bath and the deluxe master suite boasts two walk-in closets and a twin-vanity bath with a garden tub. To the right is bonus space, which you can define any way you wish.

HPK2300059

HOME PLAN

Style: Traditional

First Floor: 1,420 sq. ft.

Second Floor: 1,065 sq. ft.

Total: 2,485 sq. ft.

Bonus Space: 411 sq. ft.

Bedrooms: 4

Bathrooms: 3

Width: 57' - 8"

Depth: 49' - 0"

eplans.com

THIS PLAN OFFERS A WELL-DESIGNED, COMPACT HOME ideal for a growing family with hopes of future expansion. Upstairs houses an optional game room, and a study on the first floor doubles as an optional bedroom. The open kitchen layout serves the adjoining breakfast nook and an eating bar backs the living room. A rear screen porch makes outdoor dining a possibility. The spacious master suite sits on the first floor. A second first-floor bedroom equipped with a full bath could serve as a guest suite. Two additional family bedrooms sharing a full bath are on the second floor.

HPK2300060

HOME PLAN

Style: French
First Floor: 2,019 sq. ft.
Second Floor: 468 sq. ft.
Total: 2,487 sq. ft.
Bonus Space: 286 sq. ft.
Bedrooms: 5
Bathrooms: 3
Width: 59' - 0"
Depth: 58' - 0"

eplans.com

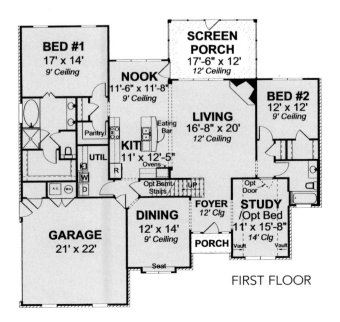

FIRST FLOOR

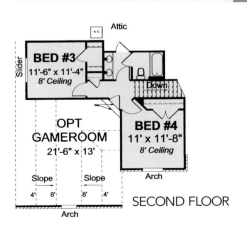

SECOND FLOOR

FIRST FLOOR

SECOND FLOOR

A STUNNING SHINGLE HOME WITH STONE ACCENTS (including a stone fireplace!), this Cape Cod-style home will complement any neighborhood. Inside, the two-story foyer presents a grand staircase and high ceilings throughout. Multipane windows light up the living room; an archway connects it to the family room. Here, a lateral fireplace allows rear views. The breakfast nook has French doors to the rear property, inviting outdoor dining. The island kitchen is designed with lots of extra space to accommodate two cooks. A butler's pantry makes entertaining a breeze. Upstairs, three bedrooms (or make one a den) share a full bath and a bonus room. The master suite is graced with a vaulted ceiling and a private bath with a Roman spa tub.

HOME PLAN

HPK2300061

Style: Country Cottage

First Floor: 1,319 sq. ft.

Second Floor: 1,181 sq. ft.

Total: 2,500 sq. ft.

Bonus Space: 371 sq. ft.

Bedrooms: 4

Bathrooms: 2 ½

Width: 60' - 0"

Depth: 42' - 0"

Foundation: Crawlspace

eplans.com

HOME PLAN

HPK2300062

Style: Traditional
First Floor: 1,808 sq. ft.
Second Floor: 698 sq. ft.
Total: 2,506 sq. ft.
Bonus Space: 217 sq. ft.
Bedrooms: 3
Bathrooms: 2 ½
Width: 62' - 8"
Depth: 49' - 0"
Foundation: Unfinished Basement

eplans.com

A POPULAR EXTERIOR WITH BRICK AND STONE is paired with an equally popular floor plan to create a home that will bring delight and comfort for many years. The foyer introduces an elegantly turned staircase and a great room with a window wall. Columns decorate the entry to the breakfast room, and a large island defines the kitchen. A mudroom offers an orderly entry through the garage, where two closets offer storage. The master suite pampers with a sloped ceiling and spacious bath with whirlpool tub, large double bowl vanity, and walk-in closet. A second-floor loft showcases a spectacular view to the great room and creates a shared computer or study area. Two additional bedrooms, each with walk-in closets, and an optional bonus room complete this family-style home.

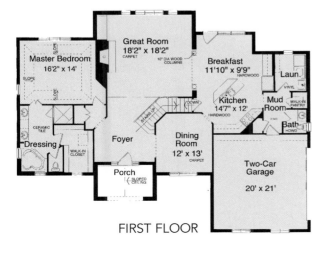

FIRST FLOOR

SECOND FLOOR

FIRST FLOOR

SECOND FLOOR

HOME PLAN

HPK2300063

Style: Craftsman

First Floor: 1,360 sq. ft.

Second Floor: 1,154 sq. ft.

Total: 2,514 sq. ft.

Bonus Space: 202 sq. ft.

Bedrooms: 3

Bathrooms: 2 ½

Width: 52' - 0"

Depth: 45' - 6"

Foundation: Crawlspace

eplans.com

THREE BEDROOMS, SPACIOUS FAMILY LIVING AREAS, and plenty of amenities make this Craftsman design a pleasure to come home to. Vaulted ceilings enhance the den and living room, and built-in bookshelves, a media center, and a fireplace highlight the family room. The kitchen, with a built-in desk and island cooktop, serves the breakfast nook and dining room with ease. Sleeping quarters—the vaulted master suite and two family bedrooms—are upstairs, along with a bonus room and the utility area.

HPK2300064

Style: French Country

First Floor: 1,834 sq. ft.

Second Floor: 681 sq. ft.

Total: 2,515 sq. ft.

Bonus Space: 365 sq. ft.

Bedrooms: 3

Bathrooms: 3 ½

Width: 50' - 8"

Depth: 66' - 8"

eplans.com

FIRST FLOOR

SECOND FLOOR

THIS RUSTIC FRENCH COUNTRY EXTERIOR
opens up to a plan full of modern amenities.
The foyer, preceded by a petite porch, leads into a gallery hall that
opens to a sunny, vaulted great room. With its fireplace and porch
access, this will be the most popular room in the house. As an
added convenience, the great room flows into the breakfast room,
with its box-bay window and built-ins. The island kitchen features a
pantry and plenty of counter space. A formal dining room is adjacent. The deluxe master suite awaits on the left of the plan, enjoying a pampering bath and double walk-in closets. Upstairs, two
bedrooms boast ample closet space and a private bath. Bonus
space awaits expansion over the garage.

FIRST FLOOR

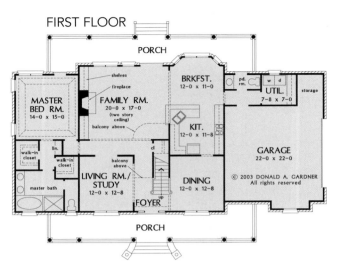

SECOND FLOOR

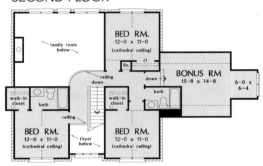

WRAPPING A TRADITIONAL BRICK EXTERIOR WITH TWO COUNTRY PORCHES creates a modern exterior that's big on Southern charm. Bold columns and a metal roof welcome guests inside to an equally impressive interior. Both the foyer and family room have two-story ceilings. The family room includes such amenities as a fireplace, built-in shelves, and access to the rear porch. A bay window expands the breakfast nook, located adjacent to the U-shaped kitchen. The living room/study and bonus room add flexibility for changing needs. The master suite, conveniently located on the first level, is complete with linen shelves, two walk-in closets, and master bath featuring a double vanity, garden tub, separate shower, and private privy. The second level holds three more bedrooms, two bathrooms, bonus space, and an overlook to the beautiful family room.

HOME PLAN

HPK2300065

Style: Farmhouse

First Floor: 1,809 sq. ft.

Second Floor: 777 sq. ft.

Total: 2,586 sq. ft.

Bonus Space: 264 sq. ft.

Bedrooms: 4

Bathrooms: 3 ½

Width: 70' - 7"

Depth: 48' - 4"

eplans.com

FIRST FLOOR

HOME PLAN

HPK2300066

Style: Country Cottage

First Floor: 2,047 sq. ft.

Second Floor: 540 sq. ft.

Total: 2,587 sq. ft.

Bonus Space: 278 sq. ft.

Bedrooms: 4

Bathrooms: 3

Width: 60' - 0"

Depth: 56' - 0"

Foundation: Crawlspace, Unfinished Walkout Basement

eplans.com

SECOND FLOOR

BEAUTIFUL COUNTRY DETAILS WILL CHARM VISITORS and passersby...not to mention the lucky owners of this fine four-bedroom home. Inside, the foyer leads to a stunning vaulted grand room. To the left, a coffered ceiling graces the kitchen and breakfast area, making any meal seem special. A formal dining room is available to host an elegant soiree. Both first-floor bedrooms—a guest room and an exquisite master suite—have inviting box-bay window seats. The upper level includes two bedrooms and bonus space that is perfect as a home office or playroom.

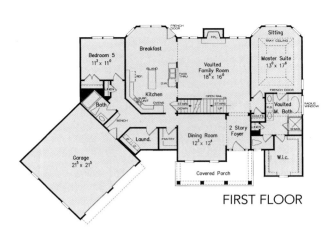

FIRST FLOOR

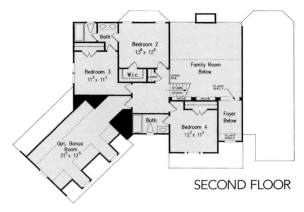

SECOND FLOOR

HPK2300067

HOME PLAN #

Style: Colonial
First Floor: 1,809 sq. ft.
Second Floor: 785 sq. ft.
Total: 2,594 sq. ft.
Bonus Space: 353 sq. ft.
Bedrooms: 5
Bathrooms: 4
Width: 72' - 7"
Depth: 51' - 5"
Foundation: Crawlspace, Unfinished Walkout Basement, Slab

eplans.com

WITH ELEMENTS OF COUNTRY STYLE, this unique Colonial-inspired home presents a rustic attitude blended with the delicate features that make this design one of a kind. Upon entry, a second-story arched window lights the foyer. Straight ahead, the family room soars with a two-story vault balanced by a cozy fireplace. A pass-through from the island kitchen keeps conversation going as the family chef whips up delectable feasts for the formal dining room or bayed breakfast nook. A bedroom at the rear provides plenty of privacy for guests, or as a home office. The master suite takes up the entire right wing, hosting a bayed sitting area and marvelous vaulted bath. Upstairs, three bedrooms access a versatile bonus room, limited only by your imagination.

HPK2300068

Style: Country Cottage

First Floor: 1,844 sq. ft.

Second Floor: 777 sq. ft.

Total: 2,621 sq. ft.

Bonus Space: 250 sq. ft.

Bedrooms: 3

Bathrooms: 2 ½

Width: 52' - 4"

Depth: 35' - 0"

Foundation: Unfinished Walkout Basement

eplans.com

A TRADITIONAL HIPPED ROOF WITH A CENTERED PEAK makes a charming statement on this beautiful three-bedroom home. Inside, multipane windows brighten the living and dining rooms, bordering the two-story foyer. Ahead, an art niche and staircase on one side, and a coat closet and powder room to the other, give way to a prominent family room. A fireplace and rear triplet of windows make this room a favorite place to relax; a serving bar from the gourmet kitchen is a thoughtful touch. Upstairs, the master suite relishes a vaulted spa bath and an immense walk-in closet. Two more bedrooms and a full bath complete the plan.

FIRST FLOOR

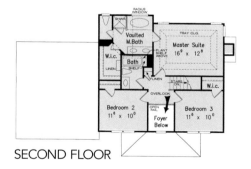

SECOND FLOOR

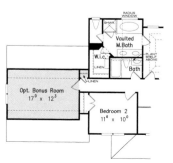

OPTIONAL LAYOUT

THIS STATELY BRICK FACADE FEATURES A COLUMNED, covered porch that ushers visitors into the large foyer. An expansive great room with a fireplace and access to a covered rear porch awaits. The centrally located kitchen is within easy reach of the great room, formal dining room, and skylit breakfast area. Split-bedroom planning places the master bedroom and elegant master bath to the right of the home. Two bedrooms with abundant closet space are placed to the left; an optional bedroom or study with a Palladian window faces the front. A large bonus room is located above the garage.

HPK2300069

HOME PLAN

Style: Traditional

Square Footage: 2,625

Bonus Space: 447 sq. ft.

Bedrooms: 4

Bathrooms: 2 ½

Width: 63' - 1"

Depth: 90' - 2"

eplans.com

B. NATHAN

© 2003 Donald A. Gardner, Inc.

HOME PLAN

HPK2300070

Style: Traditional

First Floor: 2,068 sq. ft.

Second Floor: 566 sq. ft.

Total: 2,634 sq. ft.

Bonus Space: 349 sq. ft.

Bedrooms: 4

Bathrooms: 3

Width: 68' - 0"

Depth: 61' - 4"

eplans.com

SIDELIGHTS AND A FANLIGHT FRAME THE FRONT DOOR of this cottage-style home, and French doors access the screened porch and deck. Brick detailing and columns accentuate the facade, lending strong curb appeal to any streetscape. A staircase is all that separates the kitchen and keeping room from the great room with its fireplace, built-in cabinetry, and cathedral ceiling. A decorative column distinguishes the dining room space, providing an open, unimpeded view of the rear deck. Closets, bathrooms, and cabinetry act as buffers, promoting privacy in each bedroom. The master suite and one second-floor bedroom include walk-in closets. The study/bedroom provides versatility.

FIRST FLOOR

SECOND FLOOR

FIRST FLOOR

SECOND FLOOR

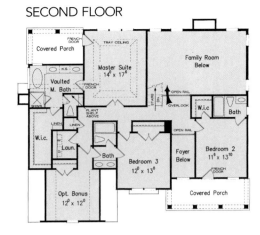

HPK2300071

Style: Cape Cod

First Floor: 1,444 sq. ft.

Second Floor: 1,191 sq. ft.

Total: 2,635 sq. ft.

Bonus Space: 186 sq. ft.

Bedrooms: 4

Bathrooms: 4

Width: 52' - 4"

Depth: 47' - 4"

Foundation: Unfinished Walkout Basement, Crawlspace, Slab

eplans.com

CAPE COD STYLE BRINGS A BEACHFRONT ATTITUDE to your neighborhood; inside, an open floor plan continues the theme of coastal bliss. From the covered porch, a two-story ceiling in the foyer flows into the hearth-warmed family room. The service-island kitchen is bathed in natural light from the breakfast nook and inviting keeping room. Easy access to the box-bayed dining room is great for entertaining. A nearby study also makes a great guest room. Upstairs, French doors open to the master suite, where a tray ceiling, private covered porch, and vaulted spa bath await. Two additional bedrooms enjoy private baths. A bonus room is available for a playroom, gym…whatever your family desires.

HOME PLAN

HPK2300072

Style: Traditional

Square Footage: 2,639

Bonus Space: 425 sq. ft.

Bedrooms: 3

Bathrooms: 2 ½

Width: 67' - 3"

Depth: 69' - 9"

eplans.com

A DRAMATIC BARREL-VAULT ENTRYWAY, GRAND COLUMNS, and arched transoms create an elegant facade. An expansive front porch and rear porches off both the family and living rooms encourage outdoor living. Inside, the open floor plan features more room definition. An abundance of windows usher in the natural light and views. Columns and a tray ceiling define the dining room, and French doors lead to the study/bedroom. A cathedral ceiling, built-in cabinetry, and a fireplace enhance the great room. The family/media room is open to the kitchen and features a staircase leading to the bonus room. The kitchen and breakfast nook are centrally located in the living area for ease of service—no matter where you eat. A vaulted ceiling crowns the master bedroom, which is complete with dual walk-in closets, a double vanity, garden tub, spacious shower with seat, and a private privy. Two family bedrooms—or make one a study—share a full bath. Note the large utility and storage room.

HOMES WITH ROOM TO GROW

STONE ACCENTS ADD A EUROPEAN FEEL TO THIS NARROW COTTAGE, perfect in an established neighborhood or out in the country. Enter beneath a keystone arch to a two-story foyer; follow an angled hall to the family room where a coffered ceiling and fireplace create a welcoming atmosphere. The kitchen works hard so you don't have to, with a serving bar, stacked ovens, and easy access to the breakfast nook and dining room, lit by a box-bay window. The keeping room is to the rear, perfect for lazy mornings, curled up with a good book. Upstairs, the master suite delights in a detailed tray ceiling, bayed sitting area, and lavish bath. Two additional bedrooms join an optional bonus area (with a charming window seat) to complete the plan.

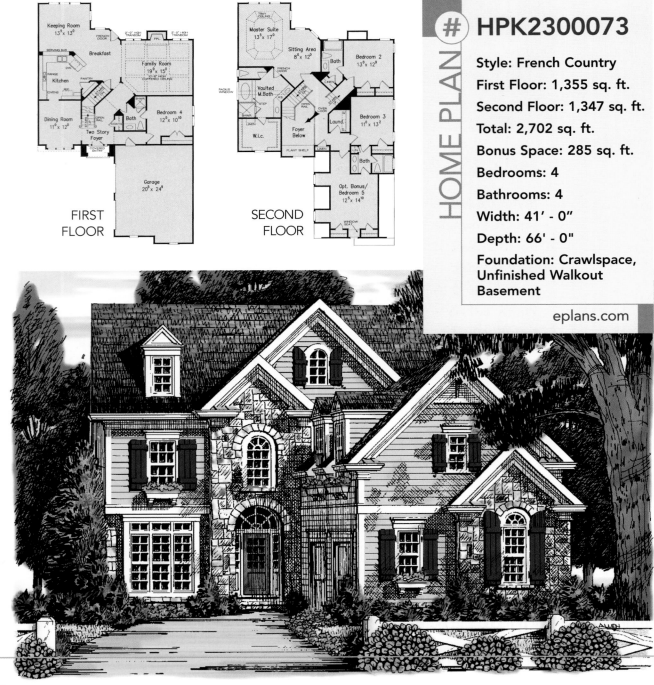

FIRST FLOOR

SECOND FLOOR

HPK2300073

HOME PLAN

Style: French Country

First Floor: 1,355 sq. ft.

Second Floor: 1,347 sq. ft.

Total: 2,702 sq. ft.

Bonus Space: 285 sq. ft.

Bedrooms: 4

Bathrooms: 4

Width: 41' - 0"

Depth: 66' - 0"

Foundation: Crawlspace, Unfinished Walkout Basement

eplans.com

WITH AN EYE TO THE FUTURE, THIS HOME OFFERS ROOM TO EXPAND or space to be creative. With a first-floor master, the homeowners are afforded a private retreat from the other family bedrooms. A sundeck off of the breakfast nook extends the living space outdoors. The second floor offers a wealth of opportunity with a large bonus space and a bedroom that can be converted to an office or a guest room. Extra storage space is an added bonus. The central loft/study area is ideal for a family computer. Upgraded ceiling treatments can be found throughout.

FIRST FLOOR

SECOND FLOOR

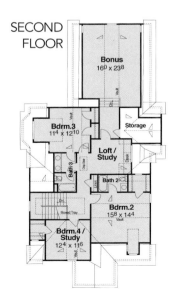

HOME PLAN # HPK2300074

Style: European Cottage

First Floor: 1,622 sq. ft.

Second Floor: 1,131 sq. ft.

Total: 2,753 sq. ft.

Bonus Space: 444 sq. ft.

Bedrooms: 4

Bathrooms: 3 ½

Width: 39' - 6"

Depth: 76' - 0"

Foundation: Crawlspace

eplans.com

FIRST FLOOR

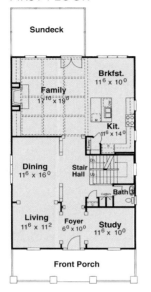

Sundeck

Brkfst.
11^6 x 10^0

Family
17^{10} x 19^0

Kit.
11^6 x 14^0

Dining
11^6 x 16^0

Stair Hall

Bath 3

Living
11^6 x 11^2

Foyer
6^0 x 10^0

Study
11^6 x 10^0

Front Porch

SECOND FLOOR

M.Bath Vaulted

M.Bdrm.
17^6 x 15^6

Bdrm.4
11^6 x 10^6

M. Closet

Bath 3

W.D. Lnd.

Upper Hall

Opt. Computer Station

Opt. Vault

Opt. Vault

Bdrm.2
10^0 x 13^2

Bath 2

Bdrm.3
10^0 x 13^2

Line of Dormer for Elev. B

BASEMENT

Opt. Rear Entry

Double Garage
28^{10} x 23^8

Recreation Rm.
28^{10} x 15^6

Storage/Severe Weather Rm.

Bath

A STYLISH CRAFTSMAN AT JUST UNDER 3,000 SQUARE FEET, this home features an open layout ideal for entertaining. Rooms are distinguished by columns, eliminating the use of unnecessary walls. At the rear of the home, the expansive family room, warmed by a fireplace, faces the adjoining breakfast area and kitchen. Access to the sundeck makes alfresco meals an option. A walk-in pantry is an added bonus. The second floor houses the family bedrooms, including the lavish master suite, two bedrooms separated by a Jack-and-Jill bath, and a fourth bedroom with a private, full bath. The second floor laundry room is smart and convenient. A centrally located, optional computer station is perfect for a family computer. A sizable recreation room on the basement level completes this plan.

HOME PLAN

HPK2300075

Style: Craftsman
First Floor: 1,440 sq. ft.
Second Floor: 1,514 sq. ft.
Total: 2,954 sq. ft.
Bedrooms: 4
Bathrooms: 3 ½
Width: 30' - 0"
Depth: 68' - 0"
Foundation: Unfinished Walkout Basement

eplans.com

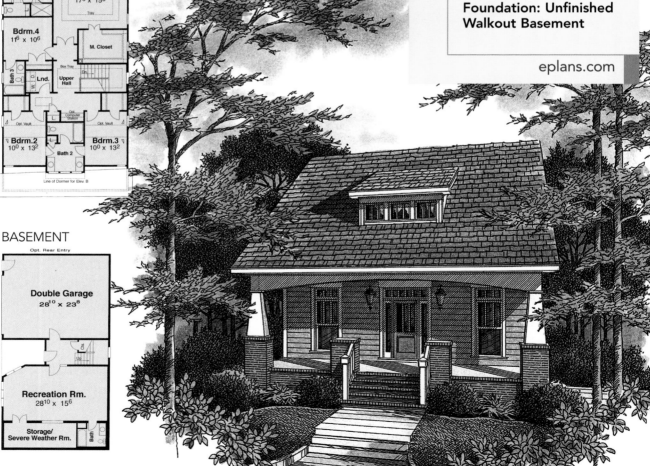

HOME PLAN

HPK2300076

Style: Farmhouse

First Floor: 2,440 sq. ft.

Second Floor: 626 sq. ft.

Total: 3,066 sq. ft.

Bonus Space: 302 sq. ft.

Bedrooms: 3

Bathrooms: 2 ½

Width: 83' - 0"

Depth: 77' - 0"

Foundation: Crawlspace

eplans.com

FIRST FLOOR

COVERED PATIO

NOOK
11/0 X 11/6 +/-
(9' CLG)

SNACK BAR

TWO STORY
GREAT RM.
17/6 X 23/6

MASTER
17/4 X 15/0
(11'-6" CLG)

GARAGE
16/6 X 25/0

MEDIA CENTER

SPA

PANTRY

BUTLER'S PANTRY

UP

DINING
11/4 X 16/0 +/-
(9' CLG)

DRAWERS BELOW

BUILT-IN

GARAGE
21/0 X 22/6

PORCH
18/6 X 6/0

OFFICE
12/0 X 11/0
(9' CLG)

SECOND FLOOR

UNFINISHED
BONUS RM.
16/6 X 15/6 +/-

BR. 2
12/5 X 12/0

GREAT RM BELOW

ATTIC STORAGE

LINEN

DN

BR. 3
11/0 X 14/2 +/-

FOYER BELOW

PLANT SHELF

MIXED EXTERIOR TEXTURES—SHINGLES, SIDING, and stone—create a distinctive look for this traditional plan. An efficient home office, brightened by two sets of windows, sits to the right of the foyer; the dining room, defined by columns, sits to the left. Directly ahead, the two-story great room offers a built-in media center and a fireplace. Nearby, the kitchen boasts an island snack bar and adjoins a nook that opens to a covered patio. Sleeping quarters consist of a first-floor master suite and two second-floor bedrooms.

HOMES WITH ROOM TO GROW

Narrow Lots—Wide Selection

The decreasing availability of land for new homes means that many of today's buildable lots are limited in size. Or perhaps you've chosen to build in an established neighborhood or in an urban environment, in place of a previous construction. Measuring at 45 feet wide—and smaller—all the homes collected in this section are suitable for building on narrow lots.

Designing for a narrow lot poses unique challenges. Because there's no room to waste, the plan must eliminate unnecessary walls and hallways. The resulting layout is usually more open, especially around causal living areas

EVEN A MODEST BATHROOM (above) can add charm and function to a home.

Andrew Lautman Photography; Tony Giammarino (2)

A PRIVATE BALCONY and plenty of windows allow this narrow-lot design to live beyond its square footage.

such as the kitchen. On the other hand, the plan must also create nurturing private spaces. Therefore, the narrow lot homes in this section also provide great master suites—a comfortable, rejuvenating place to start and end your day.

Narrow lot homes capture what we love best about affordable home building. Instead of spending money on sprawling square footage, you can finish these homes with finely detailed, quality spaces that you can appreciate at every moment.

SMARTLY COMPROMISING SQUARE FOOTAGE for custom details and a great location produced this attractive urban home.

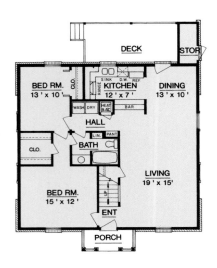

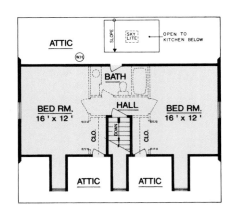

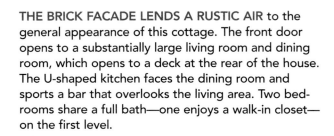

HPK2300077

HOME PLAN

Style: Farmhouse

Square Footage: 1,088

Total: 1,088 sq. ft.

Bedrooms: 2

Bathrooms: 1

Width: 34' - 0"

Depth: 44' - 0"

Foundation: Crawlspace, Slab

eplans.com

THE BRICK FACADE LENDS A RUSTIC AIR to the general appearance of this cottage. The front door opens to a substantially large living room and dining room, which opens to a deck at the rear of the house. The U-shaped kitchen faces the dining room and sports a bar that overlooks the living area. Two bedrooms share a full bath—one enjoys a walk-in closet—on the first level.

HOME PLAN

(#) HPK2300078

Style: Traditional

Square Footage: 1,140

Bedrooms: 3

Bathrooms: 2

Width: 44' - 0"

Depth: 27' - 0"

Foundation: Unfinished Basement

eplans.com

THIS STELLAR SINGLE-STORY SYMMETRICAL HOME offers plenty of living space for any family. The front porch and rear deck make outdoor entertaining delightful. The living and dining rooms are open and spacious for family gatherings. A well-organized kitchen with an abundance of cabinetry and a built-in pantry completes the functional plan. Three bedrooms reside on the left side of the plan.

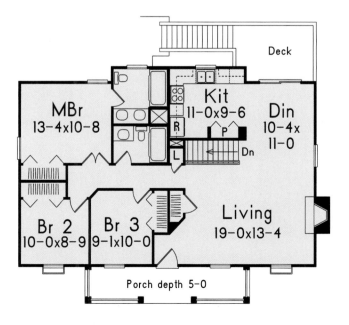

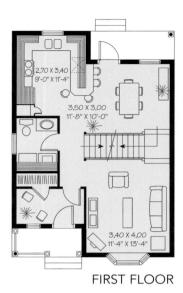

FIRST FLOOR

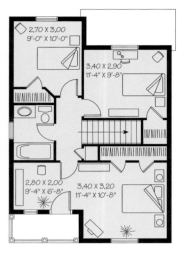

SECOND FLOOR

DOWN-HOME COMFORT ENHANCES THE UPTOWN SPIRIT of this traditional home. A charming bay window brightens the living room. A U-shaped kitchen serves a snack counter as well as the dining area, which opens to a rear porch. Upstairs, the second-floor master bedroom offers a reading area and a private balcony. A full bath serves the second-floor sleeping quarters; a powder room is conveniently located on the first floor.

HOME PLAN

HPK2300079

Style: Colonial

First Floor: 626 sq. ft.

Second Floor: 619 sq. ft.

Total: 1,245 sq. ft.

Bedrooms: 3

Bathrooms: 1 ½

Width: 22' - 0"

Depth: 32' - 0"

Foundation: Unfinished Basement

eplans.com

WITH A MASTER BEDROOM AND LIVING AREA THAT OPENS TO THE REAR, this is a home that begs for a terrific backyard. It offers great privacy while creating a sense of spaciousness with its open design. The kitchen includes a breakfast bar that opens to the living room. The living room has a corner fireplace and French doors that lead to the covered rear porch. The master bath has an oversized tub/shower and a double-sink vanity area. In addition to the master suite, this home has two other bedrooms and another full bath.

HPK2300080

Style: Farmhouse
Square Footage: 1,363
Bedrooms: 3
Bathrooms: 2
Width: 30' - 0"
Depth: 60' - 0"
Foundation: Slab

HOME PLAN

eplans.com

HOMES FOR NARROW LOTS

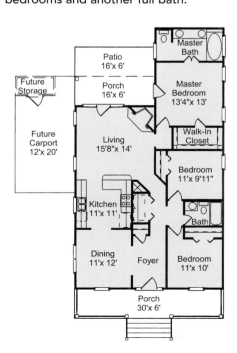

Master Bath

Patio 16'x 6'

Porch 16'x 6'

Master Bedroom 13'4"x 13'

Future Storage

Future Carport 12'x 20'

Living 15'8"x 14'

Walk-In Closet

Bedroom 11'x 9'11"

Kitchen 11'x 11'

Bath

Dining 11'x 12'

Foyer

Bedroom 11'x 10'

Porch 30'x 6'

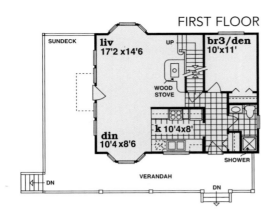

FIRST FLOOR

SUNDECK

liv
17'2 x14'6

UP

br3/den
10'x11'

WOOD
STOVE

din
10'4 x8'6

k 10'4x8'

SHOWER

DN

VERANDAH

DN

SECOND FLOOR

BALCONY

mbr
11'2x15'8

br2
10'x11'4

L

DN

VAULTED
CEILING

HOME PLAN # HPK2300081

Style: Country Cottage

First Floor: 792 sq. ft.

Second Floor: 573 sq. ft.

Total: 1,365 sq. ft.

Bedrooms: 3

Bathrooms: 2

Width: 42' - 0"

Depth: 32' - 0"

Foundation: Crawlspace, Unfinished Basement

eplans.com

THIS DISTINCTIVE VACATION HOME is designed ideally for a gently sloping lot, which allows for a daylight basement. It can, however, accommodate a flat lot nicely. An expansive veranda sweeps around two sides of the exterior and is complemented by full-height windows. Decorative woodwork and traditional multipane windows belie the contemporary interior. An open living/dining room, with a woodstove and two bay windows, is complemented by a galley-style kitchen. A bedroom, or den, on the first floor has the use of a full bath. The second floor includes a master bedroom with a balcony, and one family bedroom. Both second-floor bedrooms have dormer windows and share a full bath that has a vaulted ceiling.

REAR EXTERIOR

HOME PLAN

HPK2300082

Style: Traditional

Square Footage: 1,401

Bedrooms: 3

Bathrooms: 2

Width: 30' - 0"

Depth: 59' - 10"

Foundation: Slab

eplans.com

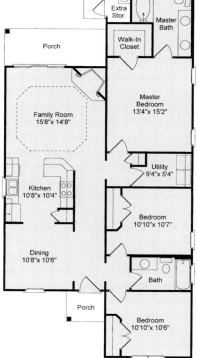

A PROMINENT FRONT GABLE AND COUNTRY-STYLE SHUTTERS lend rustic flair to this otherwise traditional home. A sensible floor plan separates living areas—located on the left side of the plan—from sleeping quarters, which sit to the right of the home. Special amenities in the living spaces include a fireplace and tray ceiling in the family room and a pantry in the kitchen; a rear covered porch offers space for outdoor activities. Each family bedroom includes a closet and access to a full bath; the master suite provides a walk-in closet and a lavish private bath.

HOMES FOR NARROW LOTS

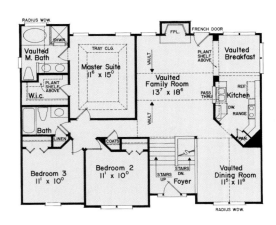

OFFERING THE BEST IN MODERN AMENITIES AND FAMILY DETAILS, this plan creates a comfortable home with room to expand. Enter from a midlevel foyer and continue up to find a hearth-warmed family room. Vaulted ceilings throughout combine with abundant natural light to visually expand the spaces, making the home appear larger than it is. The kitchen is situated to make serving a cinch, opening to the breakfast nook and dining room on either side, and with a pass-through to the family room. On the left, two secondary bedrooms that share a full bath join the luxurious master suite to complete the plan. The lower level houses a two-car garage and unfinished areas that can be completed at any time.

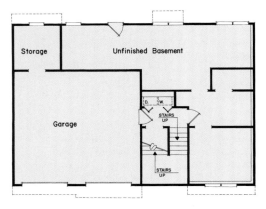

HOME PLAN

(#) HPK2300083

Design: HPK2300083

Style: Colonial

Square Footage: 1,401

Bedrooms: 3

Bathrooms: 2

Width: 43' - 0"

Depth: 33' - 6"

Foundation: Unfinished Walkout Basement

eplans.com

HOME PLAN

HPK2300084

Style: Craftsman

First Floor: 436 sq. ft.

Second Floor: 792 sq. ft.

Third Floor: 202 sq. ft.

Total: 1,430 sq. ft.

Bedrooms: 2

Bathrooms: 2

Width: 16' - 0"

Depth: 54' - 0"

Foundation: Crawlspace

eplans.com

FOR AN IN-FILL LOT, A LAKE SITE, OR SEASIDE RETREAT, this plan offers three floors of living and a very narrow footprint to make it conform to your needs. A high-pitched roofline accommodates an enchanting dormer window, and a covered porch screens the set-back entry. The lower floor at garage level holds a bedroom with full bath and laundry alcove. Built-ins include a desk and drawers along one wall. Outdoor access leads to convenient storage for lawn equipment and other essentials. The main level upstairs holds a vaulted living room with built-in media center, and L-shaped booth seating for dining, an island kitchen with double-door pantry and display shelves, and the master suite. An outdoor deck lies just beyond the living area. A cozy vaulted study loft is graced by a huge built-in bookshelf.

FIRST FLOOR

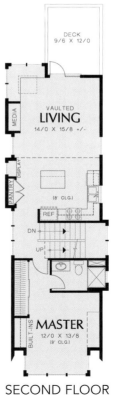

SECOND FLOOR

HERE'S A PLAN WITH LOTS OF FLEXIBILITY and open space to organize the living and dining areas to suit your needs. There's also an option of adding a fireplace. The kitchen is marked off from the living/dining area by a handy snack bar. Upstairs, a master suite with a dual-sink vanity enjoys a private bath; two family bedrooms share a bath. This plan is well-suited for a narrow lot.

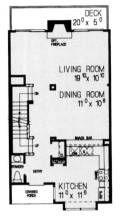

FIRST FLOOR

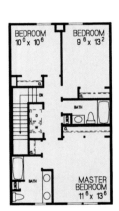

SECOND FLOOR

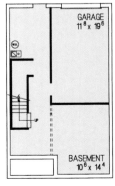

BASEMENT

REAR EXTERIOR

HPK2300085

Style: Colonial

First Floor: 685 sq. ft.

Second Floor: 760 sq. ft.

Total: 1,445 sq. ft.

Bedrooms: 3

Bathrooms: 2 ½

Width: 21' - 0"

Depth: 36' - 0"

Foundation: Unfinished Basement

HOME PLAN

eplans.com

TRADITIONAL AND CRAFTSMAN ELEMENTS shape the exterior of this lovely family home. The two-story foyer leads down the hall to a great room with a warming fireplace. The U-shaped kitchen includes a window sink and is open to the breakfast nook. A powder room is located near the garage. Upstairs, the master suite provides a private bath and walk-in closet. The two family bedrooms share a full hall bath across from the second-floor laundry room. Linen closets are available in the hall and inside the full hall bath.

HPK2300086

Style: Craftsman
First Floor: 636 sq. ft.
Second Floor: 830 sq. ft.
Total: 1,466 sq. ft.
Bedrooms: 3
Bathrooms: 2 ½
Width: 28' - 0"
Depth: 43' - 6"
Foundation: Crawlspace

eplans.com

FIRST FLOOR

SECOND FLOOR

HOME PLAN

HPK2300087

Style: Traditional

Square Footage: 1,478

Bedrooms: 2

Bathrooms: 2

Width: 42' - 0"

Depth: 55' - 8"

eplans.com

ORNATE BRICK ACCENTS AND TRANSOM WINDOWS decorate this quaint lakeside home. A gallery wall in the entry leads beyond to the great room. The breakfast area has a bay window and provides access to the rear covered porch. The master suite offers a walk-in closet, a corner whirlpool tub and its own door to the covered porch.

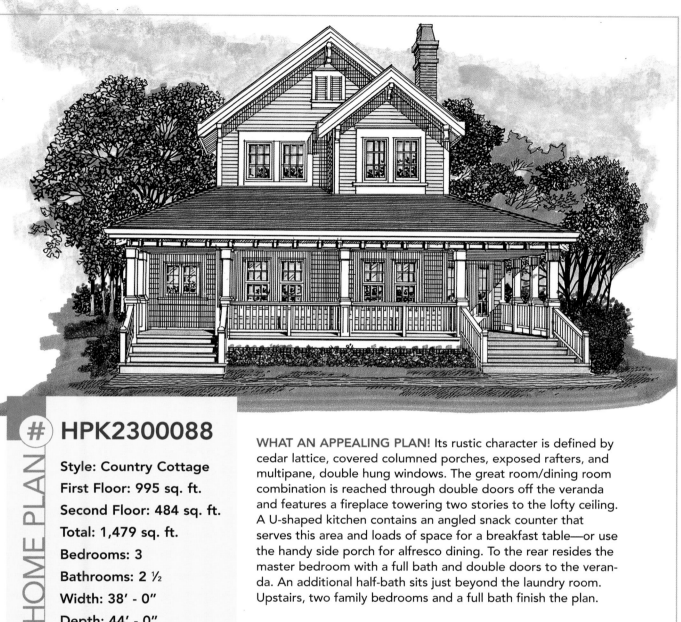

HOME PLAN

HPK2300088

Style: Country Cottage

First Floor: 995 sq. ft.

Second Floor: 484 sq. ft.

Total: 1,479 sq. ft.

Bedrooms: 3

Bathrooms: 2 ½

Width: 38' - 0"

Depth: 44' - 0"

Foundation: Crawlspace, Unfinished Basement

eplans.com

WHAT AN APPEALING PLAN! Its rustic character is defined by cedar lattice, covered columned porches, exposed rafters, and multipane, double hung windows. The great room/dining room combination is reached through double doors off the veranda and features a fireplace towering two stories to the lofty ceiling. A U-shaped kitchen contains an angled snack counter that serves this area and loads of space for a breakfast table—or use the handy side porch for alfresco dining. To the rear resides the master bedroom with a full bath and double doors to the veranda. An additional half-bath sits just beyond the laundry room. Upstairs, two family bedrooms and a full bath finish the plan.

FIRST FLOOR

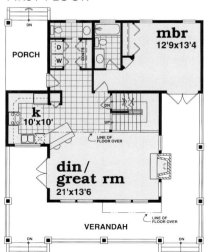

SECOND FLOOR

FIRST FLOOR

SECOND FLOOR

A TRADITIONAL NEIGHBORHOOD LOOK IS ACCENTED BY STONE AND DECORATIVE ARCHES on this stylish new design. Simplicity is the hallmark of this plan, giving the interior great flow and openness. The foyer, with a coat closet, leads directly into the two-story great room with abundant natural light and a warming fireplace. The island kitchen and dining area are to the left and enjoy rear-porch access. Upstairs, a vaulted master suite with a private bath joins two additional bedrooms to complete the plan.

HPK2300089

HOME PLAN

Style: Traditional
First Floor: 716 sq. ft.
Second Floor: 784 sq. ft.
Total: 1,500 sq. ft.
Bedrooms: 3
Bathrooms: 2 ½
Width: 36' - 0"
Depth: 44' - 0"
Foundation: Crawlspace

eplans.com

A COVERED PORCH ADDS INSTANT CURB APPEAL to any style home and this Traditional favorite is no exception. The first-floor master suite is accessible from the entryway. The open layout makes optimum use of the limited space. The kitchen easily serves the adjoining eating area and family room. A rear patio makes alfresco meals an option. Upstairs, two family bedrooms share a full bath. Bonus space on this floor makes a guest room or a gameroom an option. Extra storage space completes this level.

HOME PLAN

HPK2300090

Style: Cottage
First Floor: 1,084 sq. ft.
Second Floor: 461 sq. ft.
Total: 1,545 sq. ft.
Bonus Space: 177 sq. ft.
Bedrooms: 3
Bathrooms: 2 ½
Width: 38' - 0"
Depth: 61' - 0"
Foundation: Crawlspace

eplans.com

HOMES FOR NARROW LOTS

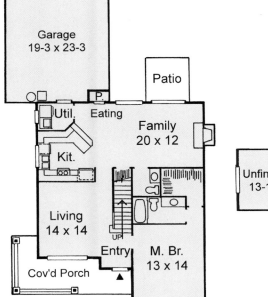

FIRST FLOOR

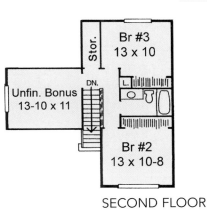

SECOND FLOOR

PETITE IN PROPORTIONS AND SCALED FOR NARROW LOTS—great first-home builders, city in-fill, and empty-nesters—this design considers modern comforts. A casual foyer connects with the vaulted family room adding warmth to the space with a fireplace. A series of windows face the large side patio, extending private living space to the outdoors. The dining room also enjoys the patio view and the convenience of the nearby C-shaped kitchen with walk-in pantry and serving bar. A short, wide hallway makes room for two family bedrooms and a full hall bath. The master suite, enhanced by a tray ceiling, is outfitted with a walk-in closet, roomy bath with dual-sink vanities, separate shower and tub, and a private toilet.

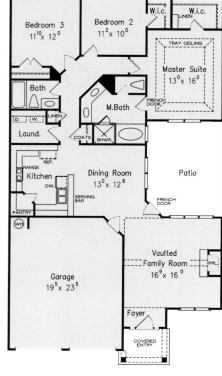

(#) HPK2300091

HOME PLAN

Style: Country Cottage

Square Footage: 1,546

Bedrooms: 3

Bathrooms: 2

Width: 37' - 0"

Depth: 65' - 5"

Foundation: Slab

eplans.com

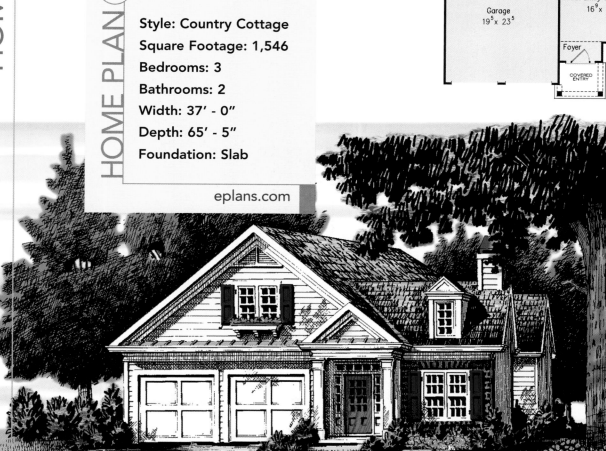

HPK2300092

Style: Traditional

First Floor: 802 sq. ft.

Second Floor: 773 sq. ft.

Total: 1,575 sq. ft.

Bedrooms: 3

Bathrooms: 2 ½

Width: 36' - 0"

Depth: 46' - 8"

Foundation: Unfinished Basement

eplans.com

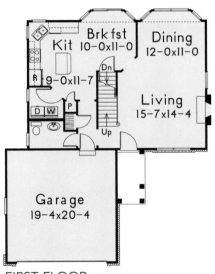

FIRST FLOOR

BRICK AND SIDING ADD CHARACTER to this traditional design. A simple and functional floor plan keeps the casual living space open on the first floor and family quarters private upstairs. An island kitchen offers plenty of counter and storage space, a nearby laundry room, pantry, and adjoining breakfast nook work in unison for a flawless use of space. The master suite enjoys a vaulted ceiling, walk-in closet, and full bath. Two secondary bedrooms share a hall bath.

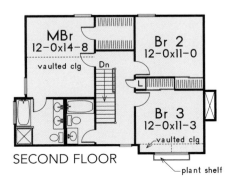

SECOND FLOOR

HOMES FOR NARROW LOTS

FIRST FLOOR

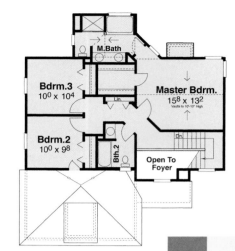

SECOND FLOOR

LOADED WITH CHARM, this mountain cottage takes on the ambiance of a country Victorian with rustic appeal. The two-story foyer opens to a sweep-back staircase, lit by a double-hung window. A spacious hearth-warmed living area views the dining room (with rear patio access) and efficient kitchen. To the left, a built-in desk is perfect as a small office or family organization center. Upstairs, a cathedral ceiling in the master suite adds drama; the private bath soothes and relaxes.

HOME PLAN

HPK2300093

Style: Country Cottage
First Floor: 737 sq. ft.
Second Floor: 840 sq. ft.
Total: 1,577 sq. ft.
Bedrooms: 3
Bathrooms: 2 ½
Width: 36' - 0"
Depth: 42' - 0"
Foundation: Unfinished Basement, Slab

eplans.com

FIRST FLOOR

10'-0" X 12'-4"
3,00 X 3,70

10'-0" X 12'-4"
3,00 X 3,70

12'-0" X 28'-4"
3,60 X 8,50

12'-0" X 14'-0"
3,60 X 4,20

SECOND FLOOR

10'-0" X 12'-4"
3,00 X 3,70

10'-0" X 10'-0"
3,00 X 3,00

12'-0" X 20'-0"
3,60 X 6,00

12'-0" X 14'-0"
3,60 X 4,20

HOME PLAN

 # HPK2300094

Style: Traditional

First Floor: 766 sq. ft.

Second Floor: 812 sq. ft.

Total: 1,578 sq. ft.

Bonus Space: 291 sq. ft.

Bedrooms: 3

Bathrooms: 2 ½

Width: 34' - 0"

Depth: 38' - 0"

Foundation: Unfinished Basement

eplans.com

HOMES FOR NARROW LOTS

SNAPPY ROOFLINES WITH STYLISH SHUTTERED WINDOWS preview the family comforts offered inside this two-story contemporary home. A master bedroom with a private bath that enjoys a shower is separated from two other family bedrooms. All three rooms have hallway access to a swanky bath with a shower and a huge corner tub. The spacious island kitchen has plenty of room for more than one cook (the walk-in pantry is especially attractive) and easily serves the adjoining dining area. A laundry opens from the kitchen and a half-bath is located down the hall. The front living room can be entered through the foyer, which comes with a roomy coat closet.

FIRST FLOOR

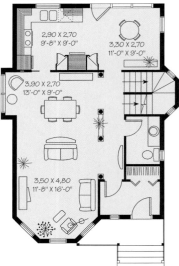

SECOND FLOOR

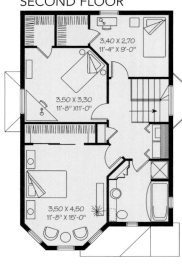

HPK2300095

Style: Victorian

First Floor: 805 sq. ft.

Second Floor: 779 sq. ft.

Total: 1,584 sq. ft.

Bedrooms: 3

Bathrooms: 1 ½

Width: 25' - 0"

Depth: 36' - 0"

Foundation: Unfinished Basement

eplans.com

THE CHARMING FRONT PORCH AND THE TWO-STORY TURRET welcome guests to this lovely home. The turret houses the living room on the first floor and the master suite on the second floor. The dining room is open to the living room and provides a box-bay window. The L-shaped kitchen features a breakfast room accessible to the backyard. A curved staircase next to the powder room leads upstairs to three bedrooms and a bath. Each family bedroom contains a walk-in closet.

(#) HPK2300096

Style: Craftsman

First Floor: 993 sq. ft.

Second Floor: 642 sq. ft.

Total: 1,635 sq. ft.

Bedrooms: 2

Bathrooms: 2 ½

Width: 28' - 0"

Depth: 44' - 0"

Foundation: Finished Walkout Basement

eplans.com

THIS MODERN THREE-LEVEL HOME IS JUST RIGHT FOR A YOUNG FAMILY. The main level features a study, kitchen, dining room, laundry, and two-story living room with a corner fireplace. A rear patio makes summertime grilling fun. The master bedroom is vaulted and features a double-bowl vanity bath and walk-in closet. Bedroom 2 offers its own full bath as well. The basement level boasts a spacious garage and storage area.

FIRST FLOOR

SECOND FLOOR

BASEMENT

FIRST FLOOR

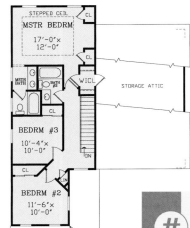

FAMILY RM
17'-0" x 10'-0"
OPT. MEDIA UNIT LOCATION

KITCHEN
13'-8" x 8'-0"

LAV.

LAUN RM

UTIL

PANT

CL

UP   UP

TWO CAR GARAGE
18'-0" x 20'-0"

LOCATION OF OPT BSMT STAIR

DINING RM
10'-4" x 11'-0"

CL

FOY

9'-4" CEIL
LIVING RM
11'-6" x 16'-0"

OPT. FIREPLACE

METER & TRASH CAN ALCOVE

PLANTER

COV. PORCH

SECOND FLOOR

STEPPED CEIL
MSTR BEDRM
17'-0" x 12'-0"

CL

CL

MSTR BATH

BATH #2

WICL

STORAGE ATTIC

CL

BEDRM #3
10'-4" x 10'-0"

DN

CL

LIN

BEDRM #2
11'-6" x 10'-0"

WITH A WRAPPING FRONT PORCH that just begs for summer's lazy days, this three-bedroom farmhouse is a step back in time. Arches and columns define the foyer, which opens to the hearth-warmed living room and dining room. At the rear, the family room and island kitchen combine to form a casual space, just right for relaxing. Utility rooms line the back of the two-car garage. Bedrooms are located upstairs, including two secondary bedrooms and a spacious master suite. An additional walk-in closet can be found in the hall and gives access to abundant attic space.

HOME PLAN

HPK2300097

Style: Traditional
First Floor: 880 sq. ft.
Second Floor: 755 sq. ft.
Total: 1,635 sq. ft.
Bedrooms: 3
Bathrooms: 2 ½
Width: 36' - 0"
Depth: 54' - 4"
Foundation: Crawlspace, Slab, Unfinished Basement

eplans.com

FIRST FLOOR

SECOND FLOOR

HOME PLAN

HPK2300098

Style: Craftsman

First Floor: 897 sq. ft.

Second Floor: 740 sq. ft.

Total: 1,637 sq. ft.

Bedrooms: 3

Bathrooms: 2 ½

Width: 30' - 0"

Depth: 42' - 6"

Foundation: Unfinished Walkout Basement

eplans.com

BASEMENT

WITH A GARAGE ON THE GROUND LEVEL, this home takes a much smaller footprint and is perfect for narrow-lot applications. Take a short flight of stairs up to the entry, which opens to a receiving hall and then to the living and dining combination. The living room features a fireplace flanked by bookshelves. The island kitchen and nook are to the rear, near a half-bath. Upstairs are two family bedrooms sharing a full bath and the vaulted master suite, with a private bath and dual walk-in closets.

STARTING WITH POSSIBILITY, THIS COUNTRY HOME OFFERS ROOM TO GROW with a versatile second floor. The quaint covered porch is a welcome sight and introduces the unusually shaped living room, which features a stepped ceiling. The kitchen is open to the dining room and is a friendly place to cook up great meals and entertain guests. Secluded are the master bedroom and two secondary bedrooms. A convenient laundry closet and full bath service this area. Upstairs, two more family bedrooms—one with a large walk-in closet—and a full bath complete this design.

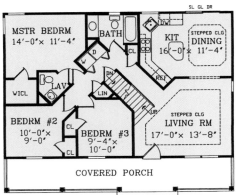

FIRST FLOOR

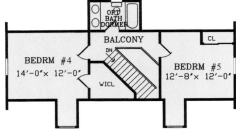

SECOND FLOOR

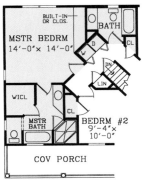

OPTIONAL LAYOUT

HOME PLAN

HPK2300099

Style: Country

First Floor: 1,040 sq. ft.

Second Floor: 597 sq. ft.

Total: 1,637 sq. ft.

Bedrooms: 5

Bathrooms: 2 ½

Width: 40' - 0"

Depth: 32' - 0"

Foundation: Slab, Unfinished Basement, Crawlspace

eplans.com

HOME PLAN

HPK2300100

Style: Traditional

First Floor: 740 sq. ft.

Second Floor: 898 sq. ft.

Total: 1,638 sq. ft.

Bedrooms: 3

Bathrooms: 2 ½

Width: 35' - 0"

Depth: 31' - 6"

Foundation: Slab

eplans.com

FIRST FLOOR

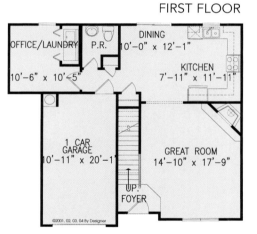

SECOND FLOOR

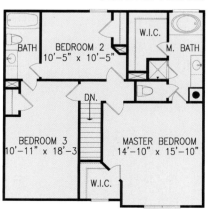

SIMPLE AND SPACIOUS...this two-story home is a great place to raise a family. A special feature is the first-floor home office, which is considerately located away from the main living areas and the second-floor bedrooms. The kitchen and dining area fit well together allowing for great flexibility. The living room enjoys a warming corner fireplace. A deluxe bath and His and Hers walk-in closets make the upstairs master suite special. On the same floor two family bedrooms share a bath. A laundry and half-bath are located near the exit to the garage.

FIRST FLOOR

SECOND FLOOR

BRACKETS AND BALUSTRADES ON FRONT AND REAR COVERED PORCHES spell old-fashioned country charm on this rustic retreat. Warm evenings will invite family and guests outdoors for watching sunsets and stars. In cooler weather, the raised-hearth fireplace will make the great room a cozy place to gather. The nearby kitchen serves both a snack bar and a breakfast nook. Two family bedrooms and a full bath complete the main level. Upstairs, a master suite with a sloped ceiling offers a window seat and a complete bath. The adjacent loft/study overlooks the great room.

HOME PLAN

(#) HPK2300101

Style: Farmhouse

First Floor: 1,093 sq. ft.

Second Floor: 580 sq. ft.

Total: 1,673 sq. ft.

Bedrooms: 3

Bathrooms: 2

Width: 36' - 0"

Depth: 52' - 0"

Foundation: Crawlspace

eplans.com

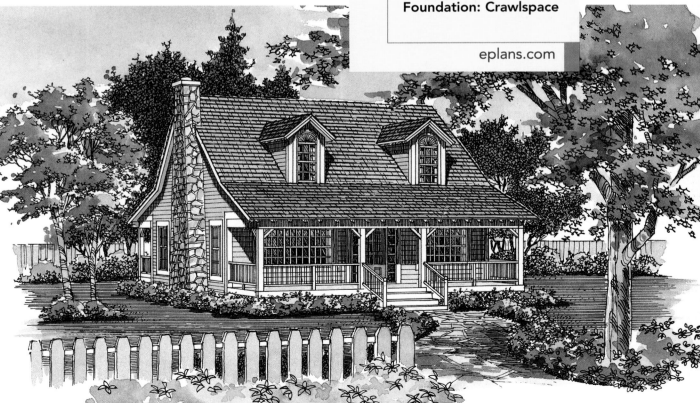

© 2001 Donald A. Gardner, Inc.

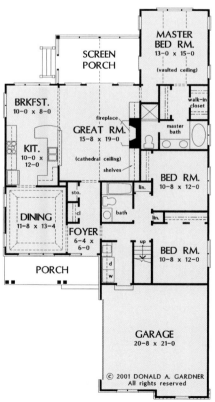

SCREEN PORCH

MASTER BED RM.
13-0 x 15-0
(vaulted ceiling)

walk-in closet

BRKFST.
10-0 x 8-0

fireplace

GREAT RM.
15-8 x 19-0
(cathedral ceiling)

master bath

KIT.
10-0 x 12-0

shelves

BED RM.
10-8 x 12-0

lin.

sto.

cl

bath

DINING
11-8 x 13-4

FOYER
6-4 x 6-0

lin.

PORCH

up

BED RM.
10-8 x 12-0

d w

GARAGE
20-8 x 21-0

HOME PLAN

HPK2300102

Style: Craftsman

Square Footage: 1,682

Bonus Space: 320 sq. ft.

Bedrooms: 3

Bathrooms: 2

Width: 40' - 0"

Depth: 78' - 4"

eplans.com

THIS ARTS AND CRAFTS COTTAGE COMBINES STONE AND STUCCO TO CREATE an Old World feel. From decorative wood brackets and columns to arched windows and shutters, the details produce architectural interest and absolute charm. This design features plenty of windows and French doors to invite nature inside. Built-in cabinetry enhances the interior and provides convenience. Topping the great room is a cathedral ceiling, and a tray ceiling completes the dining room. The master suite, which features a vaulted ceiling in the bedroom and an ample master bath, lies next to the screened porch. A bonus room, accessible from two additional bedrooms, would make a perfect game room for the family.

HOMES FOR NARROW LOTS

FIRST FLOOR

10'-8" X 10'-0"
3,20 X 3,00

9'-0" X 14'-4"
2,70 X 4,30

14'-0" X 14'-0"
4,20 X 4,20

11'-0" X 12'-0"
3,30 X 3,60

THE WRAPAROUND FRONT PORCH WELCOMES YOU HOME to this classic country farmhouse design. Two floors of family-friendly space await inside. The first level is devoted to living spaces. An island kitchen with plenty of space for helping hands has direct access to both a formal dining room and an informal niche backed by a wall of windows with views to the rear yard. Assemble the kids and some friends in the great room for a movie or a board game. Three bedrooms are situated upstairs, including the master bedroom with a large walk-in closet. The bathroom is shared by all rooms and has a dual-sink vanity, separate tub and shower, and plenty of space.

11'-8" X 11'-0"
3,50 X 3,30

13'-0" X 14'-0"
3,90 X 4,20

11'-0" X 11'-0"
3,30 X 3,30

SECOND FLOOR

HOME PLAN

(#) HPK2300103

Style: Country

First Floor: 860 sq. ft.

Second Floor: 840 sq. ft.

Total: 1,700 sq. ft.

Bedrooms: 3

Bathrooms: 1 ½

Width: 30' - 0"

Depth: 29' - 0"

Foundation: Unfinished Basement

eplans.com

HOME PLAN

HPK2300104

Style: Traditional

First Floor: 876 sq. ft.

Second Floor: 834 sq. ft.

Total: 1,710 sq. ft.

Bedrooms: 3

Bathrooms: 2 ½

Width: 35' - 0"

Depth: 39' - 8"

Foundation: Slab

eplans.com

WHEN YOU ENTER THIS CONGENIAL TWO-STORY HOME, you immediately step into the spacious great room with a charming corner fireplace. From here a wide door opens to the dining and kitchen area, marked by its open and flexible layout. Especially appealing on this floor is the back-corner home office with a close-by half-bath. Sleeping quarters are upstairs...an extraordinary master suite and two family bedrooms. Highlights of the private master bath are twin vanities, an oversize tub, and a separate shower. The other bedrooms share a bath with hall access. Extra room is available on the second level for storage.

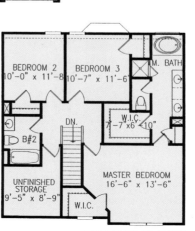

SECOND FLOOR

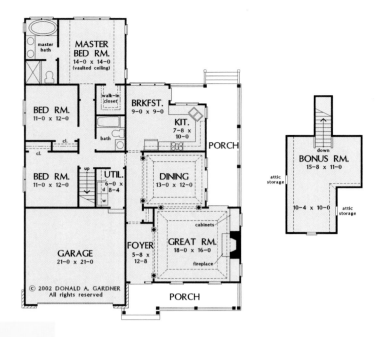

HOME PLAN

HPK2300105

Style: Country
Square Footage: 1,711
Bonus Space: 328 sq. ft.
Bedrooms: 3
Bathrooms: 2
Width: 46' - 6"
Depth: 65' - 0"

eplans.com

THIS STRIKING NARROW-LOT BUNGALOW FEATURES AN ARCHED ENTRANCE, nostalgic front porch, and hip roof. A sidelight and fanlight over the front door usher natural light into the home and columns are used to divide space without enclosing it. Featuring a fireplace and built-in cabinetry, the great room accesses both the porch and the dining room. Columns and a tray ceiling define the dining room, which also leads to the side porch through French doors. Above the garage, there is a bonus room for expansion needs. A vaulted ceiling and spacious walk-in closet highlight the master bedroom. The master bath includes a double vanity, garden tub, and separate shower.

FIRST FLOOR

110" X 138"
3,30 X 4,10

10-4" X 1-8"
3,10 X 3,50

12-0" X 158"
3,60 X 4,70

12-0" X 24-0"
3,60 X 7,20

SECOND FLOOR

13-0" X 120"
3,90 X 3,60

12-4" X 120"
3,70 X 3,60

9-8" X 9-4"
2,90 X 2,80

HOME PLAN

HPK2300106

Style: Gothic Revival

First Floor: 837 sq. ft.

Second Floor: 890 sq. ft.

Total: 1,727 sq. ft.

Bedrooms: 3

Bathrooms: 2

Width: 36' - 0"

Depth: 39' - 8"

Foundation: Unfinished Basement

eplans.com

WITH STUCCO ACCENTS, HIPPED ROOFLINES, AND GRACEFUL DETAILS, this fine two-story home will be a delight to live in. The foyer acts as an air lock, preventing cold breezes from reaching the living areas. A two-story living room is to the right of the foyer and offers a warming fireplace. At the rear of the home, the efficient open kitchen offers a worktop island with snack bar, and a window sink. Upstairs, three bedrooms—each with walk-in closets—share a spacious bath. One bedroom provides a small, private sitting room.

HOMES FOR NARROW LOTS

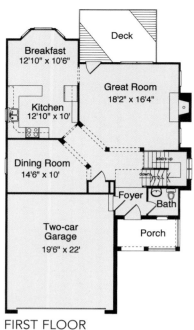

FIRST FLOOR

Deck

Breakfast
12'10" x 10'6"

Great Room
18'2" x 16'4"

Kitchen
12'10" x 10'

Dining Room
14'6" x 10'

stairs up

down

Foyer

Bath

Two-car Garage
19'6" x 22'

Porch

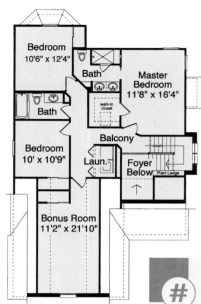

SECOND FLOOR

Bedroom
10'6" x 12'4"

Bath

Master Bedroom
11'8" x 16'4"

Bath

walk-in closet

Bedroom
10' x 10'9"

Balcony

Laun.

down

Foyer Below

Plant Ledge

Bonus Room
11'2" x 21'10"

DESIGNED FOR A NARROW LOT, this two-story home creates a package that offers maximum living space in a small footprint. The large great room features a fireplace and multiple windows. A delightful place to start the day, the bayed breakfast area enjoys plenty of sunshine. The formal dining room opens to the great room and is adorned with columns. On the second level, a master bedroom with a large walk-in closet and private bath is joined by two family bedrooms, a laundry, and a hall bath. Note the bonus room available for future expansion.

HOME PLAN

HPK2300107

Style: European Cottage

First Floor: 939 sq. ft.

Second Floor: 788 sq. ft.

Total: 1,727 sq. ft.

Bonus Space: 210 sq. ft.

Bedrooms: 3

Bathrooms: 2 ½

Width: 34' - 0"

Depth: 52' - 0"

Foundation: Unfinished Walkout Basement

eplans.com

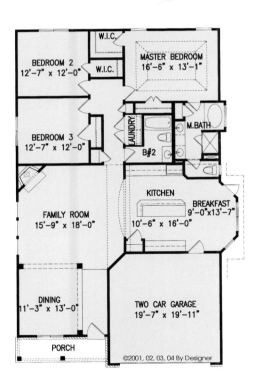

HPK2300108

HOME PLAN

Square Footage: 1,768

Bedrooms: 3

Bathrooms: 2

Width: 36' - 0"

Depth: 61' - 5"

Foundation: Slab

eplans.com

THIS COMFY FAMILY BUNGALOW WILL FIT WELL on a narrow lot. The kitchen, with a handy island counter, draws together into a spacious activity area the sunny breakfast bay and the family room, brightened by a corner fireplace. A more formal dining room is situated near the front entry. In the rear, three bedrooms—one a master suite with a posh private bath—provide ample sleeping quarters. A laundry room in the bedroom area and a front-loading two-car garage complete this plan.

HOMES FOR NARROW LOTS

FIRST FLOOR

SECOND FLOOR

THIRD FLOOR

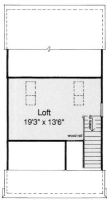

HOME PLAN

HPK2300109

Style: Adam

First Floor: 774 sq. ft.

Second Floor: 754 sq. ft.

Third Floor: 260 sq. ft.

Total: 1,788 sq. ft.

Bedrooms: 2

Bathrooms: 2 ½

Width: 20' - 0"

Depth: 40' - 0"

Foundation: Unfinished Basement

eplans.com

THE LUXURY OF DETACHED HOUSING, combined with the convenience and sophistication of city living, serves as the primary focus of this home. Provocative touches, such as a corner fireplace in the great room, a generous open floor plan, third-floor loft, and an expansive master suite, highlight the Neo-Traditional design. The warmth of the fireplace, windows across the rear (overlooking a courtyard), and angled rear entry are alluring touches. With an expansive rear patio and porch, emphasis is placed on a balance of indoor-outdoor living.

STONE ACCENTS, SET AGAINST A STUCCO FACADE WITH CONTRASTING TRIM, create a distinctive and tasteful home that will be a treasure to own for generations. The entry is lit by an arched transom window and opens on the left to a living room or formal dining room. The great room takes advantage of a two-way fireplace shared with the hearth room and includes a handy entertainment niche. An island kitchen, with a window over the sink, easily serves the bayed dinette. Bedrooms are located upstairs, situated around a central vault; two secondary bedrooms share a full bath to the right. The master suite hosts a vaulted bedroom ceiling and a bath with a sloped ceiling, spa tub, and walk-in closet. A laundry room on this level is an added convenience.

HOME PLAN

HPK2300110

Style: Traditional
First Floor: 906 sq. ft.
Second Floor: 886 sq. ft.
Total: 1,792 sq. ft.
Bonus Space: 271 sq. ft.
Bedrooms: 3
Bathrooms: 2 ½
Width: 38' - 0"
Depth: 43' - 0"
Foundation: Crawlspace, Slab, Unfinished Basement

eplans.com

HOMES FOR NARROW LOTS

FIRST FLOOR

SECOND FLOOR

FIRST FLOOR

SECOND FLOOR

FAMILY
14/8 X 13/8

NOOK
9/8 X 13/8

REF

P

DINING
13/0 X 10/0

GARAGE
20/4 X 21/4 +/-

UP

LIVING
13/0 X 12/4 +/-

BR. 3
12/0 X 10/0

BR. 2
11/0 X 10/0

LIN

DN.

D. W.

NICHE

LINEN

BONUS RM.
14/4 X 10/0 +/-

FOYER BELOW

MASTER
13/0 X 16/6 +/-
(9'-6" CLG.)

HOME PLAN

HPK2300111

Style: Traditional

First Floor: 972 sq. ft.

Second Floor: 843 sq. ft.

Total: 1,815 sq. ft.

Bonus Space: 180 sq. ft.

Bedrooms: 3

Bathrooms: 2 ½

Width: 45' - 0"

Depth: 37' - 0"

Foundation: Crawlspace

eplans.com

A BRICK ARCH AND A TWO-STORY BAY WINDOW adorn the facade of this comfortable family home. Inside, the formal bayed living room and dining room combine to make entertaining a breeze. At the rear of the home, family life is easy with the open floor plan of the family room, breakfast nook, and efficient kitchen. A fireplace graces the family room, and sliding glass doors access the outdoors from the nook. A powder room is conveniently located in the entry hall. Upstairs, three bedrooms include the master suite with a pampering bath. A full hall bath with twin vanities is shared by the family bedrooms. A bonus room is available for future development as a study, library, or fourth bedroom.

HPK2300112

Style: NW Contemporary
First Floor: 1,022 sq. ft.
Second Floor: 813 sq. ft.
Total: 1,835 sq. ft.
Bedrooms: 3
Bathrooms: 2 ½
Width: 36' - 0"
Depth: 33' - 0"
Foundation: Slab

eplans.com

THIS HOME IS QUITE A "LOOKER" WITH ITS STEEPLY SLOPING ROOFLINES and large sunburst and multipane windows. This plan not only accommodates a narrow lot, but it also fits a sloping site. The angled corner entry gives way to a two-story living room with a tiled hearth. The dining room shares an interesting angled space with this area and enjoys easy service from the efficient kitchen. The family room offers double doors to a refreshing balcony. A powder room and laundry room complete the main level. Upstairs, a vaulted master bedroom enjoys a private bath; two other bedrooms share a bath.

FIRST FLOOR

SECOND FLOOR

FIRST FLOOR

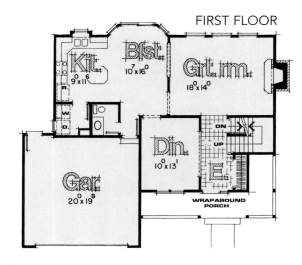

SECOND FLOOR

THIS WONDERFUL DESIGN BEGINS WITH THE WRAPAROUND PORCH. Explore further and find a two-story entry with a coat closet and plant shelf above and a strategically placed staircase alongside. The island kitchen with a boxed window over the sink is adjacent to a large bay-windowed dinette. The great room includes many windows and a fireplace. A powder room and laundry room are both conveniently placed on the first floor. Upstairs, the large master suite contains His and Hers walk-in closets, corner windows, and a bath area featuring a double vanity and whirlpool tub. Two pleasant secondary bedrooms have interesting angles, and a third bedroom in the front features a volume ceiling and an arched window.

HPK2300113

HOME PLAN

Style: Traditional

First Floor: 919 sq. ft.

Second Floor: 927 sq. ft.

Total: 1,846 sq. ft.

Bedrooms: 4

Bathrooms: 2 ½

Width: 44' - 0"

Depth: 40' - 0"

eplans.com

HOME PLAN

HPK2300114

Design: HPK2300114

Style: Bungalow

Square Footage: 1,850

Bedrooms: 3

Bathrooms: 2

Width: 44' - 0"

Depth: 68' - 0"

Foundation: Crawlspace

eplans.com

WITH ALL OF THE TANTALIZING ELEMENTS OF A COTTAGE AND THE COMFORTABLE SPACE OF A FAMILY-SIZED HOME, this Arts and Crafts one-story is the best of both worlds. Exterior accents such as stone wainscot, cedar shingles under the gable ends, and mission-style windows enhance this effect. Three bedrooms are aligned along the right of the interior, situated behind the garage, shielding them from street noise. Bedroom 3 and the master bedroom have walk-in closets; a tray ceiling decorates the master salon. Living and dining areas include a large great room, a dining room with sliding glass doors to a rear patio, and a private den with window seat and vaulted ceiling. A warming hearth lights the great room—right next to a built-in media center. The open corner kitchen features a 42-inch snack bar counter and giant walk-in pantry.

FIRST FLOOR

SECOND FLOOR

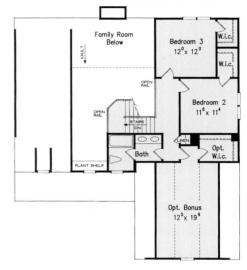

HOME PLAN

HPK2300115

Style: Colonial Revival

Main Level: 1,359 sq. ft.

Upper Level: 520 sq. ft.

Total: 1,879 sq. ft.

Bonus Space: 320 sq. ft.

Bedrooms: 3

Bathrooms: 2 ½

Width: 45' - 0"

Depth: 52' - 4"

Foundation: Crawlspace, Unfinished Walkout Basement

eplans.com

THIS FRESH-FACED COUNTRY COTTAGE TAKES THE BEST TRADITIONAL ELEMENTS AND ADDS A MODERN TWIST. The two-story foyer has a decorative plant shelf above; the vaulted dining room is adjacent, and flows into the angled kitchen. A serving bar to the vaulted breakfast nook is a convenient touch. In the family room, a vaulted ceiling is balanced by the rear fireplace, framed by windows. The first-floor master suite is a lavish retreat with a private spa bath. Upstairs, two bedrooms share a compartmented bath and optional bonus space, perfect as a playroom, home office or gym.

(#) HPK2300116

Style: Traditional

First Floor: 1,347 sq. ft.

Second Floor: 537 sq. ft.

Total: 1,884 sq. ft.

Bedrooms: 3

Bathrooms: 2 ½

Width: 32' - 10"

Depth: 70' - 10"

Foundation: Crawlspace

eplans.com

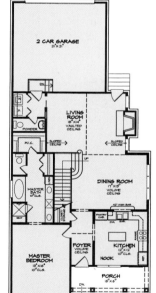

FIRST FLOOR

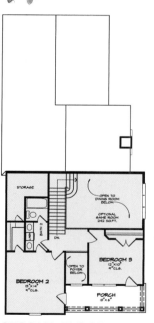

SECOND FLOOR

THIS OLD-FASHIONED TOWNHOUSE DESIGN features an attractive two-story floor plan. Two front covered porches enhance the traditional facade. Inside, the foyer introduces an island kitchen that overlooks the dining room. A formal two-story living room, located at the rear of the plan, is warmed by a fireplace. The first-floor master suite enjoys a private bath and huge walk-in closet. A powder room, laundry room, and two-car garage complete the first floor. Upstairs, two secondary bedrooms—one with a walk-in closet—share a full hall bath. Bedroom 3 features a private balcony overlooking the front property. Optional storage is available on the second floor.

FIRST FLOOR

DECK

BREAKFAST
10'-0" x 7'-0"

GREAT ROOM
18'-6" x 15'-6"

KITCHEN
12'-0" x 10'-10"

UP

DN

FOYER

DINING
9'-6" x 12'-10"

POWDER

TWO-CAR GARAGE
20'-0" x 21'-0"

PORCH

THE PLEASING CHARACTER OF THIS HOUSE DOES NOT STOP behind its facade. The foyer opens to a great room with a fireplace and also to the eat-in kitchen. Stairs lead from the great room to the second floor, where a laundry room is conveniently placed near the bedrooms. The master suite spares none of the amenities: a full bath with a double vanity, shower, tub, and walk-in closet. Bedrooms 2 and 3 share a full bath.

SECOND FLOOR

MASTER SUITE
14'-10" x 15'-8"

M. BATH

LAUN.
6'-0" x 5'-8"

W.I.C.

BEDROOM No.3
10'-0" x 12'-10"

BEDROOM NO. 2
12'-0" X 14'-0"

BATH

HPK2300117

Style: Colonial

First Floor: 830 sq. ft.

Second Floor: 1,060 sq. ft.

Total: 1,890 sq. ft.

Bedrooms: 3

Bathrooms: 2 ½

Width: 41' - 0"

Depth: 40' - 6"

Foundation: Walkout Basement

HOME PLAN

eplans.com

TRADITIONAL STYLINGS MELD WITH THE SOUTHERN FEEL of the nested gables and pediment-look entry of this four-bedroom home. A corner fireplace warms the living room, which is open to the dining and kitchen area. Secluded on the right, the master suite delights with a luxurious bath that boasts a double-sink vanity and twin walk-in closets that flank the garden tub. Two family bedrooms share a full bath on the second floor while a second full bath resides next to the fourth bedroom, making a perfect guest room.

 # HPK2300118

HOME PLAN

Style: Country Cottage
First Floor: 1,281 sq. ft.
Second Floor: 611 sq. ft.
Total: 1,892 sq. ft.
Bedrooms: 4
Bathrooms: 3
Width: 30' - 0"
Depth: 58' - 6"
Foundation: Slab

eplans.com

HOMES FOR NARROW LOTS

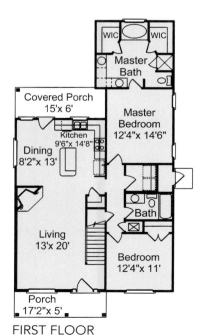

FIRST FLOOR

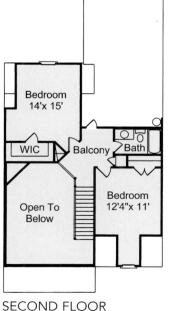

SECOND FLOOR

THE COMBINATION OF RAFTER TAILS AND STONE-AND-SIDING GABLED ROOFLINES gives this home plenty of curb appeal. Inside, a vaulted den is entered through double doors, just to the left of the foyer. A spacious vaulted great room features a fireplace and is located near the dining room. The kitchen offers an octagonal island, a corner sink with a window, and a pantry. Up the angled staircase are the sleeping quarters. Here, two secondary bedrooms share a hall bath, and the master suite is enhanced with a private bath and a walk-in closet. The three-car garage easily shelters the family fleet.

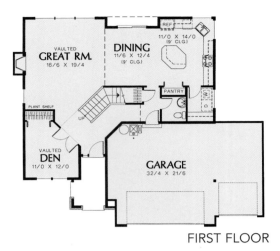

FIRST FLOOR

SECOND FLOOR

HOME PLAN

HPK2300119

Style: Traditional

First Floor: 1,097 sq. ft.

Second Floor: 807 sq. ft.

Total: 1,904 sq. ft.

Bedrooms: 3

Bathrooms: 2 ½

Width: 40' - 0"

Depth: 45' - 0"

Foundation: Crawlspace

eplans.com

HOME PLAN

HPK2300120

Style: Country

First Floor: 870 sq. ft.

Second Floor: 1,080 sq. ft.

Total: 1,950 sq. ft.

Bedrooms: 3

Bathrooms: 2 ½

Width: 32' - 0"

Depth: 47' - 0"

Foundation: Crawlspace

eplans.com

PERFECT BY THE SEA, this charming vacation retreat is a great place to call home any time of the year. A double-decker porch adds southern appeal as you approach the plan; enter directly to an expansive gathering room, with a fireplace and built-in bookshelves. An arched opening leads to the dining room, served by a beautifully planned kitchen. Past the breakfast nook, a screened porch beckons in any weather. Upstairs, the master suite (with a luxuriant bath and upper-porch access) joins two bedrooms and a convenient laundry room.

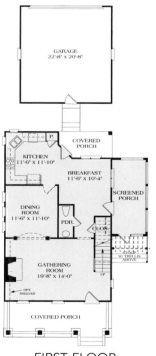

FIRST FLOOR

SECOND FLOOR

FIRST FLOOR

SECOND FLOOR

A BRICK ONE-STORY GARAGE WITH A FLOWERBOX WINDOW lends this two-story home a cottage feel. Inside, efficient use of space and flexibility adds to the appeal. A formal dining room opens from the two-story foyer, and leads to a cleverly designed kitchen. A serving bar connects the kitchen and breakfast nook. The hearth-warmed family room is just steps away. Four bedrooms—three family bedrooms and a roomy master suite—fill the second level. Note the option of turning Bedroom 4 into a sitting area for the master suite.

HOME PLAN

HPK2300121

Style: Country Cottage

First Floor: 947 sq. ft.

Second Floor: 981 sq. ft.

Total: 1,928 sq. ft.

Bedrooms: 4

Bathrooms: 2 ½

Width: 41' - 0"

Depth: 39' - 4"

Foundation: Crawlspace, Unfinished Walkout Basement, Slab

eplans.com

HOME PLAN

HPK2300122

Style: Traditional

First Floor: 1,314 sq. ft.

Second Floor: 616 sq. ft.

Total: 1,930 sq. ft.

Bedrooms: 3

Bathrooms: 2 ½

Width: 40' - 0"

Foundation: Unfinished Walkout Basement

eplans.com

FIRST FLOOR

BREAKFAST

KITCHEN

GRAND ROOM
15'-4" x 18'-4"

MASTER BEDROOM
13'-1" x 14'-1"

TWO STORY FOYER

DINING ROOM
10'-1" x 12'-3"

P.R.

M. BATH

LNDRY

W.I.C.

TWO CAR GARAGE

©2001, 02, 03, 04 By Designer

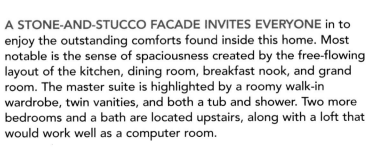

SECOND FLOOR

COMPUTER LOFT

TWO STORY FOYER

BEDROOM 2
10'-4" x 11'-4"

BEDROOM 3
13'-0" x 16'-0"

W.I.C.

A STONE-AND-STUCCO FACADE INVITES EVERYONE in to enjoy the outstanding comforts found inside this home. Most notable is the sense of spaciousness created by the free-flowing layout of the kitchen, dining room, breakfast nook, and grand room. The master suite is highlighted by a roomy walk-in wardrobe, twin vanities, and both a tub and shower. Two more bedrooms and a bath are located upstairs, along with a loft that would work well as a computer room.

WITH IRRESISTIBLE CHARM AND QUIET CURB APPEAL, this enchanting cottage conceals a sophisticated interior that's prepared for busy lifestyles. Built-in cabinetry in the great room frames a massive fireplace, which warms the area and complements the natural views. An open kitchen provides an island with a double sink and snack counter. Planned events are easily served in the formal dining room with French doors that lead to the veranda. On the upper level, a central hall with linen storage connects the sleeping quarters. The master suite boasts a walk-in closet and a roomy bath with a dual-sink vanity. Each of two secondary bedrooms has plenty of wardrobe space. Bedroom 3 leads out to the upper-level deck.

FIRST

FIRST FLOOR

SECOND FLOOR

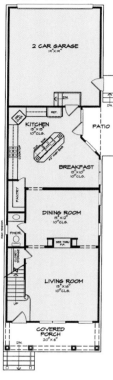

HOME PLAN

HPK2300123

Style: Traditional
First Floor: 911 sq. ft.
Second Floor: 1,029 sq. ft.
Total: 1,940 sq. ft.
Bedrooms: 3
Bathrooms: 2 ½
Width: 20' - 10"
Depth: 75' - 10"
Foundation: Crawlspace

eplans.com

HOME PLAN

HPK2300124

Style: Traditional

First Floor: 968 sq. ft.

Second Floor: 977 sq. ft.

Total: 1,945 sq. ft.

Bedrooms: 4

Bathrooms: 2 ½

Width: 40' - 0"

Depth: 46' - 0"

Foundation: Crawlspace

eplans.com

FIRST FLOOR

SECOND FLOOR

THIS TRADITIONAL HOME OFFERS LOVELY FORMAL ROOMS for entertaining. The living room has a centered fireplace and access to the front covered porch. A gourmet kitchen with a cooktop island serves the dining room. French doors open the morning nook to the outdoors; a second fireplace warms the family room. Upstairs, the master suite has a corner walk-in closet and an oversized shower. Three secondary bedrooms are connected by a stair hall.

FIRST FLOOR

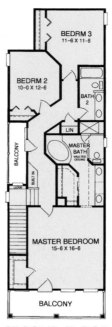

SECOND FLOOR

REMINISCENT OF THE POPULAR TOWNHOUSES OF THE PAST, this fine clapboard home is perfect for urban or river-front living. Two balconies grace the second floor—one at the front and one on the side. A two-way fireplace between the formal living and dining rooms provides visual impact. Built-in bookcases flank an arched opening between these rooms. A pass-through from the kitchen to the dining room simplifies serving, and a walk-in pantry provides storage. On the second floor, the master bedroom opens to a large balcony, and the relaxing master bath is designed with a separate shower and an angled whirlpool tub. Two secondary bedrooms and a full bath are located at the rear of the plan.

HOME PLAN

HPK2300125

Style: Traditional

First Floor: 904 sq. ft.

Second Floor: 1,058 sq. ft.

Total: 1,962 sq. ft.

Bedrooms: 3

Bathrooms: 2 ½

Width: 22' - 0"

Depth: 74' - 0"

Foundation: Slab, Crawlspace

eplans.com

THOUGH THIS HOME GIVES THE IMPRESSION OF THE NORTHWEST, it will be the winner of any neighborhood. From the foyer, the two-story living room is just a couple of steps up and features a through-fireplace. The U-shaped kitchen has a cooktop work island, an adjacent nook, and easy access to the formal dining room. A spacious family room shares the fireplace with the living room, is enhanced by built-ins, and also offers a quiet deck for stargazing. The upstairs consists of two family bedrooms sharing a full bath and a vaulted master suite complete with a walk-in closet and sumptuous bath. A two-car, drive-under garage has plenty of room for storage.

HOME PLAN

HPK2300126

Style: Craftsman

Main Level: 1,106 sq. ft.

Upper Level: 872 sq. ft.

Total: 1,978 sq. ft.

Bedrooms: 3

Bathrooms: 2 ½

Width: 38' - 0"

Depth: 35' - 0"

Foundation: Slab, Unfinished Basement

eplans.com

HOMES FOR NARROW LOTS

MAIN LEVEL

UPPER LEVEL

BASEMENT

HOME PLAN

HPK2300127

Style: Cape Cod

First Floor: 803 sq. ft.

Second Floor: 1,182 sq. ft.

Total: 1,985 sq. ft.

Bedrooms: 4

Bathrooms: 2 ½

Width: 36' - 0"

Depth: 43' - 4"

Foundation: Unfinished Walkout Basement, Crawlspace, Slab

eplans.com

FIRST FLOOR

SECOND FLOOR

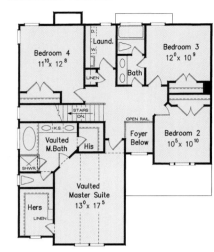

THIS NARROW-LOT HOME would be perfect nestled into an in-fill lot or standing prominently in a new development. Either way, its classic style will make it a standout. Enter to a foyer that is lit by a second-story arched window. Subtle angles direct traffic into the family room, where a warming fireplace awaits. An efficient kitchen opens to both the sunny breakfast nook and formal dining room, catering to any occasion. Upstairs, four bedrooms include a vaulted master suite with a lavish bath. A laundry room on this level is a thoughtful touch.

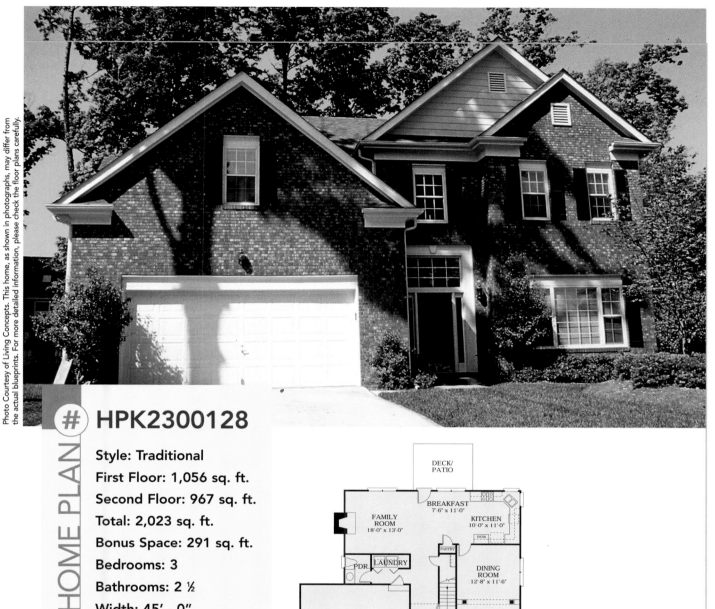

HOME PLAN (#) HPK2300128

Style: Traditional

First Floor: 1,056 sq. ft.

Second Floor: 967 sq. ft.

Total: 2,023 sq. ft.

Bonus Space: 291 sq. ft.

Bedrooms: 3

Bathrooms: 2 ½

Width: 45' - 0"

Depth: 40' - 0"

Foundation: Slab, Crawlspace

eplans.com

FIRST FLOOR

- DECK/PATIO
- BREAKFAST 7'-6" x 11'-0"
- FAMILY ROOM 18'-0" x 13'-0"
- KITCHEN 10'-0" x 11'-0"
- DESK
- PANTRY
- PDR.
- LAUNDRY
- DINING ROOM 12'-8" x 11'-6"
- GARAGE 22'-0" x 19'-8"
- FOYER
- UP
- LIVING ROOM 12'-8" x 11'-6"
- LOGGIA

SECOND FLOOR

- MASTER SUITE 13'-0" x 15'-6"
- MASTER BATH
- SUITE 2 12'-4" x 12'-0"
- W.I.C.
- DN
- BATH
- UNFIN. BONUS ROOM 14'-6" x 17'-0"
- OPEN TO BELOW
- SUITE 3 12'-8" x 12'-0"

THIS FASHIONABLE FARMHOUSE SHOWS OFF THE HEIGHT OF STYLE—but never at the expense of comfort. Inside, formal rooms flank the foyer and lead to casual living space. A family room with a fireplace opens to a breakfast area and gourmet kitchen. Upstairs, the lavish master suite offers twin vanities and a generous walk-in closet. Two additional bedrooms share a hall bath. A large bonus room includes a walk-in closet.

HOMES FOR NARROW LOTS

FIRST FLOOR

SECOND FLOOR

2 CAR GARAGE
21-4x21-4

COVERED PORCH

BREAKFAST
11-0x10-0
10 FT CLG

DINING ROOM
12-2x11-6
10 FT CLG

KITCHEN
13-4x13-6
10 FT CLG

LIVING ROOM
19-0x14-6
VOLUME CLG

BATH 3

STUDY
BEDROOM 3
12-0x13-6
10 FT CLG

FOYER
VOLUME CLG

PORCH
10 FT CLG

HERS   HIS

COVERED PORCH
9 FT CLG

MASTER BEDROOM
14-0x15-0
9 FT CLG

MSTR BATH
9 FT CLG

BATH 2
9 FT CLG

OPEN TO LIVING ROOM BELOW

BEDROOM 2
10-0x14-6
9 FT CLG

BALCONY

OPEN TO FOYER BELOW

TRADITIONAL STYLING distinguishes this narrow-lot home. As one enters the foyer, the large living room and dining room—both with volume ceilings—are visible beyond. A flex room that can be used as a guest suite or home office/study opens off the foyer. A roomy covered porch is accessed from the breakfast room and provides space for outdoor entertaining. Upstairs, the master suite has all the amenities, including access to a private second-story covered porch. Another bedroom and bath complete this efficiently designed plan.

HPK2300129

HOME PLAN

Style: Transitional
First Floor: 1,233 sq. ft.
Second Floor: 824 sq. ft.
Total: 2,057 sq. ft.
Bedrooms: 3
Bathrooms: 3
Width: 31' - 10"
Depth: 77' - 10"
Foundation: Crawlspace

eplans.com

THIS CHARMING COUNTRY DESIGN PUTS ITS BEST FOOT FORWARD by placing the two-car garage up front, thus protecting the living areas from most of the street noise. Inside, the living and dining areas flow together, defined by one simple column, letting the glow of the corner fireplace in the living area enhance any dinner party. The efficient kitchen has easy access to the garage and features a sink island and a pantry. The first-floor master suite offers a private bath and a walk-in closet, while a secondary bedroom accesses a hall bath. Upstairs, another spacious secondary bedroom provides a walk-in closet, private bath, and access to a large study area that over looks the living room below.

HOME PLAN

(#) HPK2300130

Style: Bungalow
First Floor: 1,484 sq. ft.
Second Floor: 614 sq. ft.
Total: 2,098 sq. ft.
Bedrooms: 3
Bathrooms: 3
Width: 40' - 0"
Depth: 64' - 0"
Foundation: Slab

eplans.com

HOMES FOR NARROW LOTS

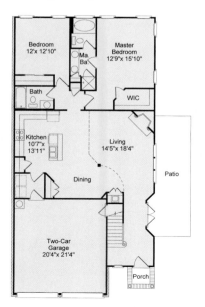

FIRST FLOOR

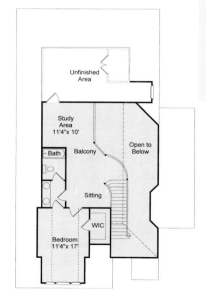

SECOND FLOOR

CRAFTSMAN STYLINGS GRACE THIS TWO-STORY TRADITIONAL HOME, designed for a narrow lot. Shingles and siding present a warm welcome; the front porch opens to the dining room and the gathering room, allowing great entertainment options. The kitchen connects to the living areas with a snack bar and works hard with an island and lots of counter space. The master suite is on this level and delights in a very private bath. Two bedrooms on the upper level have private vanities and a shared bath. Extra storage or bonus space is available for future development.

HOME PLAN #

HPK2300131

Style: Craftsman
First Floor: 1,392 sq. ft.
Second Floor: 708 sq. ft.
Total: 2,100 sq. ft.
Bedrooms: 3
Bathrooms: 2 ½
Width: 32' - 0"
Depth: 55' - 0"
Foundation: Crawlspace

eplans.com

FIRST FLOOR

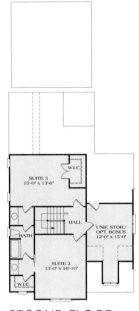

SECOND FLOOR

HOME PLAN

(#) HPK2300132

Design: HPK2300132

Style: Cottage

First Floor: 876 sq. ft.

Second Floor: 1,245 sq. ft.

Total: 2,121 sq. ft.

Bedrooms: 4

Bathrooms: 2 ½

Width: 27' - 6"

Depth: 64' - 0"

Foundation: Crawlspace, Pier (same as Piling)

eplans.com

KEY WEST CONCH STYLE BLENDS OLD WORLD CHARM WITH NEW WORLD COMFORT in this picturesque design. A glass-paneled entry lends a warm welcome and complements a captivating front balcony. Two sets of French doors open the great room to wide views and extend the living areas to the back covered porch. A gourmet kitchen is prepared for any occasion with a prep sink, plenty of counter space, an ample pantry, and an eating bar. The midlevel landing leads to two additional bedrooms, a full bath, and a windowed art niche. Double French doors open the upper-level master suite to a sundeck.

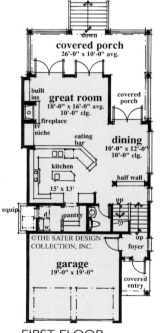

FIRST FLOOR

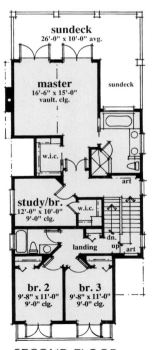

SECOND FLOOR

HOMES FOR NARROW LOTS

FIRST FLOOR

SECOND FLOOR

THIS HOME'S COVERED, ANGLED ENTRY is elegantly echoed by an angled door to a rear covered porch, thus setting the style for this amenity-filled design. Flanking the foyer to the left is the formal dining room and to the right, through double French doors, is a cozy den/parlor. The great room opens out into the comfortable breakfast nook, sharing the warmth of its corner fireplace and giving this plan a spacious feeling. Gourmets will enjoy the large island kitchen. Upstairs, the master suite is located away from two secondary bedrooms for privacy and offers a luxurious bath and a walk-in closet.

HPK2300133

Style: Farmhouse
First Floor: 1,176 sq. ft.
Second Floor: 994 sq. ft.
Total: 2,170 sq. ft.
Bedrooms: 3
Bathrooms: 2 ½
Width: 40' - 0"
Depth: 64' - 0"
Foundation: Crawlspace

HOME PLAN

eplans.com

THIS UPDATED COUNTRY COTTAGE WILL BRING CHARM to any neighborhood. Dormers and shuttered windows are dressed up with pediments for added style on the facade. Straight ahead, the hearth-warmed family room awaits with a glorious wall of windows. This room flows into the breakfast nook on the left, which features French-door access to the rear and a serving bar to the kitchen. The kitchen enjoys ample pantry space and a unique angled sink. Hidden away at the right of the plan is a comfortable guest suite. Upstairs, find the magnificent master suite, complete with a curved ribbon of windows and its own private sitting room. At the right are two additional bedrooms and a full hall bath.

(#) HPK2300134

Style: Country Cottage

First Floor: 1,042 sq. ft.

Second Floor: 1,150 sq. ft.

Total: 2,192 sq. ft.

Bedrooms: 4

Bathrooms: 3

Width: 41' - 0"

Depth: 43' - 0"

Foundation: Crawlspace, Unfinished Walkout Basement

eplans.com

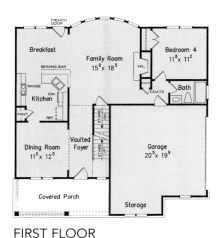

FIRST FLOOR

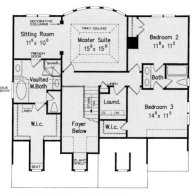

SECOND FLOOR

FIRST FLOOR

SECOND FLOOR

HOME PLAN

HPK2300135

Style: Colonial Revival
Main Level: 1,053 sq. ft.
Upper Level: 1,146 sq. ft.
Total: 2,199 sq. ft.
Bedrooms: 4
Bathrooms: 2 ½
Width: 42' - 0"
Foundation: Crawlspace, Unfinished Walkout Basement

eplans.com

FOR A TRADITIONAL COUNTRY COTTAGE WITH ALL THE AMENITIES YOU DESIRE, you can't go wrong with this beautiful four-bedroom home. From the two-story foyer, an open floor plan reveals a spacious family room, with a fireplace, a formal dining room and a casual breakfast nook. The country kitchen is defined by a serving island. The open-rail staircase leads to a resplendent master suite, complete with a vaulted bath and corner garden tub. Three additional bedrooms share a full bath. Not to be missed: the second-floor laundry room, a convenience and a luxury.

SWEEPING FRONT AND REAR RAISED COVERED PORCHES, delicately detailed railings, and an abundance of fireplaces give this farmhouse its character. Designed to accommodate a relatively narrow building site, the efficient floor plan delivers outstanding livability for the active family. Both the formal living room and dining room have corner fireplaces, as does the family room. The large, tiled country kitchen has an abundance of work space, a planning desk, and easy access to the utility room. On the second floor, the master retreat features a fireplace and an expansive bathing and dressing suite.

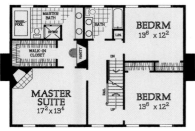

FIRST FLOOR

SECOND FLOOR

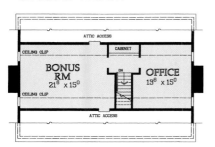

OPTIONAL LAYOUT

HOME PLAN

HPK2300136

Style: Farmhouse

First Floor: 1,120 sq. ft.

Second Floor: 1,083 sq. ft.

Total: 2,203 sq. ft.

Bonus Space: 597 sq. ft.

Bedrooms: 3

Bathrooms: 2 ½

Width: 40' - 0"

Depth: 40' - 0"

Foundation: Unfinished Basement

eplans.com

FIRST FLOOR

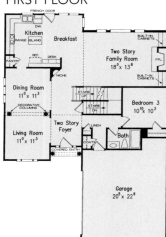

SECOND FLOOR

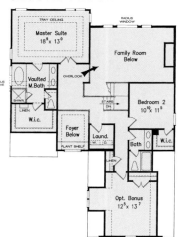

SHINGLES AND STONE DECORATE THE EXTERIOR of this charming design. Inside, decorative columns separate the living and dining rooms. The kitchen includes a pantry and a work island; the breakfast nook is conveniently nearby. Built-in cabinets flank the fireplace in the two-story family room. One family bedroom resides on the first floor, while the master suite and a second family bedroom are upstairs. An optional bonus room completes the second floor.

HOME PLAN

HPK2300137

Style: Country Cottage

First Floor: 1,293 sq. ft.

Second Floor: 922 sq. ft.

Total: 2,215 sq. ft.

Bonus Space: 235 sq. ft.

Bedrooms: 3

Bathrooms: 3

Width: 40' - 0"

Depth: 57' - 0"

Foundation: Crawlspace, Unfinished Walkout Basement

eplans.com

THE LOVELY FACADE OF THIS TOWN OR VILLAGE HOME is beautifully decorated with a double portico. A front bay window provides a stunning accent to the traditional exterior, while allowing natural light within. The formal living room features a fireplace and opens to the dining room, which leads outdoors. The gourmet kitchen has a walk-in pantry. The master suite is a relaxing space that includes a sitting bay, access to the side grounds, walk-in closet and soothing bath. A winding staircase offers an overlook to the living room.

HOME PLAN

HPK2300138

Style: Adam Style
First Floor: 1,369 sq. ft.
Second Floor: 856 sq. ft.
Total: 2,225 sq. ft.
Bedrooms: 4
Bathrooms: 2 ½
Width: 36' - 2"
Depth: 71' - 6"
Foundation: Slab

eplans.com

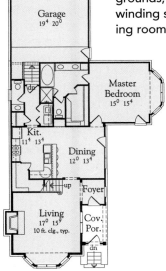

Garage
19⁴ 20⁰

Master Bedroom
15⁰ 15⁴

Kit.
11⁴ 13⁴

Dining
12⁰ 13⁴

up

Foyer

Living
17⁰ 15⁹
10 ft. clg., typ.

Cov. Por.

dn

FIRST FLOOR

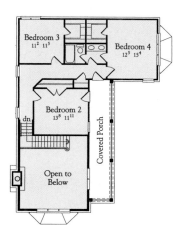

Bedroom 3
11² 11⁵

Bedroom 4
12⁵ 15⁴

dn

Bedroom 2
13⁸ 11¹¹

Open to Below

Covered Porch

SECOND FLOOR

FIRST FLOOR

Garage
21⁰ 21⁰

Kit.
12³ 12⁹

Study / Guest
10⁰ 15⁸

Dining
17⁷ 11¹⁰

up

Foyer

Living
17⁷ 15⁵
10 ft. clg., typ.

Porch

dn

SECOND FLOOR

Bedroom 2
11³ 13³

Bedroom 3
10⁰ 13³

dn

Master Bedroom
17⁷ 15⁵
9 ft. clg., typ.

Covered Balcony

HOME PLAN

HPK2300139

Style: Colonial
First Floor: 1,135 sq. ft.
Second Floor: 1,092 sq. ft.
Total: 2,227 sq. ft.
Bedrooms: 3
Bathrooms: 2 ½
Width: 28' - 8"
Depth: 74' - 2"
Foundation: Crawlspace

eplans.com

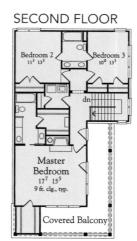

STYLISH SQUARE COLUMNS LINE THE PORCH and portico of this townhome, which has received the Builder's Choice National Design and Planning Award and the Award of Merit in Architecture. Inside, an open arrangement of the formal rooms is partially defined by a through-fireplace. Brightened by a triple window, the breakfast nook is an inviting place for family and friends to gather. A single door opens to the outside, where steps lead down to the rear property—a good place to start a walk into town. The kitchen features a food-prep island and a sizable pantry. Upstairs, the master suite offers a fireplace and access to the portico.

HPK2300140

HOME PLAN

Style: Craftsman

First Floor: 1,587 sq. ft.

Second Floor: 685 sq. ft.

Total: 2,272 sq. ft.

Bedrooms: 3

Bathrooms: 2 ½

Width: 38' - 0"

Depth: 55' - 0"

Foundation: Slab

eplans.com

WITH A NARROW PROFILE AND FOOTPRINT, this home will fit on the most compact lot without compromising space or amenities. The covered porch is set off by an open, detailed gable, making this a neighborhood-friendly facade. A formal dining room and study flank the foyer and provide ample space for entertaining. The kitchen sports a work-top island and is just a few steps from the spacious family room. The short master suite hall opens to a comfortable and private space with an adjoining sitting room and private bath. The second floor is complete with two bedrooms, loft, full bath, and plenty of storage space.

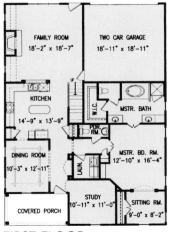

FIRST FLOOR

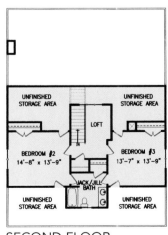

SECOND FLOOR

FIRST FLOOR

SECOND FLOOR

HPK2300141

Style: Country Cottage

First Floor: 1,290 sq. ft.

Second Floor: 985 sq. ft.

Total: 2,275 sq. ft.

Bonus Space: 186 sq. ft.

Bedrooms: 4

Bathrooms: 3

Width: 45' - 0"

Depth: 43' - 4"

Foundation: Crawlspace, Unfinished Walkout Basement, Slab

eplans.com

THIS CASUALLY ELEGANT EUROPEAN COUNTRY-STYLE HOME OFFERS MORE than just a slice of everything you've always wanted: it is designed with room to grow. Formal living and dining rooms are defined by decorative columns and open from a two-story foyer, which leads to open family space. A two-story family room offers a fireplace and shares a French door to the rear property with the breakfast room. A gallery hall with a balcony overlook connects two sleeping wings upstairs. The master suite boasts a vaulted bath, and the family hall leads to bonus space.

THE DECORATIVE PILLARS AND THE WRAPAROUND PORCH are just the beginning of this comfortable home. Inside, an angled U-shaped stairway leads to the second-floor sleeping zone. On the first floor, French doors lead to a bay-windowed den that shares a see-through fireplace with the two-story family room. The large island kitchen includes a writing desk, a corner sink, a breakfast nook, and access to the laundry room, the powder room, and the two-car garage. Upstairs, the master suite is a real treat with its French-door access, vaulted ceiling, and luxurious bath. Two other bedrooms and a full bath complete the second floor.

(#) HPK2300142

HOME PLAN

Style: Craftsman
First Floor: 1,371 sq. ft.
Second Floor: 916 sq. ft.
Total: 2,287 sq. ft.
Bedrooms: 3
Bathrooms: 2 ½
Width: 43' - 0"
Depth: 69' - 0"
Foundation: Crawlspace

eplans.com

HOMES FOR NARROW LOTS

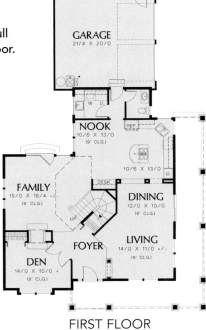

FIRST FLOOR

SECOND FLOOR

FIRST FLOOR

SECOND FLOOR

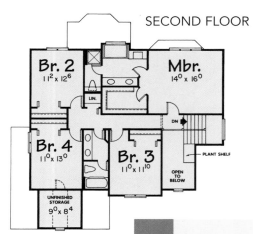

THE FARMHOUSE APPEAL of this four-bedroom home is in the wrapping, covered porch—perfect for rocking away the afternoons. The exterior detailing adds the look of yester-year, but the inside floor plan brings things up-to-date. You can easily unload a station wagon full of groceries using the quick path from garage to kitchen and then warm up by the see-through fireplace. The spacious great room is enhanced by a bay window and shares the through-fireplace with the kitchen. Upstairs, four bedrooms include a pampering master suite. The master bath includes His and Hers sinks, tub, separate shower, and spacious walk-in closet.

HOME PLAN

HPK2300143

Style: French Country

First Floor: 1,158 sq. ft.

Second Floor: 1,134 sq. ft.

Total: 2,292 sq. ft.

Bedrooms: 4

Bathrooms: 2 ½

Width: 46' - 0"

Depth: 47' - 10"

Foundation: Unfinished Basement

eplans.com

A STONE-AND-SIDING FACADE, AND AVAILABILITY OF ALTERNATE ELEVATIONS provide a unique design for this traditional Craftsman. A columned front porch transitions to a curved entry, which steps into the living room's two-story clearance. The dining and kitchen area combine to create one spacious room. The kitchen features a center island, snack bar, and L-shaped counter space. A bayed window in the dining area provides peaceful views of the rear, as does an exit to the porch. The master bedroom also offers private access to the porch. Upstairs are three more bedrooms with two additional baths, and a study with built-in cabinets and desks. A balcony provides views to the first floor.

HOME PLAN

HPK2300144

Style: Craftsman

First Floor: 1,283 sq. ft.

Second Floor: 1,010 sq. ft.

Total: 2,293 sq. ft.

Bedrooms: 4

Bathrooms: 3 ½

Width: 38' - 0"

Depth: 59' - 0"

Foundation: Unfinished Walkout Basement

eplans.com

HOMES FOR NARROW LOTS

FIRST FLOOR

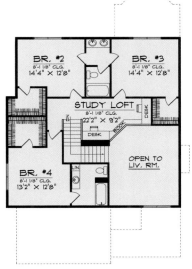

SECOND FLOOR

FIRST FLOOR

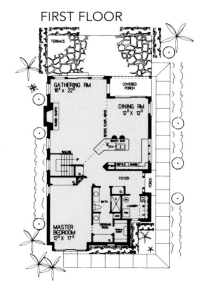

SECOND FLOOR

HOME PLAN

HPK2300145

Style: Cape Cod

First Floor: 1,387 sq. ft.

Second Floor: 929 sq. ft.

Total: 2,316 sq. ft.

Bedrooms: 4

Bathrooms: 3

Width: 30' - 0"

Depth: 51' - 8"

Foundation: Crawlspace

eplans.com

REAR EXTERIOR

PERFECT FOR A NARROW LOT, this shingle-and-stone Nantucket Cape home caters to the casual lifestyle. The side entrance gives direct access to the wonderfully open living areas: gathering room with fireplace and an abundance of windows; island kitchen with angled, pass-through snack bar; and dining area with sliding glass doors to a covered eating area. Note also the large deck that further extends the living potential. Also on this floor is the large master suite with a compartmented bath, private dressing room, and walk-in closet. Upstairs, you'll find the three family bedrooms. Of the two bedrooms that share a bath, one features a private balcony.

FIRST FLOOR

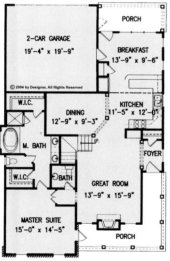

- PORCH
- 2-CAR GARAGE 19'-4" x 19'-9"
- BREAKFAST 13'-9" x 9'-6"
- © 2004 by Designer, All Rights Reserved
- W.I.C.
- DINING 12'-9" x 9'-3"
- KITCHEN 11'-5" x 12'-0"
- M. BATH
- FOYER
- W.I.C.
- BATH
- GREAT ROOM 13'-9" x 15'-9"
- MASTER SUITE 15'-0" x 14'-5"
- PORCH

SECOND FLOOR

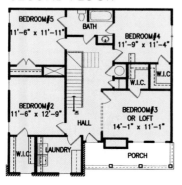

- BEDROOM #5 11'-6" x 11'-11"
- BATH
- BEDROOM #4 11'-9" x 11'-4"
- W.I.C.
- W.I.C.
- BEDROOM #2 11'-6" x 12'-9"
- HALL
- BEDROOM #3 OR LOFT 14'-1" x 11'-1"
- W.I.C.
- LAUNDRY
- PORCH

HPK2300146

HOME PLAN

Style: Traditional

First Floor: 1,260 sq. ft.

Second Floor: 1,057 sq. ft.

Total: 2,317 sq. ft.

Bedrooms: 5

Bathrooms: 2 ½

Width: 35' - 0"

Depth: 56' - 0"

Foundation: Slab

eplans.com

AT HOME IN THE CITY, this narrow-lot design takes advantage of street views. A rear-loading, two-car garage is accessed via a rear porch and breakfast room. The adjoining C-shaped kitchen is only steps from the formal dining room. A warming fireplace can be enjoyed in the great room (and even from the dining room). A first-floor master suite provides convenience and comfort. Two walk-in closets, dual-sink vanity, soaking tub, and enclosed shower pamper and dissolve stress. The second floor is home to four bedrooms—or three bedrooms and a loft. A roomy laundry area is located on the second floor.

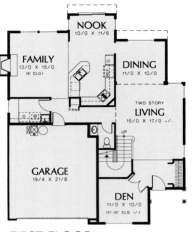

FIRST FLOOR

SECOND FLOOR

THIS ATTRACTIVE DESIGN COMBINES TRADITIONAL CHARM with a very livable floor plan. A coat closet is conveniently placed just inside the front entrance, which leads to an open living room and dining room area. The family room with fireplace opens to the near-by kitchen and breakfast nook. A den, or home office, is well situated inside the front entrance. The sleeping zone is located on the second floor which includes three family bedrooms sharing a full bath and a large master suite with an attractive dormer window and master bath.

HPK2300147

HOME PLAN

Style: Traditional
First Floor: 1,255 sq. ft.
Second Floor: 1,074 sq. ft.
Total: 2,329 sq. ft.
Bedrooms: 4
Bathrooms: 2 ½
Width: 40' - 0"
Depth: 51' - 0"
Foundation: Crawlspace

eplans.com

Photo by Robert Starling. This home, as shown in photographs, may differ from the actual blueprints. For more detailed information, please check the floor plans carefully.

FIRST FLOOR

MASTER SUITE 14'-8" x 20'-0"

COVERED VERANDA

GATHERING ROOM 24'-2" x 13'-0"

DECK

MASTER BATH

W.I.C.

KITCHEN 13'-6" x 12'-6"

STOR.

LAUN.

FOYER

PDR.

PORTICO

DINING ROOM 12'-0" x 12'-0"

GARAGE 19'-4" x 19'-2"

SECOND FLOOR

SUITE 2 17'-6" x 13'-6"

EVENING DECK

W.I.C.

BATH

CAPTAINS QUARTERS 14'-8" x 17'-8"

UNFIN. 16'-2" x 10'-8"

ACCESS

SUITE 3 12'-4" x 11'-8"

OPEN TO BELOW

W.I.C.

HOME PLAN

HPK2300148

Style: Traditional

First Floor: 1,563 sq. ft.

Second Floor: 772 sq. ft.

Total: 2,335 sq. ft.

Bedrooms: 3

Bathrooms: 2 ½

Width: 45' - 0"

Depth: 55' - 8"

Foundation: Crawlspace

eplans.com

GRACEFUL, ELEGANT LIVING TAKES PLACE in this charming cottage, which showcases a stone-and-stucco facade. Inside, the formal dining room features a columned entrance and a tray ceiling; nearby, the kitchen boasts a central island and a bay window. The expansive gathering room includes a fireplace and opens to the covered rear veranda, which extends to a side deck. The master suite, also with a tray ceiling, offers a walk-in closet and lavish private bath. Upstairs, two family bedrooms—both with walk-in closets—share a full bath and the captain's quarters, which opens to a deck.

HOMES FOR NARROW LOTS

FIRST FLOOR

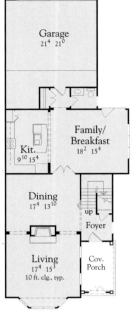

SECOND FLOOR

HPK2300149

Style: Southern Colonial

First Floor: 1,237 sq. ft.

Second Floor: 1,098 sq. ft.

Total: 2,335 sq. ft.

Bedrooms: 3

Bathrooms: 2 ½

Width: 29' - 4"

Depth: 73' - 0"

Foundation: Slab

eplans.com

THE CURB APPEAL OF THIS HOME CAN BE FOUND IN THE DAZZLING DETAILS: a bay window, twin sconces illuminating a columned porch, a pretty portico, and classic shutters. The foyer opens to the formal living and dining rooms, subtly defined by a central fireplace. The gourmet kitchen overlooks a spacious family/breakfast area, which leads outdoors. The second floor includes a lavish master suite with a spa-style tub and a private covered balcony. The secondary sleeping area is connected by a gallery hall and a stair landing.

(#) HPK2300150

HOME PLAN

Style: SW Contemporary

First Floor: 1,463 sq. ft.

Second Floor: 872 sq. ft.

Total: 2,335 sq. ft.

Bedrooms: 3

Bathrooms: 3

Width: 44' - 0"

Depth: 58' - 10"

Foundation: Crawlspace, Unfinished Basement

eplans.com

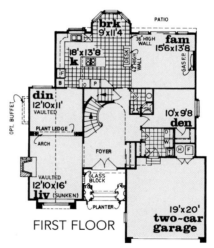

FIRST FLOOR

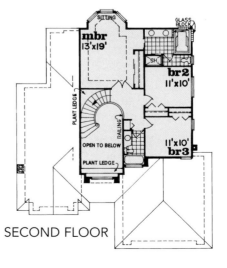

SECOND FLOOR

TWO DIFFERENT FACADES ARE AVAILABLE FOR THIS HOME: a California stucco or a traditional brick-and-siding version. The interior plan begins with a vaulted foyer hosting a sweeping curved staircase spilling into a sunken living room with a masonry fireplace and vaulted ceiling. The kitchen features a pantry, center cooking island, built-in desk, and sunny breakfast bay. A den with a walk-in closet and nearby bath can easily double as a guest room. The master suite on the second floor boasts a drop ceiling, bayed sitting area, and lavish bath. The family bedrooms share a full bath.

HOMES FOR NARROW LOTS

A TRADITIONAL DESIGN WITH UNTRADITIONAL AMENITIES, this mid-size home is sure to please. The front-facing den, enhanced by French doors, is bathed in natural light. The great room sits at the heart of the home with an optional media center in the corner and a central fireplace along the right wall. The open design leads nicely into the adjoining dining room and kitchen. An island cooktop/serving bar conveniently serves the area. A future deck is accessible from the breakfast nook. Upstairs, the spacious master suite boasts a dual-sink vanity, a spa tub, a separate shower, a compartmented toilet, and an enormous walk-in closet. Two additional family bedrooms share a full bath. A bonus room and a practical second-floor laundry room complete this level.

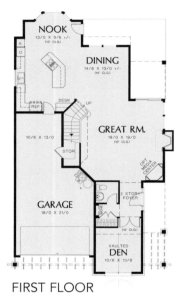

FIRST FLOOR

SECOND FLOOR

HOME PLAN

HPK2300151

Style: Craftsman

First Floor: 1,204 sq. ft.

Second Floor: 1,264 sq. ft.

Total: 2,468 sq. ft.

Bonus Space: 213 sq. ft.

Bedrooms: 3

Bathrooms: 2 ½

Width: 35' - 0"

Depth: 63' - 0"

Foundation: Crawlspace

eplans.com

**THE UNASSUMING
FACADE OF THIS TRADITIONAL HOME** offers
few clues about how ideal this deisgn is for entertaining. The lack
of unnecessary walls achieves a clean, smart layout that flows
seamlessly. A side deck accessed from the living room and breakfast area extends the gathering outside. Upstairs houses all of
the family bedrooms, including the master suite, enhanced by a
spacious private deck. Two additional family bedrooms share a
full bath. A fourth bedroom boasts a full bath and could be used
as a recreation/exercise/guest room. The central study/loft area
is perfect for a family computer.

HOME PLAN

HPK2300152

Style: Craftsman

First Floor: 1,294 sq. ft.

Second Floor: 1,220 sq. ft.

Total: 2,514 sq. ft.

Bonus Space: 366 sq. ft.

Bedrooms: 4

Bathrooms: 3 ½

Width: 38' - 0"

Depth: 76' - 0"

Foundation: Unfinished
Walkout Basement

eplans.com

FIRST FLOOR

SECOND FLOOR

OPTIONAL LAYOUT

HOMES FOR NARROW LOTS

FIRST FLOOR

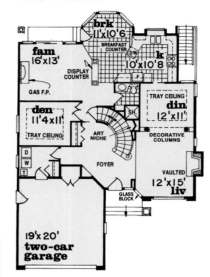

SECOND FLOOR

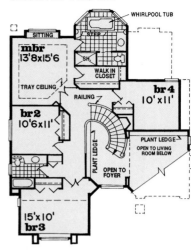

HOME PLAN (#) HPK2300153

Style: Mediterranean

First Floor: 1,383 sq. ft.

Second Floor: 1,156 sq. ft.

Total: 2,539 sq. ft.

Bedrooms: 4

Bathrooms: 2 ½

Width: 40' - 0"

Depth: 59' - 0"

Foundation: Unfinished Basement, Crawlspace

eplans.com

THIS WELL-PLANNED STUCCO HOME is suited for a narrow lot. Its interior begins with a two-story foyer that displays a sweeping, curved staircase, an art niche, and a plant ledge. The vaulted ceiling in the living room is enhanced by a full-height window and a fireplace. Columns separate the living and dining rooms; the dining room has a tray ceiling. The step-saving kitchen is adjacent to a carousel breakfast room with a French door to the rear yard. A gas fireplace warms the family room, which features a room-divider display counter and sliding glass doors. A den with a tray ceiling rounds out the first floor. The master suite boasts a tray ceiling, window seat, raised whirlpool tub, and separate shower. Three family bedrooms share a full bath.

FIRST FLOOR

SECOND FLOOR

HPK2300154

HOME PLAN

Style: European Cottage

First Floor: 1,152 sq. ft.

Second Floor: 1,434 sq. ft.

Total: 2,586 sq. ft.

Bedrooms: 4

Bathrooms: 3

Width: 44' - 0"

Depth: 44' - 0"

Foundation: Unfinished Basement

eplans.com

TALL, ROBUST COLUMNS FLANK THE IMPRESSIVE TWO-STORY ENTRY of this European-style home. Views can be had in the living room—in the turret—and with the open dining area just steps away, entertaining will be a splendid affair. The kitchen features a breakfast bar and adjoining sun room. Upstairs, the master suite is enhanced by a large sitting area, bumped-out bay window, and a relaxing bath. Three family bedrooms and a full bath complete this level.

FIRST FLOOR

SECOND FLOOR

THE WELL-BALANCED USE OF STUCCO AND STONE combined with box-bay window treatments and a covered entry make this English Country home especially inviting. The two-story foyer opens on the right to formal living and dining rooms, bright with natural light. A spacious U-shaped kitchen adjoins a breakfast nook with views of the outdoors. This area flows nicely into the two-story great room, which offers a through-fireplace to the media room. A plush retreat awaits the homeowner upstairs with a master suite that offers a quiet, windowed sitting area with views to the rear grounds. Two family bedrooms share a full bath and a balcony hall that has a dramatic view of the great room below.

HPK2300155

HOME PLAN

Style: European Cottage

First Floor: 1,395 sq. ft.

Second Floor: 1,210 sq. ft.

Total: 2,605 sq. ft.

Bonus Space: 225 sq. ft.

Bedrooms: 3

Bathrooms: 2 ½

Width: 47' - 0"

Foundation: Unfinished Basement

eplans.com

HPK2300156

Style: Prairie

First Floor: 1,198 sq. ft.

Second Floor: 1,570 sq. ft.

Total: 2,768 sq. ft.

Bedrooms: 4

Bathrooms: 3 ½

Width: 38' - 0"

Depth: 75' - 0"

Foundation: Crawlspace

eplans.com

HOME PLAN

IDEAL FOR A NARROW CITY-LOT, THIS URBAN IN-FILL HOME IS A CITY DWELLER'S DREAM. The open, first-floor layout offers easy interaction between rooms. Access to a rear deck from the living room and breakfast area makes outdoor dining a possibility. The sleeping quarters are housed upstairs, including the master suite and three additional family bedrooms. Bedroom 4 boasts a private, full bath, a linen storage closet, and the command center control panel for the home automation system. The second floor laundry room is an added convenience.

FIRST FLOOR

SECOND FLOOR

WITH NO SHORTAGE OF CURB APPEAL, the elaborate front porch rivals the entrance to any home in the neighborhood. The interior reveals an open floor plan with most of the common living areas on the first floor. The exception is a second-floor game room, complete with a wet bar and built-in bookshelves. The lavish master suite boasts a spacious walk-in closet and a private fireplace. Two additional bedrooms on the second floor share a full bath. A bedroom on the first floor is ideal for guests or in-laws.

FIRST FLOOR

SECOND FLOOR

HOME PLAN

(#) HPK2300157

Style: Farmhouse

First Floor: 1,491 sq. ft.

Second Floor: 1,368 sq. ft.

Total: 2,859 sq. ft.

Bedrooms: 4

Bathrooms: 3

Width: 35' - 0"

Depth: 56' - 0"

Foundation: Crawlspace

eplans.com

HOME PLAN

HPK2300158

Style: Southern Colonial

First Floor: 1,440 sq. ft.

Second Floor: 1,440 sq. ft.

Total: 2,880 sq. ft.

Bonus Space: 140 sq. ft.

Bedrooms: 4

Bathrooms: 2 ½

Width: 30' - 0"

Depth: 56' - 0"

Foundation: Unfinished Basement

eplans.com

THE IMPRESSIVE EXTERIOR gives way to an interior without boundaries. The lack of unnecessary walls creates a feeling of spaciousness. Access to the sundeck from the family room extends the living space, encouraging entertaining. The second floor houses the master suite and three additional family bedrooms. Bedrooms 2 and 3 enjoy private access to a front-facing covered porch. A second-floor laundry room is an added convenience. The finished basement, boasting a sizable recreation room, completes this plan.

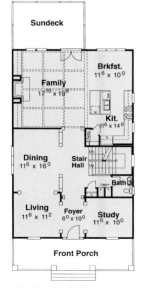

FIRST FLOOR

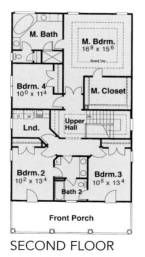

SECOND FLOOR

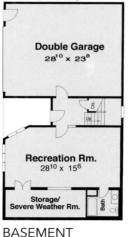

BASEMENT

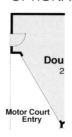

OPTIONAL LAYOUTS

HOMES FOR NARROW LOTS

FIRST FLOOR

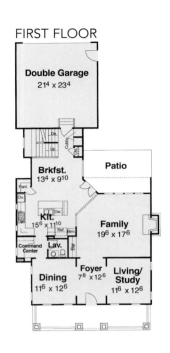

SECOND FLOOR

BOLD COLUMNS DISTINGUISH THE COVERED PORCH on this traditional home. Inside, the minimal use of walls is refreshing and opens the floor plan by adjoining living spaces. Access to the rear patio from the breakfast area makes alfresco meals a possibility. The second floor houses the spacious master suite, enhanced by a tray ceiling and private balcony. Two adjacent family bedrooms are separated by a Jack-and-Jill bath. A short hallway leads to the second-floor laundry room. The family computer station sits outside of bedroom 4—equipped with a full, private bath—useful as an ideal guest suite.

HOME PLAN

HPK2300159

Style: Prairie

First Floor: 1,379 sq. ft.

Second Floor: 1,794 sq. ft.

Total: 3,173 sq. ft.

Bedrooms: 4

Bathrooms: 3 ½

Width: 38' - 0"

Depth: 80' - 0"

Foundation: Unfinished Walkout Basement

eplans.com

HPK2300160

Style: Prairie
First Floor: 1,379 sq. ft.
Second Floor: 1,794 sq. ft.
Total: 3,173 sq. ft.
Bedrooms: 4
Bathrooms: 3 ½
Width: 38' - 0"
Depth: 80' - 0"
Foundation: Unfinished Basement

eplans.com

FIRST FLOOR

SECOND FLOOR

A SERIES OF TAPERING COLUMNS ANCHORED WITH BRICK, a wide covered porch, and deep eaves are Craftsman-style trademarks. The foyer is flanked by more formal spaces. To the back of the plan, the family room offers a deck view and fireplace. The kitchen is outfitted with a large island and convenient breakfast nook. The second floor is home to three family bedrooms—one with a private bath—and a computer station. The master suite opens through double doors and enjoys a private balcony, walk-in closet, and super bath.

First Time's the Charm—Modest Homes for New Builders

Few experiences measure up to the joy of building a new home, especially if it is for the first time. Starter homes mark the beginning of a new time in the life of a small family or individual, and our designers mean to celebrate the occasion with homes that will feel just right for a long time.

First-time builders generally appreciate amenities such as a clustered bedroom plan—with a nearby nursery or study—and a casual kitchen with breakfast nook. A nearby family or gathering room opens up the heart of the plan, and lets cozy private spaces exist at the corners. Another space-saving strategy is to forgo formal spaces, such as separate dining rooms, in favor of flexible-use spaces like living rooms and dens. A kitchen with a peninsula can accommodate cooks as well as diners. Finally, judicious use of balconies and porches add character and low-cost square footage to the home.

Mark Samu

A TRADITIONAL KITCHEN LAYOUT works best. But be sure invest in good lighting design and surfaces.

SMALLER HOMES may lack all the built-in amenities of larger designs. Keeping rooms simple and open to traffic will help them work their best.

Selecting a design for the first time requires a lot of imagination and a bit of instinct. This section offers 74 plans, ordered by square footage, for you to start from—and thousands more are available at www.eplans.com. Each design promises a winning blend of style and function—a home you'll love for years to come.

RECOVER UNDERUTILIZED SPACES but go "with the flow" of existing design elements. The result can be surprisingly attractive.

THE DETAILS OF THE EXTERIOR OF THIS SMALL, ATTRACTIVE COLONIAL-STYLE home include wood siding, shuttered windows, a gabled room and a stunning entry with sidelights. At the front of the house, the family room offers a fireplace to warm the cold night air. Beyond lies the dining room and U-shaped kitchen, which share a door to the sun deck. Two family bedrooms located at the middle of the home share a bathroom that contains a laundry. To the left of the house is the master bedroom with two closets, an optional plant shelf, and a bathroom with dual sinks and a linen closet.

 # HPK2300161

Style: Traditional

Square Footage: 1,208

Bedrooms: 3

Bathrooms: 2

Width: 48' - 0"

Depth: 29' - 0"

Foundation: Unfinished Basement

HOME PLAN

eplans.com

THIS ECONOMICAL-TO-BUILD BUNGALOW works well as a small family home or a retirement cottage. The covered porch leads to a vaulted living room with a fireplace. Behind this living space is the L-shaped kitchen with a walk-in pantry and an island with a utility sink. An attached breakfast nook has sliding glass doors to a rear patio. Three bedrooms each have ample wall closets. The master bedroom has a private full bath, and the family bedrooms share a main bath. Both baths have bright skylights. A two-car garage sits to the front, protecting the bedrooms from street noise.

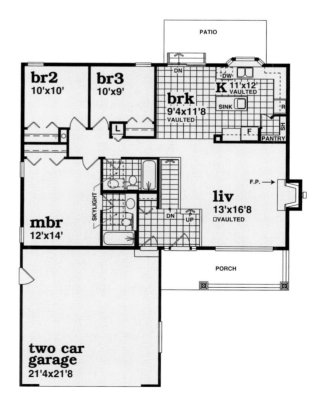

HOME PLAN

HPK2300162

Style: Ranch

Square Footage: 1,260

Bedrooms: 3

Bathrooms: 2

Width: 42' - 0"

Depth: 52' - 0"

Foundation: Unfinished Basement

eplans.com

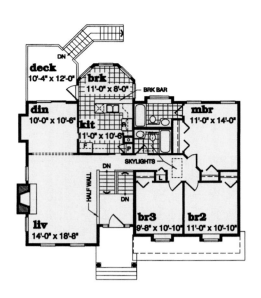

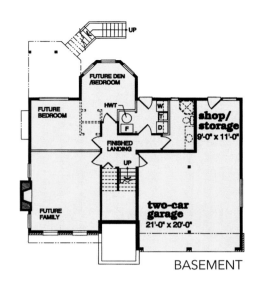

BASEMENT

(#) HPK2300163

Style: Traditional

Square Footage: 1,363

Basement: 848 sq. ft.

Bedrooms: 3

Bathrooms: 2

Width: 44' - 0"

Depth: 43' - 0"

Foundation: Unfinished Basement

eplans.com

A COLUMNED, COVERED ENTRY CHARMS THE EXTERIOR OF THIS THREE-BEDROOM, split-entry home. Inside, a one-and-a-half-story foyer boasts a dual staircase—one up to the main-floor living area and the other down to the basement. The living area includes a gas fireplace and windows on all walls, ensuring natural light. The adjacent dining room with a buffet alcove exits through a sliding glass door to the rear patio. The roomy kitchen has a raised snack bar, built-in pantry, and access to a bayed eating area surrounded by windows. A skylight brightens the hall to the three bedrooms. Look for His and Hers closets and a private bath in the master suite. Future expansion is reserved for space on the lower level.

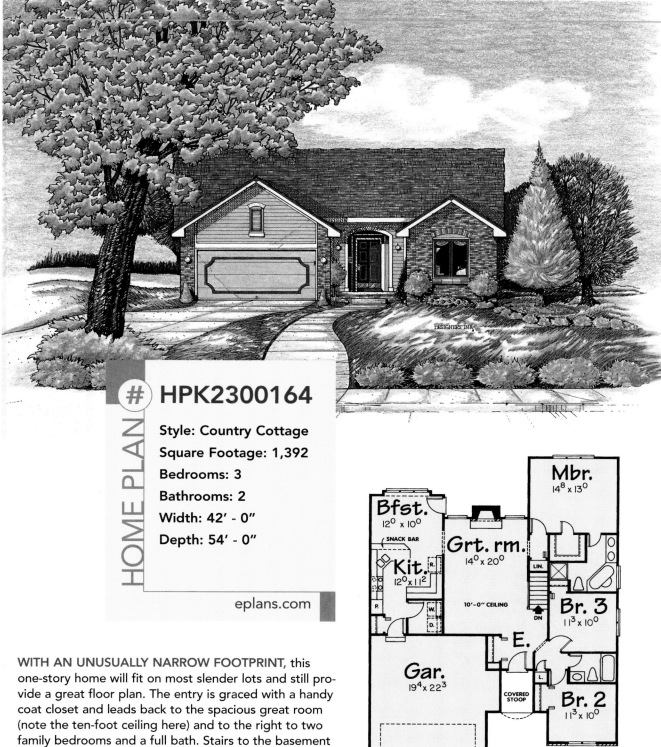

(#) HPK2300164

HOME PLAN

Style: Country Cottage

Square Footage: 1,392

Bedrooms: 3

Bathrooms: 2

Width: 42' - 0"

Depth: 54' - 0"

eplans.com

WITH AN UNUSUALLY NARROW FOOTPRINT, this
one-story home will fit on most slender lots and still provide a great floor plan. The entry is graced with a handy
coat closet and leads back to the spacious great room
(note the ten-foot ceiling here) and to the right to two
family bedrooms and a full bath. Stairs to the basement
level are found just beyond the entry hall. The breakfast
room and kitchen dominate the left side of the plan.
Separating them is a snack-bar counter for quick meals.
Pampered amenities in the secluded master bedroom
include a walk-in closet, windowed corner whirlpool tub,
dual sinks and a separate shower. A service entrance
through the kitchen to the garage leads to a convenient
laundry area and broom closet.

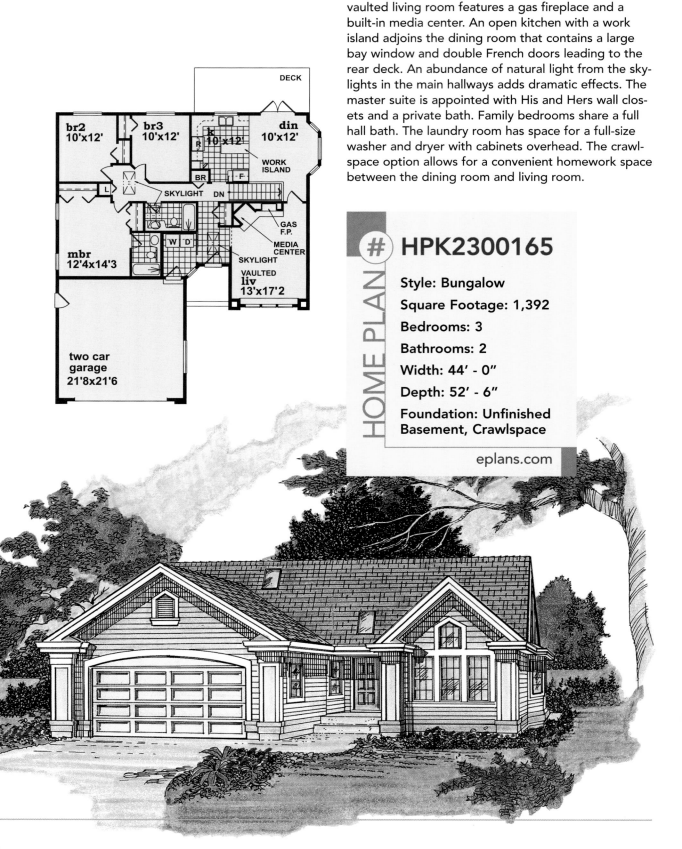

DECK

br2
10'x12'

br3
10'x12'

k
10'x12'

din
10'x12'

WORK
ISLAND

L

BR

F

R

SKYLIGHT

DN

GAS
F.P.

MEDIA
CENTER

mbr
12'4x14'3

W

D

SKYLIGHT

VAULTED
liv
13'x17'2

two car
garage
21'8x21'6

TRADITIONAL CORNER COLUMNS ADD PRESTIGE TO THIS THREE-BEDROOM RANCH HOME. The vaulted living room features a gas fireplace and a built-in media center. An open kitchen with a work island adjoins the dining room that contains a large bay window and double French doors leading to the rear deck. An abundance of natural light from the skylights in the main hallways adds dramatic effects. The master suite is appointed with His and Hers wall closets and a private bath. Family bedrooms share a full hall bath. The laundry room has space for a full-size washer and dryer with cabinets overhead. The crawl-space option allows for a convenient homework space between the dining room and living room.

HOME PLAN

HPK2300165

Style: **Bungalow**

Square Footage: **1,392**

Bedrooms: **3**

Bathrooms: **2**

Width: **44' - 0"**

Depth: **52' - 6"**

Foundation: **Unfinished Basement, Crawlspace**

eplans.com

HOME PLAN

HPK2300166

Style: **Bungalow**

Square Footage: **1,484**

Bedrooms: **3**

Bathrooms: **2**

Width: **38' - 0"**

Depth: **70' - 0"**

Foundation: **Crawlspace**

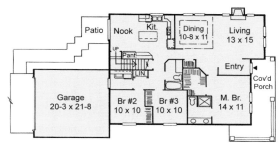

HOME PLAN

HPK2300167

Style: **Craftsman**

Square Footage: **1,544**

Bedrooms: **2**

Bathrooms: **2**

Width: **40' - 0"**

Depth: **60' - 0"**

Foundation: **Finished Walkout Basement**

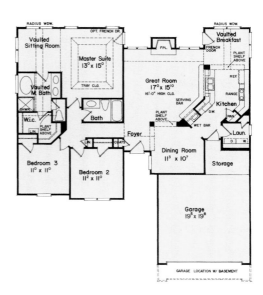

HPK2300168

Style: Traditional

Square Footage: 1,575

Bedrooms: 3

Bathrooms: 2

Width: 50' - 0"

Depth: 52' - 6"

Foundation: Crawlspace, Unfinished Walkout Basement

eplans.com

OPT. BASEMENT STAIR LOCATION

GENTLE ARCHED LINTELS HARMONIZE WITH THE HIGH HIPPED ROOF to create an elevation that is both welcoming and elegant. This efficient plan minimizes hallway space in order to maximize useable living areas. A favorite feature of this home is the "elbow-bend" galley kitchen that has easy access to the dining room and breakfast room—plus a full-length serving bar open to the great room. The master suite has a cozy sitting room and a compartmented bath. Two family bedrooms share a full hall bath.

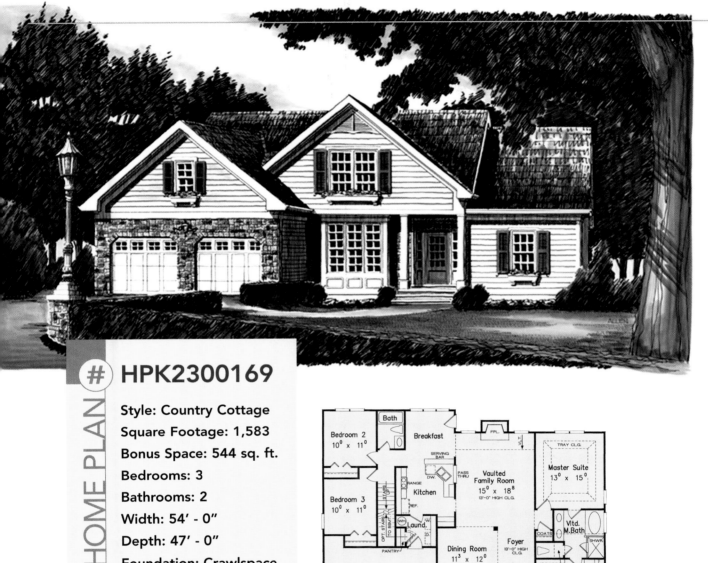

HOME PLAN

(#) HPK2300169

Style: Country Cottage

Square Footage: 1,583

Bonus Space: 544 sq. ft.

Bedrooms: 3

Bathrooms: 2

Width: 54' - 0"

Depth: 47' - 0"

Foundation: Crawlspace, Unfinished Walkout Basement, Slab

eplans.com

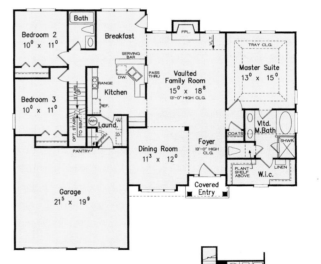

THIS COMFORTABLE COTTAGE IS WELL SUITED TO AN ALPINE ENVIRONMENT, yet, with its flexible interior and superior architecture, can be built anywhere. Open living and dining space is anchored by a decorative column and a fireplace surrounded by views. A well-planned kitchen features a food-preparation island and a serving bar. A triple window in the breakfast area brightens the kitchen; a French door allows access to the rear property. To the right of the plan, the master suite boasts a vaulted bath, a plant shelf, and a walk-in closet. Two secondary bedrooms share a full bath.

MULTIPLE GABLES, A TRANSOM OVER THE ENTRY DOOR, and a brick-and-stone exterior combine to create an exciting front on this beautiful one-story home. The open foyer offers a view through the great room to the rear yard. A dramatic fireplace and sloped ceiling decorate the fashionable great room. The spacious kitchen and breakfast room feature a favorable indoor/outdoor relationship. The first-floor master bedroom with a tray ceiling, private bath, and extra-large walk-in closet pampers homeowners with its size and luxury. Two additional bedrooms complete this spectacular home.

 # HPK2300170

HOME PLAN

Style: Transitional

Square Footage: 1,593

Bedrooms: 3

Bathrooms: 2

Width: 60' - 0"

Depth: 48' - 10"

Foundation: Unfinished Basement

eplans.com

Master Bedroom 15'3" x 12
9' ceiling height
Bath
walk-in closet
Hall
Bedroom 11' x 10'2"
Bath
Foyer
Bedroom 10'6" x 11'
slope ceiling
Porch
Great Room 18'2" x 17'
Dining 12'4' x 12'
Porch 11'4" x 10'9"
Kitchen 17'4" x 9'6"
pantry
Storage 7' x 14'8"
Laun.
Two-car Garage 20' x 22'

Deck

built in bench

Master Bedroom
11' x 13'

Breakfast
13' x 9'4"

Library/
Bedroom
11'8" x 12'10"

Great Room
15' x 16'4"

built-in bookcases

Kitchen
13' x 12'3"

walk-in closet

Bath

Laun.

stairs down

Bath

Dining Room
10'4" x 11'

Foyer

Bedroom
11'8" x 10'

stairs up

Two Car Garage
21'3" x 23'8"

Porch

HPK2300171

Style: Craftsman

Square Footage: 1,594

Bedrooms: 2

Bathrooms: 2

Width: 52' - 8"

Depth: 55' - 5"

Foundation: Unfinished Basement

eplans.com

HOME PLAN

THIS HOME BOASTS TRANSITIONAL TRENDS with its charming exterior. The columned entrance introduces the formal dining room and leads to the massive great room with a sloped ceiling and cozy fireplace. On the right, you will find French doors leading to a library/bedroom featuring built-in bookcases—another set of French doors accesses the rear deck. A family bedroom nearby shares a full bath. The gourmet kitchen enjoys an angled sink counter and a breakfast area with a bay window and built-in bench. The secluded master bedroom includes a walk-in closet, a full bath with dual vanities, and private access to the laundry room. This plan includes an optional layout for a third bedroom.

HOMES FOR FIRST-TIME BUILDERS

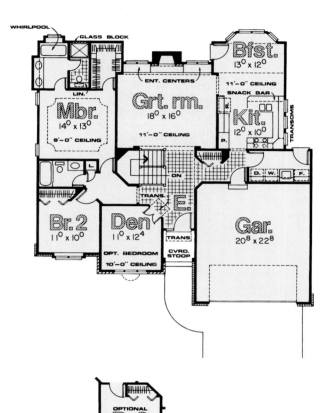

Volume ceilings add a distinctive touch to this efficient plan. The great room is complete with a fireplace framed by two built-in entertainment centers crowned with windows. The kitchen has a snack bar adjacent to the breakfast room, which features a gorgeous bay to highlight both formal and informal meals. The master bedroom has a detailed ceiling, walk-in closet and spa-style bath. A den—or make it a third bedroom—and a family bedroom with a full hall bath complete this plan.

HPK2300172

Style: Cottage
Square Footage: 1,622
Bedrooms: 2
Bathrooms: 2
Width: 51' - 0"
Depth: 52' - 0"

HOME PLAN

eplans.com

HOME PLAN

(#) HPK2300173

Style: European Cottage

First Floor: 1,177 sq. ft.

Second Floor: 457 sq. ft.

Total: 1,634 sq. ft.

Bonus Space: 249 sq. ft.

Bedrooms: 3

Bathrooms: 2 ½

Width: 41' - 0"

Depth: 48' - 0"

Foundation: Crawlspace, Unfinished Walkout Basement

eplans.com

FIRST FLOOR

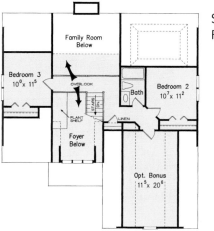

SECOND FLOOR

INFLUENCED BY EARLY AMERICAN ARCHITECTURE, THIS PETITE RENDITION offers all of the amenities you love in a space designed for small lots. A two-story foyer is lit by surrounding sidelights and a multi-pane dormer window. The dining room flows conveniently into the efficient kitchen, which opens to the breakfast nook, brightened by sliding glass doors. The vaulted family room is warmed by an extended-hearth fireplace. Past a well-concealed laundry room, the master suite pampers with a vaulted spa bath and immense walk-in closet. Two bedrooms upstairs access future bonus space.

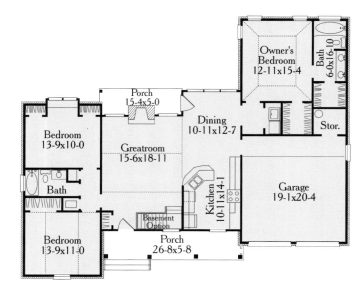

(#) HPK2300174

Style: Traditional

Square Footage: 1,643

Bedrooms: 3

Bathrooms: 2

Width: 62' - 2"

Depth: 51' - 4"

Foundation: Crawlspace, Slab, Unfinished Basement

eplans.com

TWO COVERED PORCHES LEND A RELAXING CHARM to this three-bedroom ranch home. Inside, the focal point is a warming fireplace with windows framing each side. The vaulted ceiling in the great room adds spaciousness to the adjoining kitchen and dining areas. A tray ceiling decorates the master suite, which also sports two walk-in closets. Two family bedrooms are located on the opposite side of the house.

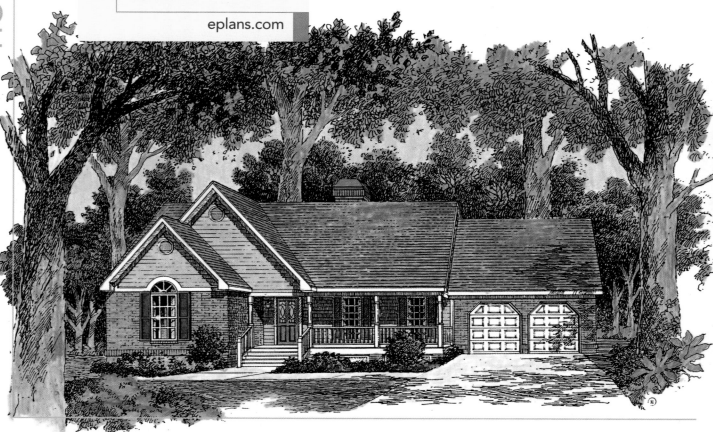

LARGE MULTIPANE WINDOWS AND STEEPLY SLOP-ING ROOFLINES lend a calming elegance to this two-story farmhouse. Inside, the great room features a warming fireplace and a bumped-out window. French doors access the three-season porch, a great place to escape to after a busy day. The U-shaped kitchen conveniently accesses a powder room to the left and the dining area to the right. Three bedrooms are nestled on the second floor—two family bedrooms sharing a full bath and a master suite with an oversized whirlpool tub, separate shower, and twin vanity sinks. Laundry facilities sit on the second level for convenience. An unfinished storage area will protect all the family heirlooms.

HOME PLAN

 # HPK2300175

Style: **Farmhouse**
First Floor: **846 sq. ft.**
Second Floor: **804 sq. ft.**
Total: **1,650 sq. ft.**
Bonus Space: **274 sq. ft.**
Bedrooms: **3**
Bathrooms: **2 ½**
Width: **50' - 0"**
Depth: **37' - 0"**

eplans.com

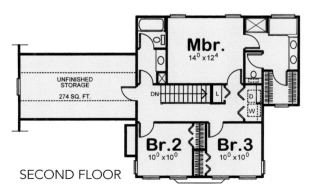

FIRST FLOOR

SECOND FLOOR

ASYMMETRICAL GABLES, A COLUMNED PORCH, AND AN ABUNDANCE OF WINDOWS brighten the exterior of this compact home. An efficient kitchen boasts a pantry and a serving bar that it shares with the formal dining room and the vaulted family room. A sunny breakfast room and nearby laundry room complete the living zone. Be sure to notice extras such as the focal-point fireplace in the family room and a plant shelf in the laundry room. The sumptuous master suite offers a door to the backyard, a vaulted sitting area, and a pampering bath. Two family bedrooms share a hall bath.

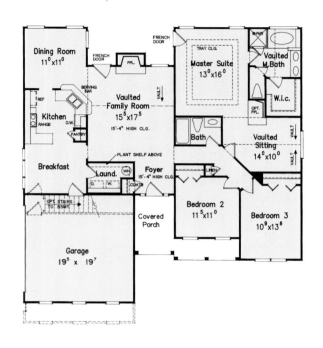

HPK2300176

HOME PLAN

Style: Southern Colonial

Square Footage: 1,671

Bedrooms: 3

Bathrooms: 2

Width: 50' - 0"

Depth: 51' - 0"

Foundation: Slab, Crawlspace, Unfinished Walkout Basement

eplans.com

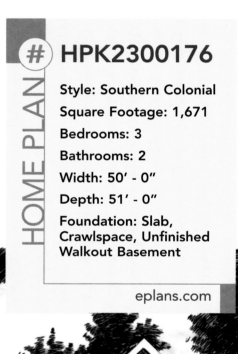

HOME PLAN (#) HPK2300177

Style: Colonial Revival

First Floor: 882 sq. ft.

Second Floor: 793 sq. ft.

Total: 1,675 sq. ft.

Bonus Space: 416 sq. ft.

Bedrooms: 3

Bathrooms: 2 ½

Width: 49' - 6"

Depth: 35' - 4"

Foundation: Crawlspace, Slab, Unfinished Walkout Basement

eplans.com

THIS FETCHING COUNTRY HOME FEATURES A SECOND-FLOOR ROOM-TO-GROW OPTION that is both savvy and stylish. The first floor places formal living spaces to the front of the design and casual living spaces to the rear of the plan. Upstairs, the master suite is enhanced with a bath that contains a walk-in closet.

FIRST FLOOR

SECOND FLOOR

OPTIONAL LAYOUT

A FINE BRICK PRESENTATION, THIS HOME BOASTS BRICK QUOINS, keystone lintels, muntin windows, and a covered porch entryway. Sleeping quarters flank either end of the general living areas. On the right side of the plan are two family bedrooms, which share a full bath. On the left side, a vaulted master suite resides, complete with a garden tub and His and Hers sinks and walk-in closets. In the center of the plan is a large living room with a fireplace, a bayed nook with rear-deck access, a dining room with a pillared entrance, and a large kitchen. Storage space is provided just off the garage.

HOME PLAN

**HPK2300178**

Style: Traditional

Square Footage: 1,675

Bedrooms: 3

Bathrooms: 2

Width: 57' - 5"

Depth: 59' - 6"

Foundation: Slab, Crawlspace, Unfinished Basement

eplans.com

HOME PLAN

HPK2300179

Style: Farmhouse

First Floor: 1,100 sq. ft.

Second Floor: 584 sq. ft.

Total: 1,684 sq. ft.

Bedrooms: 3

Bathrooms: 2

Width: 36' - 8"

Depth: 45' - 0"

FIRST FLOOR

SECOND FLOOR

HOME PLAN

HPK2300180

Style: Traditional

Square Footage: 1,700

Bonus Space: 333 sq. ft.

Bedrooms: 3

Bathrooms: 2

Width: 49' - 0"

Depth: 65' - 4"

DON'T LET THE BRICKS AND CLASSIC COLUMNS FOOL YOU—this is one home that's fully prepared for the new age. A spacious great room offers an entertainment center, a massive fireplace and, best of all, access to a private side patio. Casual dining space opens to the kitchen, which features a walk-in pantry. Three tall windows and a vaulted ceiling enhance the master suite. Separate lavatories and a garden tub highlight the private bath.

HPK2300181

HOME PLAN

Style: **Country Cottage**
Square Footage: **1,701**
Bedrooms: **3**
Bathrooms: **2**
Width: **45' - 0"**
Depth: **68' - 2"**
Foundation: **Slab**

eplans.com

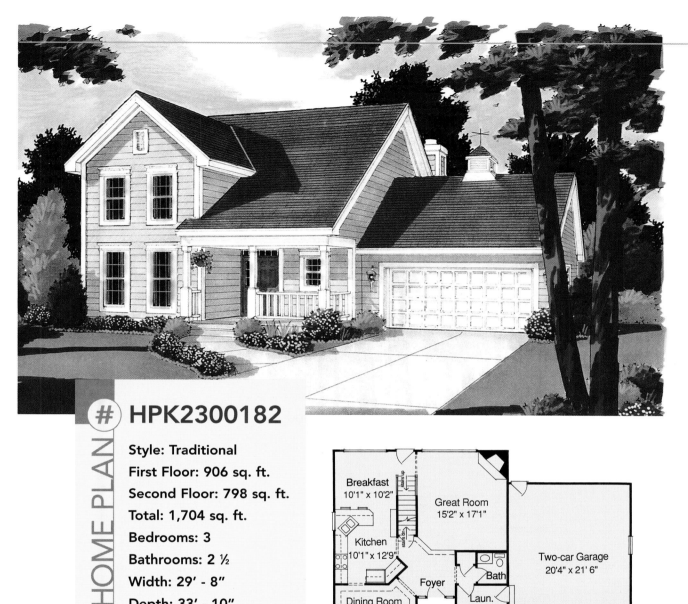

HPK2300182

Style: Traditional

First Floor: 906 sq. ft.

Second Floor: 798 sq. ft.

Total: 1,704 sq. ft.

Bedrooms: 3

Bathrooms: 2 ½

Width: 29' - 8"

Depth: 33' - 10"

Foundation: Unfinished Basement

eplans.com

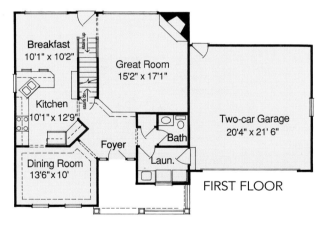

FIRST FLOOR

SECOND FLOOR

ELEMENTS OF FARMHOUSE STYLE GRACE THE FACADE of this rustic design. Inside, the floor plan is all modern. A huge great room in the rear is complemented by both a formal dining room and a casual breakfast room with a snack bar through to the kitchen. A corner fireplace in the great room warms a cozy gathering area. The two-car garage is easily accessed through a service entrance near the laundry. Bedrooms on the second floor consist of a master suite and two family bedrooms. The master suite enjoys a private bath; family bedrooms share a full bath.

A GRAND DOUBLE BANK OF WINDOWS LOOKING IN ON THE FORMAL DINING ROOM MIRRORS the lofty elegance of the extra-tall vaulted ceiling inside. From the foyer, an arched entrance to the great room visually frames the fireplace on the back wall. The wrap-around kitchen has plenty of counter and cabinet space, along with a handy serving bar. The luxurious master suite features a front sitting room for quiet times and a large spa-style bath. Two family bedrooms share a hall bath.

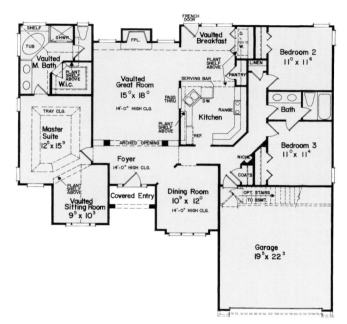

HOME PLAN

(#) HPK2300183

Style: Mediterranean

Square Footage: 1,715

Bedrooms: 3

Bathrooms: 2

Width: 55' - 0"

Depth: 49' - 0"

Foundation: Unfinished Walkout Basement, Slab, Crawlspace

eplans.com

DELIGHTFULLY DIFFERENT, THIS BRICK ONE-STORY HOME has everything for the active family. The foyer opens to a formal dining room, accented with four columns, and a great room with a fireplace and French doors to the rear deck. The efficient kitchen has an attached light-filled breakfast nook. The master bath features a tray ceiling, His and Hers walk-in closets, a double-sink vanity, and a huge garden tub. The two-car garage is accessed through the laundry room.

DECK

BEDROOM NO. 3
11'-6" X 11'-0"

BREAKFAST
11'-4" X 8'-6"

GREAT ROOM
14'-0" X 17'-6"

KITCHEN
11'-4" X 10'-0"

MASTER
BEDROOM
12'-4" X 15'-6"

BATH

FOYER
6'-6" X 6'-6"

DN

HIS

MASTER
BATH

BEDROOM NO. 2
11'-0" X 14'-8"

DINING ROOM
11'-4" X 10'-6"

PWDR.

HERS

LAUNDRY

TWO-CAR GARAGE
20'-4" X 19'-4"

HOME PLAN

HPK2300184

Style: Traditional

Square Footage: 1,733

Bedrooms: 3

Bathrooms: 2 ½

Width: 55' - 6"

Depth: 57' - 6"

Foundation: Walkout Basement

eplans.com

HOME PLAN #

HPK2300185

Style: Traditional

First Floor: 884 sq. ft.

Second Floor: 860 sq. ft.

Total: 1,744 sq. ft.

Bedrooms: 4

Bathrooms: 2 ½

Width: 50' - 0"

Depth: 32' - 0"

Foundation: Slab, Unfinished Walkout Basement, Crawlspace

FIRST FLOOR

SECOND FLOOR

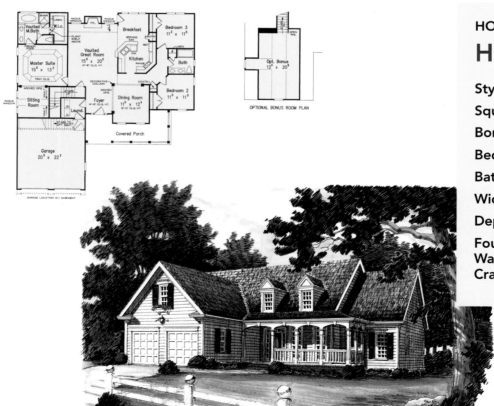

HOME PLAN #

HPK2300186

Style: Country Cottage

Square Footage: 1,749

Bonus Space: 327 sq. ft.

Bedrooms: 3

Bathrooms: 2

Width: 54' - 0"

Depth: 56' - 6"

Foundation: Unfinished Walkout Basement, Slab, Crawlspace

A SUNBURST WINDOW SET WITHIN A BRICK EXTERIOR AND MULTIGABLED ROOF lends a vibrant aura to this three-bedroom home. The slope-ceilinged great room features a fireplace with French doors at each side. The nearby bay-windowed dining room accesses the rear porch—a perfect place for a barbecue grill. Conveniently placed near the garage for fast unloading, the U-shaped kitchen is sure to please. The master suite enjoys a walk-in closet and a luxurious bath including a separate shower, whirlpool tub, and twin-sink vanity. The two family bedrooms benefit from front-facing windows and share a full bath.

HOME PLAN

HPK2300187

Style: Traditional

Square Footage: 1,755

Bedrooms: 3

Bathrooms: 2

Width: 78' - 6"

Depth: 47' - 7"

Foundation: Unfinished Basement

eplans.com

HOMES FOR FIRST-TIME BUILDERS

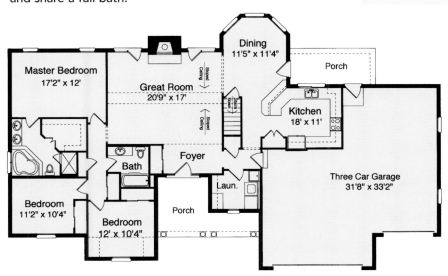

Master Bedroom
17'2" x 12'

Dining
11'5" x 11'4"

Great Room
20'9" x 17'

Porch

Kitchen
18' x 11'

Foyer

Bath

Laun.

Three Car Garage
31'8" x 33'2"

Bedroom
11'2" x 10'4"

Bedroom
12' x 10'4"

Porch

FIRST FLOOR

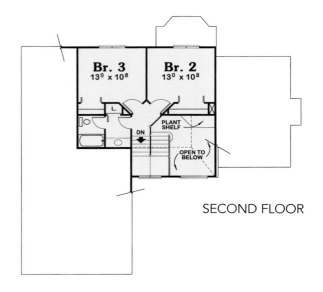

SECOND FLOOR

HANDSOME DETAILING AND UNIQUE WINDOWS ARE HALLMARKS ON THE ELEVATION of this two-story design. Triple-arch windows in the front and rear of the great room create an impressive view. Counter space is coordinated in the island kitchen to make it easy to prepare meals. A compartmentalized master bath provides a convenient dressing area and vanity space. In the entry, a U-shaped staircase with a window leads to a second-floor balcony, two bedrooms, and a full bath.

HOME PLAN

(#) HPK2300188

Style: New American
First Floor: 1,314 sq. ft.
Second Floor: 458 sq. ft.
Total: 1,772 sq. ft.
Bedrooms: 3
Bathrooms: 2 ½
Width: 52' - 0"
Depth: 51' - 4"

eplans.com

(#) HPK2300189

Style: European Cottage

Square Footage: 1,779

Bedrooms: 3

Bathrooms: 2

Width: 57' - 0"

Depth: 56' - 4"

Foundation: Unfinished Walkout Basement, Crawlspace

eplans.com

EUROPEAN STYLE SHINES FROM THIS HOME'S FACADE in the form of its stucco detailing, hipped rooflines, fancy windows, and elegant entryway. Inside, decorative columns and a plant shelf define the formal dining room, which works well with the vaulted family room. The efficient kitchen offers a serving bar to both the family room and the deluxe breakfast room. Located apart from the family bedrooms for privacy, the master suite is sure to please with its many amenities, including a vaulted sitting area and a private covered porch. The two secondary bedrooms share a full hall bath.

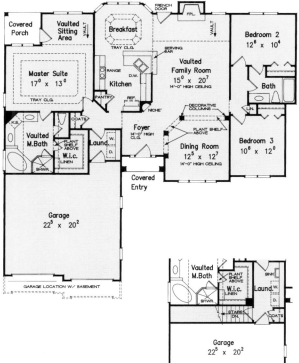

OPTIONAL LAYOUT

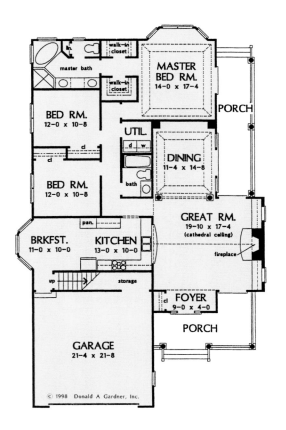

THIS LOVELY HOME INCORPORATES
STYLE AND PRACTICALITY in an economical
and charming package. A cathedral ceiling
enhances the great room, which also displays
a fireplace and built-ins. An optional
loft/study above the kitchen overlooks the
great room. The kitchen serves the breakfast
bay, the dining room, and the great room.
Sleeping arrangements include a delightful
master suite, with two walk-in-closets, and
two family bedrooms that share a hall bath.
A bonus room over the garage offers room
for future expansion.

HPK2300190

HOME PLAN

Style: Country Cottage
Square Footage: 1,795
Bonus Space: 368 sq. ft.
Bedrooms: 3
Bathrooms: 2
Width: 45' - 0"
Depth: 72' - 4"

eplans.com

© 1998 Donald A. Gardner, Inc.

THIS TRADITIONAL DESIGN FEATURES A GARDEN ROOM with twin skylights, a sloped ceiling, and two walls of windows. The kitchen provides plenty of counter space and easily serves the formal dining room, which opens through double doors to the garden room. A balcony overlooks the great room, which is warmed by a fireplace. All four bedrooms including the master suite with its full bath and plentiful storage space, are on the upper level.

HOME PLAN

HPK2300191

Style: Traditional
First Floor: 837 sq. ft.
Second Floor: 977 sq. ft.
Total: 1,814 sq. ft.
Bedrooms: 4
Bathrooms: 2 ½
Width: 58' - 4"
Depth: 41' - 4"

eplans.com

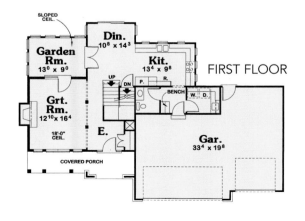

FIRST FLOOR

SECOND FLOOR

HOMES FOR FIRST-TIME BUILDERS

THIS COMPACT ONE-STORY HAS PLENTY OF LIVING IN IT. The master suite features an optional sun-washed sitting area with views to the rear of the home. A vaulted great room with fireplace conveniently accesses the kitchen via a serving bar. Meals can also be taken in the cozy breakfast area. For formal occasions the dining room creates opulence with its decorative columns. Two family bedrooms flank the right of the home with a shared bath, linen storage, and easy access to laundry facilities.

HOME PLAN

(#) HPK2300192

Style: Country Cottage

Square Footage: 1,832

Bonus Space: 68 sq. ft.

Bedrooms: 3

Bathrooms: 2 ½

Width: 59' - 6"

Depth: 52' - 6"

Foundation: Crawlspace, Slab, Unfinished Walkout Basement

eplans.com

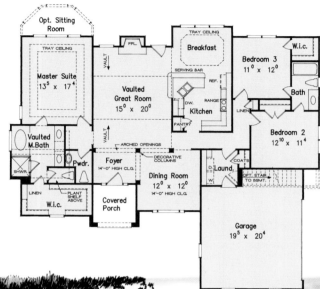

HOME PLAN

HPK2300193

Style: Craftsman

Square Footage: 1,860

Bedrooms: 3

Bathrooms: 2

Width: 64' - 2"

Depth: 44' - 2"

Foundation: Finished Walkout Basement

eplans.com

Deck

Master Bedroom
12' x 14'6"
10'10" CEILING

WALK-IN CLOSET

Dressing

Great Room
16'6" x 21'2"
11'1" CEILING HT

TV ALCOVE

ALCOVE 8'6" x 6'6"

STAIRS DOWN

Breakfast
12'9" x 13'

Porch
11'8" x 11'

Kitchen
12'6" x 10'11"

Laun.

HANGING SPACE

Hall

Bath

PANTRY

Bedroom
10' x 12'

Bedroom
11'3" x 11'1"

Foyer

Dining Room
10'10" x 12'2"

Garage
19'8" x 23'2"

Porch

A BRICK, STONE, AND CEDAR-SHAKE FACADE provide color and texture to the exterior of this delightful one-level home. A spacious great room is decorated with a wood-burning fireplace, high ceiling, and French doors. Grand openings to both the breakfast room and dining room offer expanded space for formal or informal occasions. A breakfast bar offers additional seating and a comfortable gathering place. A covered porch provides a pleasant retreat and is located for convenient access from the kitchen and breakfast area. Alcoves in the great room and master bedroom are created for furniture placement. An angled entry in the master suite introduces a spectacular bath with a whirlpool tub and double-bowl vanity.

FIRST FLOOR

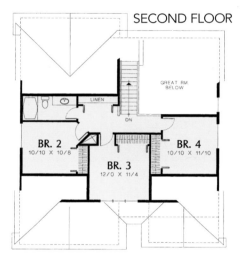

SECOND FLOOR

A FINE EXAMPLE OF A CRAFTSMAN BUNGALOW, this four-bedroom home will be a delight to own. The efficient kitchen offers a serving island to the dining area, while the glow from the corner fireplace in the great room adds cheer to the entire area. Located on the first floor for privacy, the vaulted master bedroom features a walk-in closet, a private bath with a dual-bowl vanity, and access to the rear yard. Upstairs, three secondary bedrooms share a full hall bath and a large linen closet. The two-car garage will easily shelter the family fleet.

HPK2300194

HOME PLAN

Style: Country Cottage
First Floor: 1,198 sq. ft.
Second Floor: 668 sq. ft.
Total: 1,866 sq. ft.
Bedrooms: 4
Bathrooms: 2 ½
Width: 40' - 0"
Depth: 47' - 0"
Foundation: Crawlspace

eplans.com

© 1993 Donald A. Gardner Architects, Inc.

DORMERS CAST LIGHT AND INTEREST INTO THE FOYER for a grand first impression that sets the tone in this home full of today's amenities. The great room, articulated by columns, features a cathedral ceiling and is conveniently located adjacent to the breakfast room and kitchen. Tray ceilings and circle-top picture windows accent the front bedroom and dining room. A secluded master suite, highlighted by a tray ceiling in the bedroom, includes a bath with a skylight, a garden tub, a separate shower, a double-bowl vanity, and a spacious walk-in closet.

HOME PLAN

HPK2300195

Style: Country Cottage

Square Footage: 1,879

Bonus Space: 360 sq. ft.

Bedrooms: 3

Bathrooms: 2

Width: 66' - 4"

Depth: 55' - 2"

eplans.com

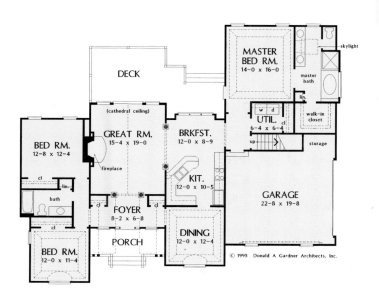

© 1995 Donald A Gardner Architects, Inc.

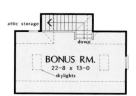

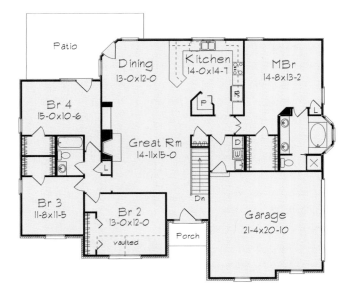

(#) HPK2300196

Style: Traditional

Square Footage: 1,882

Bedrooms: 4

Bathrooms: 2

Width: 58' - 0"

Depth: 47' - 6"

Foundation: Unfinished Basement

eplans.com

AN ELEGANT BRICK FACADE AND ARCH-TOPPED WINDOWS give this home plenty of curb appeal. Its compact shape and side-loading garage make it perfect for a corner lot. Inside, the great room is enhanced by a fireplace and opens to the rear patio via the dining room. The deluxe master bath is distinguished by the large tub and double-sink vanity, and spacious closets are found in all four bedrooms. The delightful kitchen easily serves the dining area and great room.

HOME PLAN

(#) # HPK2300197

Style: Country Cottage

Square Footage: 1,884

Bedrooms: 3

Bathrooms: 2 ½

Width: 50' - 0"

Depth: 55' - 4"

Foundation: Slab, Crawlspace, Unfinished Walkout Basement

eplans.com

ARCHED OPENINGS, DECORATIVE COLUMNS, and elegant ceiling details throughout highlight this livable floor plan. The country kitchen includes a spacious work area, preparation island, serving bar to the great room, and a breakfast nook with a tray ceiling. Set to the rear for gracious entertaining, the dining room opens to the great room. Note the warming fireplace and French-door access to the backyard in the great room. The master suite is beautifully appointed with a tray ceiling, bay window, compartmented bath, and walk-in closet. Two family bedrooms, a laundry room, and a powder room complete this gracious design.

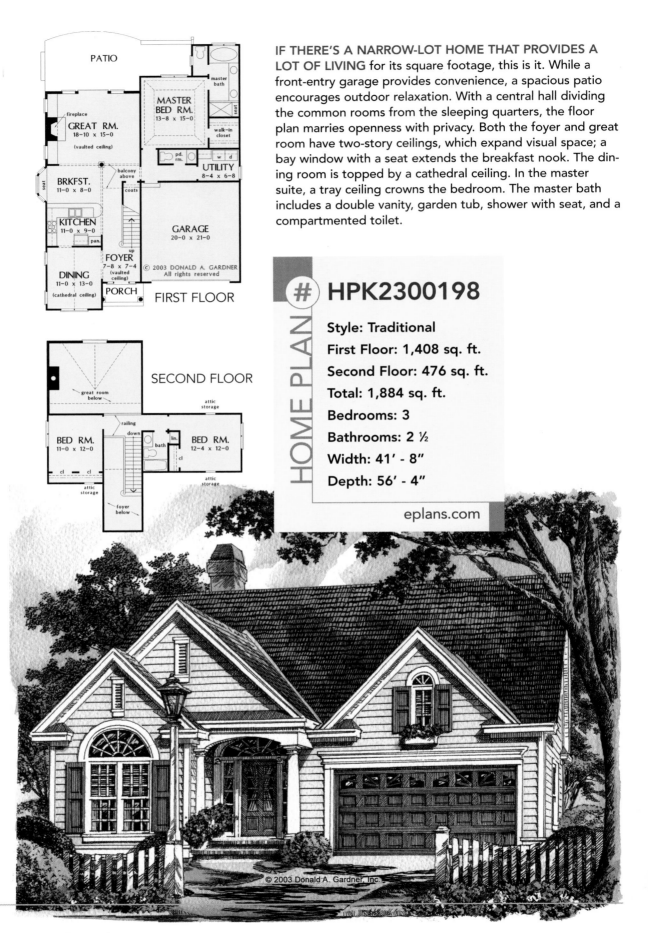

PATIO

MASTER BED RM.
13-8 x 15-0

master bath

seat

fireplace

GREAT RM.
18-10 x 15-0
(vaulted ceiling)

walk-in closet

BRKFST.
11-0 x 8-0

balcony above

seat

coats

pd. rm.

w d

UTILITY
8-4 x 6-8

KITCHEN
11-0 x 9-0

pan.

up

GARAGE
20-0 x 21-0

FOYER
7-8 x 7-4
(vaulted ceiling)

© 2003 DONALD A. GARDNER
All rights reserved

DINING
11-0 x 13-0
(cathedral ceiling)

PORCH

FIRST FLOOR

great room below

attic storage

BED RM.
11-0 x 12-0

railing

down

lin.

bath

cl

BED RM.
12-4 x 12-0

cl   cl

attic storage

attic storage

foyer below

SECOND FLOOR

IF THERE'S A NARROW-LOT HOME THAT PROVIDES A LOT OF LIVING for its square footage, this is it. While a front-entry garage provides convenience, a spacious patio encourages outdoor relaxation. With a central hall dividing the common rooms from the sleeping quarters, the floor plan marries openness with privacy. Both the foyer and great room have two-story ceilings, which expand visual space; a bay window with a seat extends the breakfast nook. The dining room is topped by a cathedral ceiling. In the master suite, a tray ceiling crowns the bedroom. The master bath includes a double vanity, garden tub, shower with seat, and a compartmented toilet.

HOME PLAN

HPK2300198

Style: Traditional
First Floor: 1,408 sq. ft.
Second Floor: 476 sq. ft.
Total: 1,884 sq. ft.
Bedrooms: 3
Bathrooms: 2 ½
Width: 41' - 8"
Depth: 56' - 4"

eplans.com

© 2003 Donald A. Gardner, Inc.

SPECIAL ARCHITECTURAL ASPECTS turn this quaint home into much more than just another one-story ranch design. A central great room acts as the hub of the plan and is graced by a fireplace flanked on either side by windows. It is separated from the kitchen by a convenient serving bar. Formal dining is accomplished to the front of the plan in a room with a tray ceiling. Casual dining takes place in the breakfast room with its full wall of glass. Two bedrooms to the left share a full bath. The master suite and one additional bedroom are to the right.

HOME PLAN

HPK2300199

Style: Traditional

Square Footage: 1,932

Bedrooms: 4

Bathrooms: 3

Width: 63' - 0"

Depth: 45' - 0"

Foundation: Unfinished Walkout Basement, Crawlspace

eplans.com

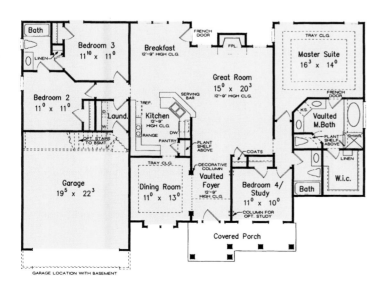

FIRST FLOOR

SECOND FLOOR

HPK2300200

Style: Farmhouse
First Floor: 1,305 sq. ft.
Second Floor: 636 sq. ft.
Total: 1,941 sq. ft.
Bedrooms: 4
Bathrooms: 2 ½
Width: 42' - 4"
Depth: 46' - 10"
Foundation: Crawlspace, Slab, Unfinished Basement

eplans.com

CRAFTSMAN-STYLE WINDOWS DECORATE THE FACADE OF THIS BEAUTIFUL BUNGALOW DESIGN. Inside, the formal dining room, to the left of the foyer, can double as a study; the family room offers a sloping ceiling and a fireplace option. In the breakfast nook, a window seat and sliding glass doors that open to the covered patio provide places to enjoy the outdoors. The master bedroom dominates the right side of the plan, boasting a walk-in closet and private bath. Upstairs, two secondary bedrooms—both with walk-in closets, and one with a private bath—sit to either side of a game room.

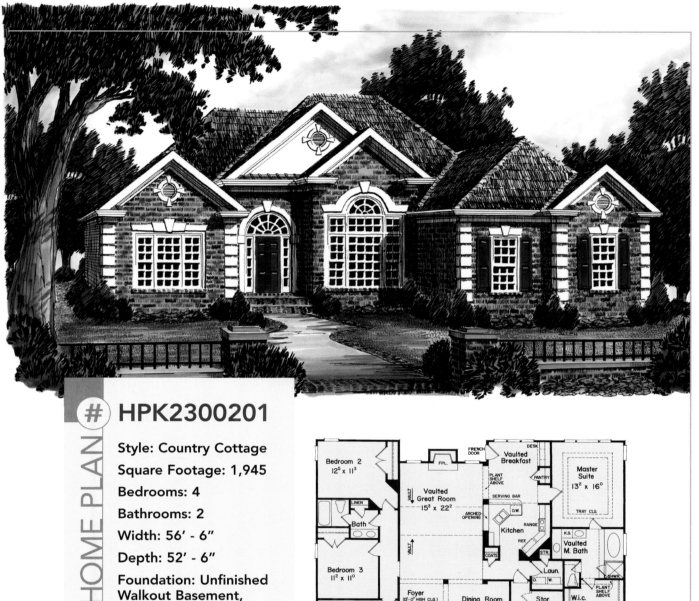

(#) HPK2300201

Style: Country Cottage

Square Footage: 1,945

Bedrooms: 4

Bathrooms: 2

Width: 56' - 6"

Depth: 52' - 6"

Foundation: Unfinished Walkout Basement, Crawlspace, Slab

eplans.com

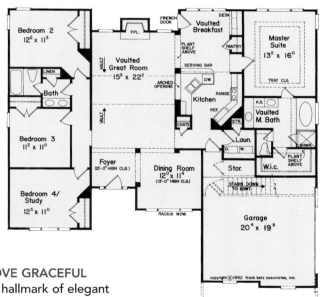

CORNER QUOINS AND KEYSTONES ABOVE GRACEFUL WINDOW TREATMENTS have long been a hallmark of elegant European-style exteriors—this home has all that and more. This becomes apparent upon entering the foyer, which is beautifully framed by columns in the dining room and the entrance to the vaulted great room. The left wing holds three secondary bedrooms—one doubles as a study—and a full bath. To the right of the combined kitchen and vaulted breakfast room, you will find the private master suite. A relaxing master bath and a large walk-in closet complete this splendid retreat.

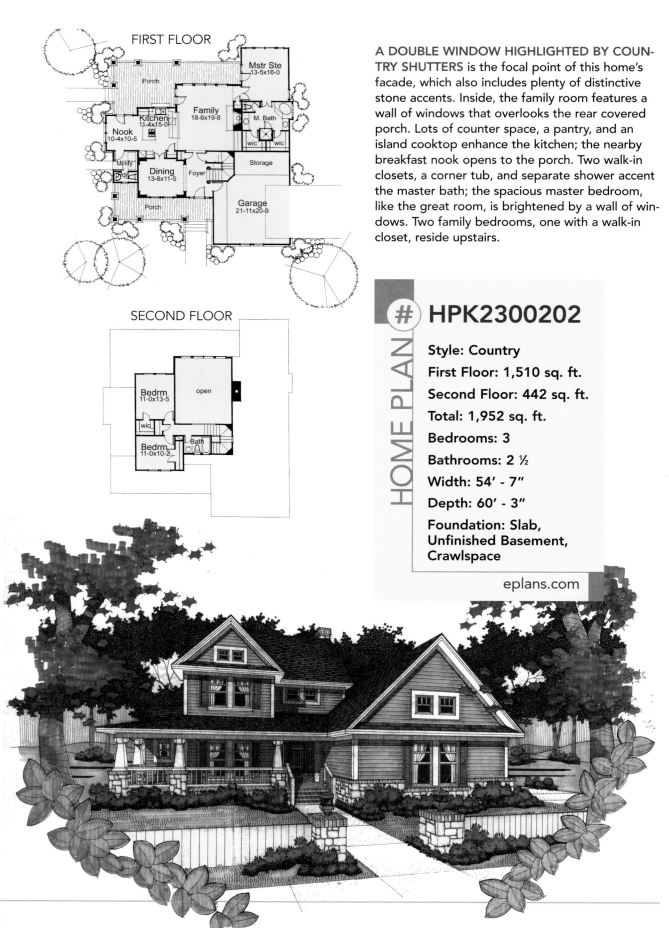

FIRST FLOOR

Porch

Mstr Ste
13-5x16-0

Kitchen
11-4x15-0

Nook
10-4x10-5

Family
18-6x19-8

M. Bath

wic   wic

Utility

Dining
13-8x11-5

Foyer

Storage

Porch

Garage
21-11x20-9

SECOND FLOOR

Bedrm
11-0x13-5

open

w.i.c

Bedrm
11-0x10-2

Bath

A DOUBLE WINDOW HIGHLIGHTED BY COUNTRY SHUTTERS is the focal point of this home's facade, which also includes plenty of distinctive stone accents. Inside, the family room features a wall of windows that overlooks the rear covered porch. Lots of counter space, a pantry, and an island cooktop enhance the kitchen; the nearby breakfast nook opens to the porch. Two walk-in closets, a corner tub, and separate shower accent the master bath; the spacious master bedroom, like the great room, is brightened by a wall of windows. Two family bedrooms, one with a walk-in closet, reside upstairs.

HPK2300202

HOME PLAN

Style: Country

First Floor: 1,510 sq. ft.

Second Floor: 442 sq. ft.

Total: 1,952 sq. ft.

Bedrooms: 3

Bathrooms: 2 ½

Width: 54' - 7"

Depth: 60' - 3"

Foundation: Slab, Unfinished Basement, Crawlspace

eplans.com

HOME PLAN

 # HPK2300203

Style: Southern Colonial

Square Footage: 1,955

Bedrooms: 3

Bathrooms: 2 ½

Width: 56' - 4"

Depth: 67' - 4"

Foundation: Crawlspace, Slab, Unfinished Basement

eplans.com

DOUBLE PILLARS, BEAUTIFUL TRANSOMS, AND SIDELIGHTS set off the entry door and draw attention to this comfortable home. The foyer leads to a formal dining room and a great room with two pairs of French doors framing a warming fireplace. The kitchen enjoys a large island/snack bar and a walk-in pantry. Privacy is assured in the master suite—a large walk-in closet and full bath with a separate shower and large tub add to the pleasure of this wing. Two family bedrooms share a full bath at the front of the design.

FIRST FLOOR

FAMILY
15/0 X 13/0
(9' CLG.)

NOOK
8/6 X 11/0 +/-
(9' CLG.)

8/6 X 15/2
(9' CLG.)

BLT-IN

BLT-IN

STORAGE

UP

DINING
12/0 X 10/0
(9' CLG.)

P. REF

GARAGE
20/0 X 24/0 +/-

VAULTED
LIVING
12/0 X 12/6

SECOND FLOOR

SHLVS

MASTER
15/6 X 16/0

SPA

D W

DN.

BR. 3
10/6 X 13/8 +/-

BR. 2
10/2 X 12/8

A SENSIBLE FLOOR PLAN, WITH LIVING SPACES ON THE FIRST FLOOR AND BEDROOMS on the second floor, is the highlight of this Craftsman home. Elegance reigns in the formal living room, with a vaulted ceiling and columned entry; this room is open to the dining room, which is brightened by natural light from two tall windows. Ideal for informal gatherings, the family room boasts a fireplace flanked by built-in shelves. The efficient kitchen includes a central island and double sink, and the nearby nook features easy access to the outdoors through sliding glass doors. The master suite includes a lavish bath with a corner spa tub and compartmented toilet; two additional bedrooms, one with a walk-in closet, share a full bath.

HPK2300204

HOME PLAN

Style: Craftsman

First Floor: 970 sq. ft.

Second Floor: 988 sq. ft.

Total: 1,958 sq. ft.

Bedrooms: 3

Bathrooms: 2 ½

Width: 40' - 0"

Depth: 43' - 0"

Foundation: Crawlspace

eplans.com

HOME PLAN

#️⃣ HPK2300205

Style: Southern Colonial

First Floor: 1,071 sq. ft.

Second Floor: 924 sq. ft.

Total: 1,995 sq. ft.

Bonus Space: 280 sq. ft.

Bedrooms: 3

Bathrooms: 2 ½

Width: 55' - 10"

Foundation: Crawlspace, Unfinished Walkout Basement, Slab

eplans.com

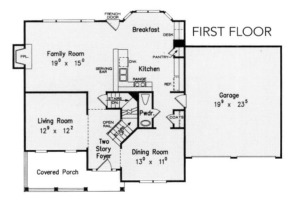

FIRST FLOOR

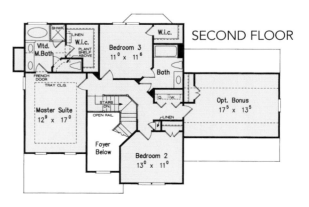

SECOND FLOOR

MOVE-UP BUYERS CAN ENJOY ALL THE LUXURIES of this two-story home highlighted by an angled staircase separating the dining room from casual living areas. A private powder room is tucked away behind the dining room—convenient for formal dinner parties. A bay window and built-in desk in the breakfast area are just a few of the plan's amenities. The sleeping zone occupies the second floor—away from everyday activities—and includes a master suite and two secondary bedrooms.

THE WIDE FRONT STEPS, COLUMNED PORCH, and symmetrical layout give this charming home a Georgian appeal. The large kitchen, with its walk-in pantry, island/snack bar, and breakfast nook, will gratify any cook. The central great room offers radiant French doors on both sides of the fireplace. Outside those doors is a comfortable covered porch with two skylights. To the left of the great room reside four bedrooms—three secondary bedrooms and a master bedroom. The master bedroom enjoys a walk-in closet, twin-vanity sinks, a separate shower and tub, and private access to the rear porch.

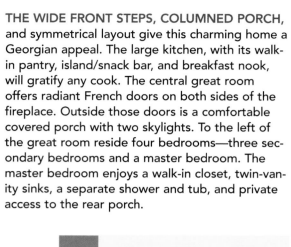

HOME PLAN

(#) HPK2300206

Style: Colonial

Square Footage: 1,997

Bedrooms: 4

Bathrooms: 2 ½

Width: 56' - 4"

Depth: 67' - 4"

Foundation: Crawlspace, Slab, Unfinished Basement

eplans.com

DECK

VAULTED
MASTER
16/2 X 13/0

SCISSOR VAULTED
LIVING/DINING
15/2 X 20/2

D. W.

PAN.

GARAGE
19/6 X 20/0

REF

DEN
11/0 X 10/0
(10' CLG.)

DN.

MAIN LEVEL

BR. 2
10/6 X 12/8 +

BR. 3
10/8 X 11/0

REC. RM.
14/10 X 12/8

CRAWLSPACE

UP

STORAGE

LOWER LEVEL

HOME PLAN

HPK2300207

Style: Country Cottage
Main Level: 1,230 sq. ft.
Lower Level: 769 sq. ft.
Total: 1,999 sq. ft.
Bedrooms: 3
Bathrooms: 2 ½
Width: 40' - 0"
Depth: 52' - 6"
Foundation: Finished Walkout Basement

eplans.com

THIS PETITE COUNTRY COTTAGE DESIGN is enhanced with all the modern amenities. Inside, through a pair of double doors, the family den is illuminated by a large window. The kitchen, which features efficient pantry space, opens to the living/dining area. This spacious room is highlighted by a scissor vaulted ceiling, and features a warming fireplace and nook space. The living/dining room also overlooks a large rear deck, which is accessed through a back door. Secluded on the ground level for extra privacy, the vaulted master bedroom includes a private full bath and a walk-in closet. A laundry room, two-car garage, and powder room all complete this floor. Downstairs, two additional family bedrooms share a hall bath. The recreation room is an added bonus. Extra storage space is also available on this floor.

FIRST FLOOR

SECOND FLOOR

A CAREFUL BLEND OF SIDING AND STONE LENDS EYE-CATCHING APPEAL to this traditional plan. Vaulted ceilings grace the great room, master bath, and dining room. The efficient kitchen offers pantry storage and a serving bar to the breakfast room. The master suite features a tray ceiling and a deluxe private bath. A bedroom/study is located on the first floor. Two second-floor bedrooms easily access a full bath. An optional bonus room offers plenty of room to grow—making it perfect for a guest suite, home office, or exercise room.

HOME PLAN

HPK2300208

Style: Country Cottage

First Floor: 1,559 sq. ft.

Second Floor: 475 sq. ft.

Total: 2,034 sq. ft.

Bonus Space: 321 sq. ft.

Bedrooms: 4

Bathrooms: 3

Width: 50' - 0"

Depth: 56' - 4"

Foundation: Crawlspace, Slab, Unfinished Walkout Basement

eplans.com

HOME PLAN

(#) HPK2300209

Style: Contemporary

First Floor: 1,347 sq. ft.

Second Floor: 690 sq. ft.

Total: 2,037 sq. ft.

Bedrooms: 4

Bathrooms: 2

Width: 55' - 0"

Depth: 41' - 0"

Foundation: Unfinished Basement

eplans.com

REAR EXTERIOR

FIRST FLOOR

SECOND FLOOR

PERFECT FOR WATERFRONT PROPERTY, this home boasts windows everywhere. Inside, open planning can be found in the living room, which offers a corner fireplace for cool evenings and blends beautifully into the dining and kitchen areas. All areas enjoy window views. A laundry room is conveniently nestled between the kitchen and the two-car garage. The master suite features a walk-through closet and sumptuous bath. Upstairs, three uniquely shaped bedrooms share a full bath.

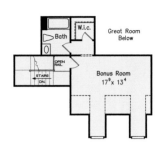

(#) HPK2300210

Style: Country Cottage

Square Footage: 2,050

Bonus Space: 418 sq. ft.

Bedrooms: 4

Bathrooms: 3

Width: 60' - 0"

Depth: 56' - 0"

Foundation: Crawlspace, Unfinished Walkout Basement, Slab

eplans.com

THIS HOME PLAN IS SO COMPREHENSIVE, you won't believe that there is bonus space included. A covered porch accesses a foyer with adjoining open formal dining area, leading to the stunning great room, past decorative columns. The master suite is partitioned to the right of the great room, and features a stylish tray ceiling and luscious vaulted bath behind a French door. A separate bedroom is hidden away with its own bath. An ultra-functional kitchen lies to the left of the great room, with an open space adjoining the breakfast area to the latter. The nook opens to the patio via a French door, and affords a panoramic outdoor view through a bayed window. Around a built-in desk and walk-in pantry are the laundry, and two bedrooms with shared bath. The staircase and interior access to the garage are located back through the kitchen.

LIGHT POURS IN THROUGH MANY WINDOWS on this home's facade. The handsome two-story foyer with a balcony creates a spacious entrance area. The U-shaped kitchen provides easy serving access to the dining room and breakfast nook. A vaulted ceiling, private dressing area and large walk-in closet complement the master bedroom. Skylights flood both the hall bath and master bath with natural light. A conveniently located second-floor laundry room resides near the bedrooms.

(#) HPK2300211

Style: Traditional

First Floor: 1,098 sq. ft.

Second Floor: 960 sq. ft.

Total: 2,058 sq. ft.

Bedrooms: 3

Bathrooms: 2 ½

Width: 50' - 0"

Depth: 36' - 0"

Foundation: Crawlspace, Slab, Unfinished Basement

eplans.com

FIRST FLOOR

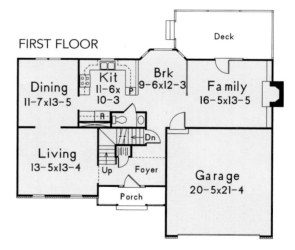

SECOND FLOOR

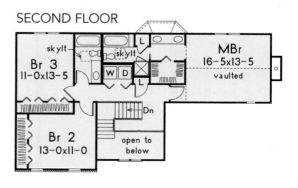

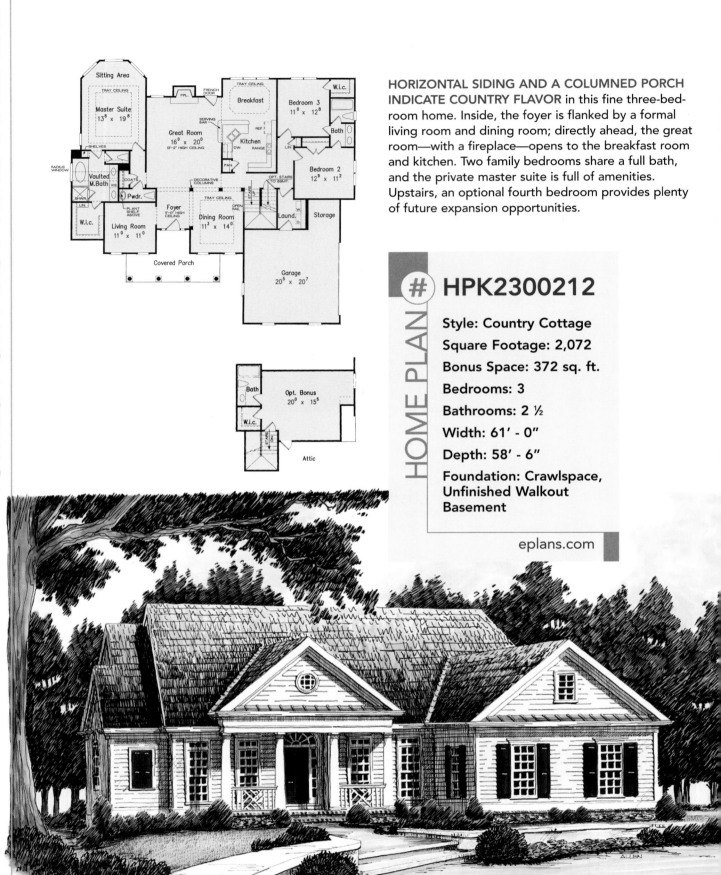

HORIZONTAL SIDING AND A COLUMNED PORCH INDICATE COUNTRY FLAVOR in this fine three-bedroom home. Inside, the foyer is flanked by a formal living room and dining room; directly ahead, the great room—with a fireplace—opens to the breakfast room and kitchen. Two family bedrooms share a full bath, and the private master suite is full of amenities. Upstairs, an optional fourth bedroom provides plenty of future expansion opportunities.

HPK2300212

Style: Country Cottage
Square Footage: 2,072
Bonus Space: 372 sq. ft.
Bedrooms: 3
Bathrooms: 2 ½
Width: 61' - 0"
Depth: 58' - 6"
Foundation: Crawlspace, Unfinished Walkout Basement

HOME PLAN

eplans.com

THIS FOUR-BEDROOM, THREE-BATH HOME offers the finest in modern amenities. The huge family room, which opens up to the patio with 12-foot pocket sliding doors, provides space for a fireplace and media equipment. Two family bedrooms share a full bath; one bedroom has a private bath with patio access, making it the perfect guest room. The master suite, located just off the kitchen and nook, is private yet easily accessible. The double-door entry, bed wall with glass above, step-down shower and private toilet room, walk-in linen closet, and lavish vanity make this a very comfortable master suite!

HOME PLAN

HPK2300213

Style: Italianate
Square Footage: 2,089
Bedrooms: 4
Bathrooms: 3
Width: 61' - 8"
Depth: 50' - 4"
Foundation: Slab

eplans.com

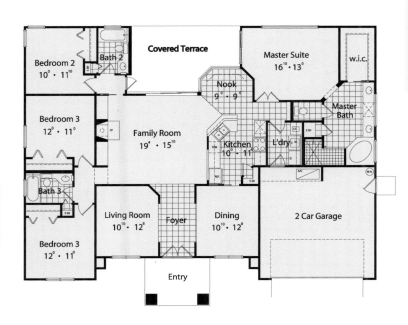

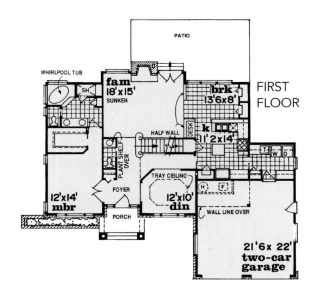

FIRST FLOOR

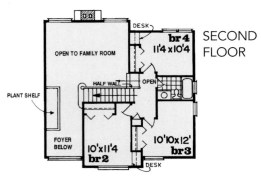

SECOND FLOOR

A PORTICO ENTRY, GRACEFUL ARCHES, AND BRICK DETAILING provide appeal and a low-maintenance exterior for this design. A half-circle transom over the entry lights the two-story foyer, and a plant shelf lines the hallway to the sunken family room. This living space holds a vaulted ceiling, masonry fireplace, and French-door access to the railed patio. The nearby kitchen has a center prep island, built-in desk overlooking the family room, and extensive pantries in the breakfast area. The formal dining room has a tray ceiling and access to the foyer and the central hall. The master suite is on the first level for privacy and convenience. It features a walk-in closet and lavish bath with twin vanities, a whirlpool tub, and separate shower. Three family bedrooms, two of which feature built-in desks, are on the second floor.

HOME PLAN

HPK2300214

Style: Traditional
First Floor: 1,445 sq. ft.
Second Floor: 652 sq. ft.
Total: 2,097 sq. ft.
Bedrooms: 4
Bathrooms: 2 ½
Width: 56' - 8"
Depth: 48' - 4"
Foundation: Crawlspace, Unfinished Basement

eplans.com

HOME PLAN

(#) HPK2300215

Style: French Country

First Floor: 1,626 sq. ft.

Second Floor: 475 sq. ft.

Total: 2,101 sq. ft.

Bedrooms: 3

Bathrooms: 2 ½

Width: 59' - 0"

Depth: 60' - 8"

Foundation: Unfinished Basement

eplans.com

FIRST FLOOR

AN EXTERIOR WITH A RICH, SOLID LOOK AND AN EXCITING ROOFLINE is very important to the discriminating buyer. An octagonal and vaulted master bedroom and a sunken great room with a balcony above provide this home with all the amenities. The island kitchen is easily accessible to both the breakfast area and the bayed dining area. The tapered staircase leads to two family bedrooms, each with its own access to a full dual-vanity bath. Both bedrooms have a vast closet area with double doors.

SECOND FLOOR

COME HOME TO THIS DELIGHTFUL BUNGALOW, created with you in mind. From the covered front porch, the foyer opens to the dining room on the left and vaulted family room ahead. An elongated island in the well-planned kitchen makes meal preparation a joy. A sunny breakfast nook is perfect for casual pursuits. Tucked to the rear, the master suite enjoys ultimate privacy and a luxurious break from the world with a vaulted bath and garden tub. Secondary bedrooms share a full bath upstairs; a bonus room is ready to expand as your needs change.

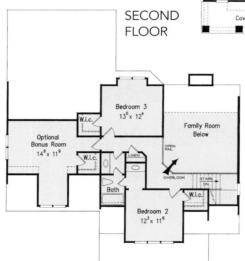

HOME PLAN

HPK2300216

Style: Craftsman

First Floor: 1,561 sq. ft.

Second Floor: 578 sq. ft.

Total: 2,139 sq. ft.

Bonus Space: 238 sq. ft.

Bedrooms: 3

Bathrooms: 2 ½

Width: 50' - 0"

Depth: 56' - 6"

Foundation: Crawlspace, Unfinished Walkout Basement, Slab

eplans.com

HOME PLAN

HPK2300217

Style: Colonial

Square Footage: 2,150

Bedrooms: 3

Bathrooms: 2 ½

Width: 64' - 0"

Depth: 64' - 3"

Foundation: Walkout Basement

eplans.com

THIS ATTRACTIVE BRICK COTTAGE HOME WITH AN ARCHED COVERED ENTRY gives family and friends a warm welcome. The jack-arch window detailing adds intrigue to the exterior. The foyer, dining room, and great room are brought together, defined by decorative columns. To the right of the foyer, a bedroom with a complete bath could double as a home office or children's den. The spacious kitchen has a centered work island and an adjacent keeping room with a fireplace—ideal for families that like to congregate at mealtimes. The abundance of windows throughout the back of the home provides a grand view of the back property. The master suite enjoys privacy to the rear of the home. A garden tub, large walk-in closet, and two vanities make a perfect homeowner retreat.

REAR EXTERIOR

THIS CLASSIC COTTAGE BOASTS A STONE-AND-WOOD EXTERIOR with a welcoming arch-top entry that leads to a columned foyer. An extended-hearth fireplace is the focal point of the family room, and a nearby sunroom with covered porch access opens up the living area to the outdoors. The gourmet island kitchen opens through double doors from the living area; the breakfast area looks out to a porch. Sleeping quarters include a master wing with a spacious, angled bath, and a sitting room or den that has its own full bath—perfect for a guest suite. On the opposite side of the plan, two family bedrooms share a full bath.

HPK2300218

HOME PLAN

Style: Country Cottage
Square Footage: 2,170
Bedrooms: 4
Bathrooms: 3
Width: 62' - 0"
Depth: 61' - 6"
Foundation: Walkout Basement

eplans.com

HPK2300219

HOME PLAN

Style: Neoclassic

Square Footage: 2,189

Bedrooms: 3

Bathrooms: 2

Width: 56' - 0"

Depth: 72' - 0"

Foundation: Slab

eplans.com

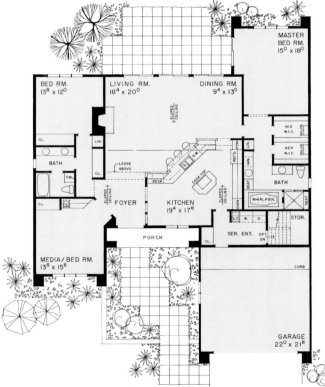

SIMPLICITY IS THE KEY TO THE STYLISH GOOD LOOKS of this home's facade. Inside, the kitchen opens directly off the foyer and contains an island and a work counter with eating space on the living-area side. The master bedroom sports sliding glass doors to the terrace. Its dressing area is enhanced with double walk-in closets and lavatories. A whirlpool tub and seated shower are additional amenities. Two family bedrooms are found on the opposite side of the house.

HPK2300220

Style: Traditional

Square Footage: 2,193

Bonus Space: 400 sq. ft.

Bedrooms: 4

Bathrooms: 2

Width: 64' - 6"

Depth: 59' - 0"

Foundation: Slab, Unfinished Walkout Basement, Crawlspace

eplans.com

FROM THE HIPPED AND GABLED ROOF TO THE GRACIOUS ENTRYWAY, style is a common element in the makeup of this home. Inside, the foyer is flanked by a formal living room (or make it a guest bedroom) and a formal dining room, defined by columns. Directly ahead lies the spacious family room, offering a warming fireplace. The sleeping quarters are separated for privacy. The master suite has a lavish bath and tray ceiling.

THERE IS MORE TO THIS EARLY AMERICAN HOME than a warm, inviting exterior. Inside, fireplaces warm each of the first-floor rooms—living room, country kitchen, and master bedroom. To the right of the foyer is the private master suite enhanced by a walk-in closet and a pampering bath that includes a soothing whirlpool tub, twin vanities, and a bath seat. To the rear of the plan, an L-shaped food preparation area conveniently connects via an island snack bar to a large country kitchen perfect for informal gatherings. The formal living room and the laundry room complete this level. The second floor holds two secondary bedrooms, a full bath, and a lounge/study with a built-in desk.

HOME PLAN

HPK2300221

Style: Federal

First Floor: 1,536 sq. ft.

Second Floor: 679 sq. ft.

Total: 2,215 sq. ft.

Bedrooms: 3

Bathrooms: 2 ½

Width: 53' - 0"

Depth: 44' - 0"

Foundation: Unfinished Basement

eplans.com

HOMES FOR FIRST-TIME BUILDERS

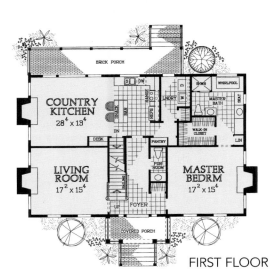

FIRST FLOOR

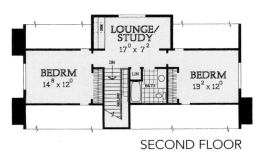

SECOND FLOOR

THE MASTER SUITE OF THIS ONE-STORY TRADITIONAL WILL BE A HAVEN for any homeowner. Separate tray ceilings split a generous sitting room from the main bedroom and a fireplace warms both areas. The vaulted master bath includes a three-sided mirror, a corner whirlpool tub, His and Hers sinks, and a walk-in closet with built-in linen storage. The master suite also includes French-door access to the rear yard. The rest of the home is equally impressive. Radius windows highlight the central living room, arches create a dramatic entrance to the dining room, and the open kitchen area includes a cooktop island, a sunny breakfast area, and a serving bar to the vaulted family room with its cozy fireplace. Two bedrooms and a full bath with dual basins complete this amenity-filled design.

HOME PLAN

HPK2300222

Style: European Cottage

Square Footage: 2,236

Bedrooms: 3

Bathrooms: 2 ½

Width: 63' - 0"

Depth: 67' - 0"

Foundation: Crawlspace, Unfinished Walkout Basement

eplans.com

HOME PLAN

HPK2300223

Style: Victorian Eclectic

First Floor: 1,128 sq. ft.

Second Floor: 1,130 sq. ft.

Total: 2,258 sq. ft.

Bedrooms: 4

Bathrooms: 2 ½

Width: 48' - 0"

Depth: 53' - 0"

Foundation: Crawlspace, Unfinished Basement

eplans.com

FIRST FLOOR

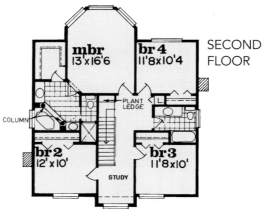

SECOND FLOOR

A GAZEBO PORCH, TOPPED WITH A TURRET ROOF, and nostalgic wood detailing grace this four-bedroom Victorian design. Double front doors open to a spacious living room and adjoining dining room. The living room has a warming fireplace. The kitchen, with a center prep island and raised eating bar, serves a sunny breakfast bay and the family room. A door leads out to a rear patio. The family room shares the warmth of its hearth with the kitchen and breakfast bay. All four bedrooms are on the second floor. The master suite features a bay window, walk-in closet, and a bath with a corner whirlpool tub that's adorned by columns. Three family bedrooms share a full bath. A small study area is located at the top of the stairs.

FIRST FLOOR

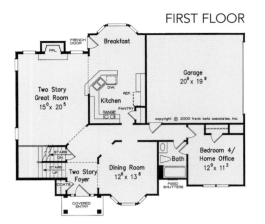

SECOND FLOOR

CAPE COD STYLE AND GEORGIAN SENSIBILITIES set this stunning home apart from the rest. Upon entry, a lovely bayed dining room is to the right. The two-story great room includes a fireplace framed by windows. In the kitchen, a step-saving shape allows easy meal preparation. A bedroom/home office would also make a great guest room. Upstairs, the master suite is rich with natural light. The master bath has a vaulted ceiling and pampering spa tub. Two more bedrooms share a full bath. Located for ultimate convenience, a laundry room near the bedrooms encourages organization.

HOME PLAN

 # HPK2300224

Style: Cape Cod

First Floor: 1,233 sq. ft.

Second Floor: 1,045 sq. ft.

Total: 2,278 sq. ft.

Bedrooms: 4

Bathrooms: 3

Width: 49' - 0"

Depth: 42' - 0"

Foundation: Crawlspace, Unfinished Walkout Basement

eplans.com

CHEERFUL WINDOW SHUTTERS AND A COVERED FRONT PORCH welcome you home at day's end. A two-story foyer sets the tone for indulgence inside, with the formal dining room opening off immediately to the right. A vaulted family room awaits at the other end, affording ambient sunlight through a radius transom. The adjacent kitchen connects to a screened porch through the breakfast area and a French door. A family bedroom is on the other side of the kitchen, with the laundry, a full bath, closets and garage access nearby. The left wing of the plan is reserved for the palatial master suite, with beamed ceilings in the bedroom, and a vaulted bath. Upstairs comes with two family bedrooms with respective walk-in closets, attic space, and a bonus room.

HOME PLAN

HPK2300225

Style: Country Cottage
First Floor: 1,774 sq. ft.
Second Floor: 525 sq. ft.
Total: 2,299 sq. ft.
Bonus Space: 300 sq. ft.
Bedrooms: 4
Bathrooms: 3
Width: 56' - 0"
Depth: 63' - 4"
Foundation: Crawlspace, Unfinished Walkout Basement, Slab

eplans.com

HOMES FOR FIRST-TIME BUILDERS

FIRST FLOOR

SECOND FLOOR

AN ECLECTIC MIX OF BUILDING MATERIALS—STONE, STUCCO, AND SIDING—sings in tune with the European charm of this one-story home. Within, decorative columns set off the formal dining room and the foyer from the vaulted family room; the formal living room is quietly tucked behind French doors. The gourmet kitchen provides an angled snack bar and a sunny breakfast room. Two family bedrooms each have a walk-in closet and private access to a shared bath. The master suite holds an elegant tray ceiling, a bay sitting area, and a lush bath.

HOME PLAN

HPK2300226

Style: Country Cottage

Square Footage: 2,322

Bedrooms: 3

Bathrooms: 2 ½

Width: 62' - 0"

Depth: 61' - 0"

Foundation: Crawlspace, Slab, Unfinished Walkout Basement

eplans.com

HOME PLAN

HPK2300227

Style: Traditional

First Floor: 1,208 sq. ft.

Second Floor: 1,137 sq. ft.

Total: 2,345 sq. ft.

Bedrooms: 3

Bathrooms: 3

Width: 38' - 6"

Depth: 51' - 4"

Foundation: Crawlspace, Unfinished Walkout Basement

eplans.com

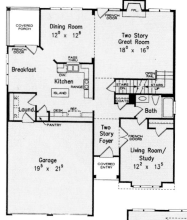

FIRST FLOOR

SECOND FLOOR

A HIPPED ROOF, SIDING, AND STONE ACCENTS BRING A NEOCLASSICAL ELEMENT to this traditional family home. Inside, the two-story great room is inviting, with a fireplace and lots of natural light. The living room/study is entered through French doors and is set in a box-bay window. A country kitchen serves the dining room and breakfast area with ease; covered-porch access beckons outdoor meals. The second-floor master suite enjoys a sitting area and a vaulted bath with a garden tub. Two bedrooms, one with a sitting area and a walk-in closet, share a full bath.

FIRST FLOOR

SECOND FLOOR

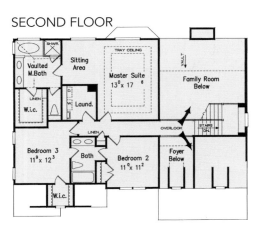

RUSTIC DETAILS COMPLEMENT BRICK AND SIDING on the exterior of this home. The interior features vaulted living and family rooms and a convenient kitchen separating the dining and breakfast rooms. The living room provides a fireplace flanked by radius windows, and a French door in the breakfast room opens to the rear property. A bedroom to the back could be used as a study. Second-floor bedrooms include a master suite with a sitting area.

HOME PLAN

HPK2300228

Style: Country Cottage

First Floor: 1,279 sq. ft.

Second Floor: 1,071 sq. ft.

Total: 2,350 sq. ft.

Bedrooms: 4

Bathrooms: 3

Width: 50' - 0"

Depth: 42' - 6"

Foundation: Crawlspace, Unfinished Walkout Basement

eplans.com

FIRST FLOOR

Hearth Room
15'2" x 21

Breakfast
15'2" x 9'

Dining
13' x 15'
sloped / sloped

Kitchen
16'6" x 9'

Great Room
16' x 23'10"

Laun.

Hall

Dressing

walk-in closet

Raised Foyer

Three-car Garage
25' x 30'

Master Bedroom
13'2" x 16'

Porch

SECOND FLOOR

Bedroom
12'10" x 11'6"

Bedroom
11' x 11'6"

Bath

Balcony

Great Room Below

Bonus Room
11'1" x 22'6"

HPK2300229

Style: Craftsman

First Floor: 1,784 sq. ft.

Second Floor: 566 sq. ft.

Total: 2,350 sq. ft.

Bonus Space: 336 sq. ft.

Bedrooms: 3

Bathrooms: 2 ½

Width: 59' - 0"

Depth: 67' - 0"

Foundation: Unfinished Basement

HOME PLAN

eplans.com

AN ATTRACTIVE COMBINATION OF STYLES creates a lovely exterior for this transitional home. The first floor offers a raised foyer and open great room leading to the dining room with a sloped ceiling. Exposed on two sides, a fireplace warms the formal gathering area. A less formal space is created in the island kitchen and breakfast/hearth room combination. The master bedroom is located on the main floor, featuring a sloped ceiling through the private bath with a large walk-in closet, dressing area, dual vanities and an angled soaking tub.

HOMES FOR FIRST-TIME BUILDERS

HOME PLAN
HPK2300230

Style: Country Cottage
First Floor: 1,120 sq. ft.
Second Floor: 1,250 sq. ft.
Total: 2,370 sq. ft.
Bedrooms: 3
Bathrooms: 2 ½
Width: 41' - 4"
Depth: 51' - 0"
Foundation: Crawlspace, Unfinished Walkout Basement, Slab

FIRST FLOOR

SECOND FLOOR

HOME PLAN
HPK2300231

Style: Country Cottage
Square Footage: 2,403
Bonus Space: 285 sq. ft.
Bedrooms: 3
Bathrooms: 2 ½
Width: 60' - 0"
Depth: 67' - 0"
Foundation: Crawlspace, Slab, Unfinished Walkout Basement

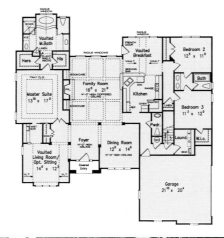

HOME PLAN

(#) HPK2300232

Style: Farmhouse

Square Footage: 2,424

Bedrooms: 3

Bathrooms: 2 ½

Width: 68' - 0"

Depth: 64' - 0"

Foundation: Unfinished Basement

eplans.com

THIS UNIQUE ONE-STORY PLAN SEEMS TAILOR-MADE for a small family or for empty-nesters. Formal areas are situated well for entertaining—living room to the right and formal dining room to the left. A large family room to the rear accesses a rear wood deck and is warmed in the cold months by a welcome hearth. The U-shaped kitchen features an attached morning room for casual meals near the laundry and a washroom. The master suite sits to the right of the plan and has a walk-in closet and a fine bath. A nearby den opens to a private porch. Two family bedrooms on the other side of the home share a full bath.

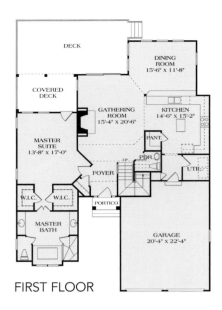

FIRST FLOOR

SECOND FLOOR

WITH HINTS OF CAPE COD AND A DASH OF COUNTRY, this unique home makes a perfect vacation retreat or a comfortable full-time home. The foyer leads into the welcoming two-story gathering room, graced with a fireplace and sliding glass doors to the deck. The island kitchen is open to the gathering room, for effortless entertaining, and serves the dining room with the help of a snack bar. The master suite is located on this level and enjoys deck access, dual amenities, and a lavish bath with a tub set in a flower-box window. Two bedrooms share a full bath upstairs, joined by the "captain's quarters" that would provide a great home office or guest room (with a private evening deck). Extra storage is a thoughtful touch.

HOME PLAN

HPK2300233

Style: **Cottage**

First Floor: **1,494 sq. ft.**

Second Floor: **954 sq. ft.**

Total: **2,448 sq. ft.**

Bedrooms: **3**

Bathrooms: **2 ½**

Width: **45' - 0"**

Depth: **60' - 2"**

Foundation: **Crawlspace**

eplans.com

THIS ELEGANT TRADITIONAL HOME IS DISTINGUISHED by its brick exterior and arched entryway with keystone accent. The entryway opens on the right to a formal dining room with an attractive tray ceiling. On the left, a private study—or make it a fourth bedroom—boasts a vaulted ceiling and a picture window with sunburst transom. Family living space includes a vaulted great room with a corner fireplace and a gourmet kitchen with an adjacent breakfast room. Special features in the kitchen include a breakfast bar, center island, menu desk and pantry. The fabulous master suite enjoys a bay window, large bath, walk-in closet and vaulted ceiling. Two family bedrooms sharing a full hall bath complete the plan. An unfinished basement provides room for future expansion.

HOME PLAN

HPK2300234

Style: Traditional

Square Footage: 2,483

Bedrooms: 3

Bathrooms: 2

Width: 69' - 0"

Depth: 53' - 8"

Foundation: Unfinished Basement

eplans.com

Easy Living—Designs That Let Empty-Nesters Rule the Roost

These are homes for people who have earned their chance to relax and enjoy life. Although the size of these designs remains under 3,000 square feet, the master suites are more sumptuous—and located on the first level for easy enjoyment. In place of a third or fourth bedroom the plan designates a study or recreation room. Dine-in kitchens and sunny breakfast nooks provide for everyday occasions. If a separate dining room exists, it opens casually into the rest of the home.

Some of our best traditional designs have been collected here; traditional, but with a twist. With classic features such as gables, dormers, porches, and verandas, these homes are designed to look like they've been in the family for generations. Some favor a country style; others sport a more cosmopolitan attitude.

Take a look at one of our larger empty-nest designs, plan HPK2300301 on page 303, for an example of a home that lives well every day and makes room for visiting children. And there are 52 other plans to consider, all hand-chosen by our knowledgeable staff.

IN LIEU OF A FORMAL dining room, create elegant casual-dining spaces like this nook.

Mark Samu (2)

AN OLD-FASHIONED SITTING ROOM can become the home's entertainment space.

FIRST FLOOR

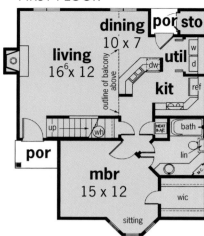

THIS PLAN EASILY FITS INTO ESTABLISHED NEIGHBORHOODS, with a canted bay window, traditional trim, and stucco finish. An upper-level bedroom—with private bath—overlooks the vaulted living room or can be finished off for more privacy. The appealing master suite features a sunny sitting area and walk-in closet. The efficient kitchen offers angles and looks out over the dining area and the cozy living room. Note the warming fireplace in the living room.

HPK2300235

HOME PLAN

Style: Country Cottage

First Floor: 814 sq. ft.

Second Floor: 267 sq. ft.

Total: 1,081 sq. ft.

Bedrooms: 2

Bathrooms: 2

Width: 28' - 0"

Depth: 34' - 6"

Foundation: Unfinished Basement, Crawlspace, Slab

eplans.com

SECOND FLOOR

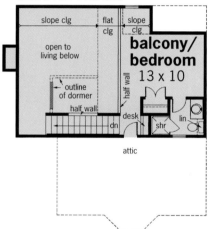

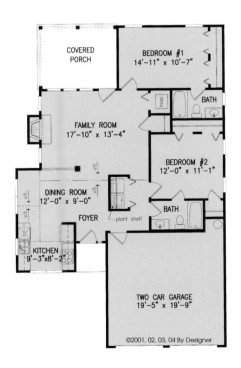

COVERED PORCH

BEDROOM #1
14'-11" x 10'-7"

BATH

FAMILY ROOM
17'-10" x 13'-4"

BEDROOM #2
12'-0" x 11'-1"

DINING ROOM
12'-0" x 9'-0"

FOYER

plant shelf

BATH

KITCHEN
9'-3"x8'-2"

TWO CAR GARAGE
19'-5" x 19'-9"

©2001, 02, 03, 04 By Designer

HPK2300236

HOME PLAN

Square Footage: 1,093

Bedrooms: 2

Bathrooms: 2

Width: 35' - 0"

Depth: 56' - 0"

Foundation: Slab

eplans.com

THIS HANDSOME BUNGALOW offers many splendid features. A cozy fireplace in the family room, a rear covered porch, and a plant shelf in the laundry are some of the highlights. The plan includes two bedrooms, both with private baths, and a spacious dining room, off the well-equipped kitchen. A front-loading, two-car garage also comes with the plan.

HOMES FOR EMPTY-NESTERS

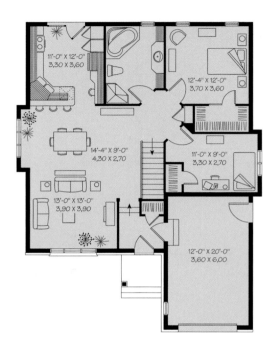

11'-0" X 12'-0"
3.30 X 3.60

12'-4" X 12'-0"
3.70 X 3.60

14'-4" X 9'-0"
4.30 X 2.70

11'-0" X 9'-0"
3.30 X 2.70

13'-0" X 13'-0"
3.90 X 3.90

12'-0" X 20'-0"
3.60 X 6.00

UNDER HIPPED ROOFS AND BEHIND A RUSTIC BRICK FACADE is a cozy living area your family will want to call home. An unexpectedly extravagant bath with both a shower and tub is sure to soothe. Two bedrooms, the larger with a walk-in closet, are on the right side of the house. The family chef will go wild with the walls of counter space and cabinets. A peninsula counter with a snack bar separates the kitchen from the combined dining and living rooms. Large windows on two sides of this area will let in plenty of sunshine. A front-entry, one-car garage completes this plan.

HPK2300237

HOME PLAN

Style: Contemporary

Square Footage: 1,138

Bedrooms: 2

Bathrooms: 1

Width: 34' - 0"

Depth: 48' - 0"

Foundation: Unfinished Basement

eplans.com

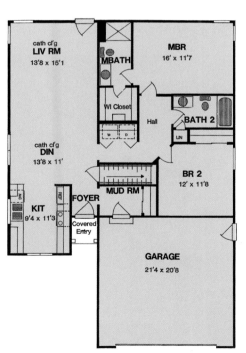

HPK2300238

Square Footage: 1,212

Bedrooms: 2

Bathrooms: 2

Width: 36' - 0"

Depth: 53' - 0"

Foundation: Unfinished Basement

HOME PLAN

eplans.com

LOOKING FOR A HOME THAT IS ROOMY, YET AFFORDABLE? This two-bedroom bungalow with a two-car garage could be the right fit. The master bedroom enjoys a private bath and a large walk-in closet; the second bedroom has easy hall access to another bath. A mudroom, with an entry through the garage, is one of the more thoughtful features for helping to make cleaning easier. A front covered entry is perfect for welcoming guests. The kitchen, dining area, and living room flow smoothly together in a way that enhances the sense of space. A French door in the living room opens to the backyard.

FIRST FLOOR

A GLASS-DOOR ENTRANCE WELCOMES VISITORS into the picturesque charm of this countryside home. A large wraparound porch leads to a relaxing outdoor lounge area—perfect for summer afternoons. The island kitchen opens to an eating area across from the living room. A powder room, laundry area, and the one-car garage complete this floor. Upstairs, two family bedrooms are linked by a full bath.

SECOND FLOOR

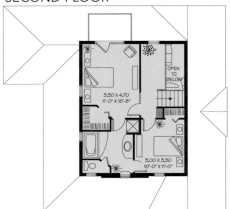

HOME PLAN

(#) **HPK2300239**

Style: Farmhouse

First Floor: 694 sq. ft.

Second Floor: 558 sq. ft.

Total: 1,252 sq. ft.

Bedrooms: 2

Bathrooms: 1 ½

Width: 28' - 0"

Depth: 40' - 0"

Foundation: Unfinished Basement

eplans.com

THIS COMPACT HOME HAS A LOT MORE PACKED INSIDE ITS WALLS than it might appear from the outside. It enjoys three bedrooms, one of them an amenity-filled master suite; two baths; a well-equipped laundry; and a two-car garage. The grand room, with a warming fireplace, soars two stories high to a vaulted ceiling. It easily opens to the kitchen and a breakfast nook, which opens to a rear deck or patio.

HOMES FOR EMPTY-NESTERS

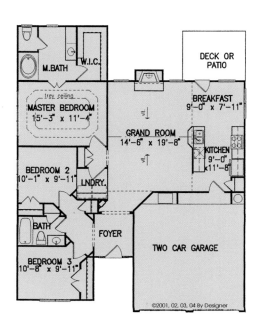

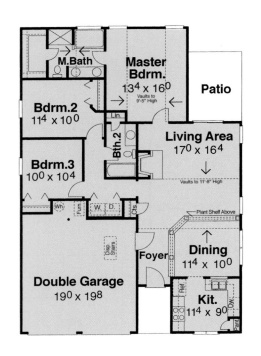

M.Bath

Master Bdrm.
13⁴ x 16⁰
Vaults to 9'-5" High

Patio

Bdrm.2
11⁴ x 10⁰

Bth.2

Living Area
17⁰ x 16⁴
Vaults to 11'-8" High

Bdrm.3
10⁰ x 10⁴

Lin.

Cls.

Wh.   Furn.   W. D.   Cls.

Plant Shelf Above

Disp.
Stairs

Foyer   Dining
11⁴ x 10⁰

Double Garage
19⁰ x 19⁸

Ref.

Kit.
11⁴ x 9⁰

DW.

2nd

SIMPLE COUNTRY COTTAGE CHARM IS EXPRESSED WITH CARRIAGE-STYLE GARAGE DOORS on this narrow-lot design. The foyer opens to a living room with a full vaulted ceiling, rising to soaring heights for a feeling of expanded space. The dining area is elegantly defined by columns and a ceiling-height plant shelf. The country-style kitchen features wide windows facing the front property. Bedrooms are designed for privacy; the master suite hosts a dramatic vaulted ceiling and a private spa bath. Not to be missed: a rear patio that is perfect for summer barbecues.

HPK2300241

Square Footage: 1,365

Bedrooms: 3

Bathrooms: 2

Width: 37' - 0"

Depth: 53' - 0"

Foundation: Unfinished Basement, Slab

HOME PLAN

eplans.com

OPTIONAL
LAYOUT

HPK2300242

Style: Bungalow

Square Footage: 1,393

Bonus Space: 206 sq. ft.

Bedrooms: 2

Bathrooms: 2

Width: 32' - 0"

Depth: 70' - 0"

Foundation: Crawlspace, Unfinished Walkout Basement

HPK2300243

Style: Craftsman

Square Footage: 1,393

Bonus Space: 160 sq. ft.

Bedrooms: 2

Bathrooms: 2

Width: 32' - 0"

Depth: 63' - 0"

Foundation: Unfinished Walkout Basement, Slab

HOMES FOR EMPTY-NESTERS

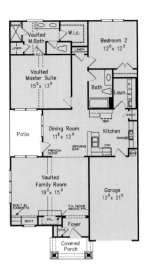

HOME PLAN #

HPK2300244

Style: Craftsman

Square Footage: 1,407

Bedrooms: 2

Bathrooms: 2

Width: 32' - 0"

Depth: 61' - 7"

Foundation: Slab, Unfinished Walkout Basement

HOME PLAN #

HPK2300245

Square Footage: 1,420

Bedrooms: 2

Bathrooms: 2

Width: 40' - 0"

Depth: 58' - 0"

Foundation: Crawlspace

HOMEOWNERS CAN WAIT OUT RAINY DAYS ON THE FRONT COVERED PORCH of this home and likewise enjoy sunny afternoons on the rear deck. They'll find spacious shelter inside in the large great room, easily accessible from the kitchen with a breakfast nook. With a corner fireplace and rear deck access, the great room will be buzzing with activity. Two secondary bedrooms—make one a library—share a full hall bath. The master suite is graciously appointed with a private bath and walk-in closet.

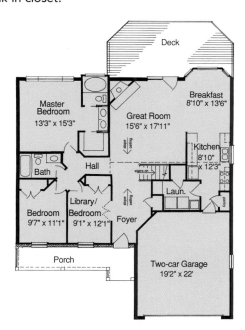

HOME PLAN

HPK2300246

Style: Country Cottage

Square Footage: 1,422

Bedrooms: 3

Bathrooms: 2

Width: 45' - 0"

Depth: 51' - 4"

Foundation: Unfinished Walkout Basement

eplans.com

HOMES FOR EMPTY-NESTERS

MODERN AMENITIES AND AN ELEGANT FLOOR PLAN define the interior of this design, which offers a classic Craftsman exterior. The vaulted great room, with a fireplace and built-in media center, shares a snack bar with the gourmet kitchen. The nearby breakfast nook includes sliding glass doors. The dining room also boasts a vaulted ceiling; add an optional wall and French doors to convert this room to a cozy den. The master suite, secluded to the right, contains a walk-in closet with built-in shelves, along with a private bath. Two secondary bedrooms, to the left of the plan, share a full bath and linen closet.

HPK2300247

HOME PLAN

Style: Craftsman

Square Footage: 1,771

Bedrooms: 3

Bathrooms: 2

Width: 50' - 0"

Depth: 70' - 0"

Foundation: Crawlspace

eplans.com

HPK2300248

Style: Country Cottage

Square Footage: 1,437

Bedrooms: 2

Bathrooms: 2

Width: 37' - 0"

Depth: 64' - 5"

Foundation: Slab

eplans.com

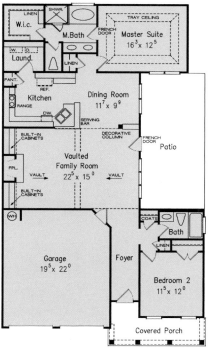

A TWO-CAR GARAGE TOPPED BY TWIN DORMERS, AND A COVERED AND PILLARED FRONT PORCH capture a timeless essence on the facade of this country home. In one story you get two bedrooms and two full baths, perfect for a small family, empty-nesters, or even as a vacation home. The long foyer leads directly into a great room filled with amenities such as a fireplace flanked by built-in shelves, decorative colums, French-door access to a vast side patio, and a vaulted ceiling. From there you can enter the dining room, wisely placed adjacent to the kitchen with convenient serving bar. The master suite leaves nothing to be desired; pass through the French doors into the master bath and discover the dual-sink vanity and access to a spacious walk-in closet.

THIS TRANSITIONAL-STYLE HOME IS A GREAT NARROW-LOT DESIGN. Inside, the foyer opens to the great room/dining area combination—here, a corner fireplace warms crisp evenings. The kitchen easily serves the dining area and optional screened porch, which is great for seasonal outdoor meals. The first-floor master suite includes a whirlpool bath and a walk-in closet. The laundry room leads to the two-car garage. Optional basement-level fixtures include a spacious recreation room, a hall bath, and two additional bedrooms—one easily converts to a library. Basement storage and unexcavated space is reserved for future developments.

FIRST FLOOR

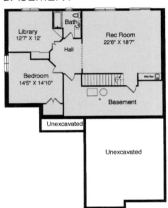

BASEMENT

HOME PLAN

HPK2300249

Style: Transitional

Square Footage: 1,462

Bedrooms: 3

Bathrooms: 2 ½

Width: 46' - 0"

Depth: 59' - 4"

Foundation: Finished Walkout Basement

eplans.com

Vaulted Master Suite 16⁰ x 13⁵

Vaulted M.Bath

W.i.c.

Patio

Dining Room 12⁰ x 12⁰

Kitchen

Vaulted Family Room 19² x 14⁹

Garage 12⁰ x 21⁶

Bath

Foyer

Bedroom 2 12⁰ x 10⁹

Covered Entry

copyright © 2004 frank betz associates, inc.

OPTIONAL LAYOUT

HOME PLAN

HPK2300250

Square Footage: 1,472

Bedrooms: 2

Bathrooms: 2

Width: 32' - 0"

Depth: 63' - 0"

Foundation: Crawlspace, Unfinished Walkout Basement

HOME PLAN

HPK2300251

Square Footage: 1,502

Bedrooms: 2

Bathrooms: 2

Width: 32' - 0"

Depth: 67' - 8"

Foundation: Slab

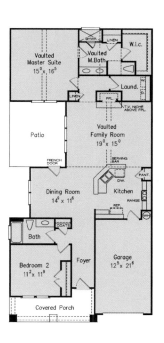

Vaulted Master Suite 15⁰ x 16⁵

Vaulted M.Bath

W.i.c.

Laund.

Patio

Vaulted Family Room 19⁰ x 15⁰

Dining Room 14⁰ x 11⁶

Kitchen

Bath

Bedroom 2 11² x 11⁹

Foyer

Garage 12⁵ x 21⁶

Covered Porch

OPTIONAL LAYOUT

HOMES FOR EMPTY-NESTERS

HOME PLAN #

HPK2300252

Style: Country Cottage

Square Footage: 1,532

Bedrooms: 3

Bathrooms: 2

Width: 38' - 0"

Depth: 66' - 0"

Foundation: Unfinished Basement, Slab

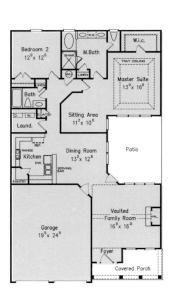

HOME PLAN #

HPK2300253

Style: Country Cottage

Square Footage: 1,546

Bedrooms: 2

Bathrooms: 2

Width: 37' - 0"

Depth: 64' - 0"

Foundation: Slab

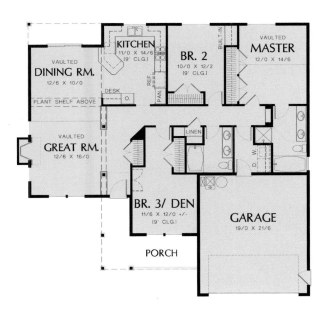

HOME PLAN

HPK2300254

Style: Traditional

Square Footage: 1,557

Bedrooms: 3

Bathrooms: 2

Width: 50' - 0"

Depth: 50' - 0"

Foundation: Crawlspace

eplans.com

A WRAPAROUND PORCH sets off this sweet country facade. The gallery foyer opens to a vaulted great room with a fireplace and leads to the formal dining room. Advanced amenities such as a vaulted ceiling and a plant shelf complement views of nature through tall windows and sliding glass doors. A planning desk, pantry, and peninsula counter highlight the gourmet kitchen, which boasts a window over the sink. A flex room easily converts from a secondary bedroom to a den or home office. A second bedroom enjoys a view of the rear property; nearby, a full bath offers two sinks.

CLEAN LINES CHARACTERIZE THE ELEVATION of this sophisticated ranch home. The volume entry with transom windows offers expansive views of the great room. Just off the entry, the formal living room serves as an optional third bedroom. Flexibility is also designed into the dining room and great room, which share a 10-foot ceiling. A thoughtfully designed kitchen with a pantry and corner sink serves the sunny breakfast area, which accesses a covered deck. The master suite includes a volume ceiling and a master bath with a whirlpool tub and skylight. One secondary bedroom is provided—or add one more by making the living room a bedroom.

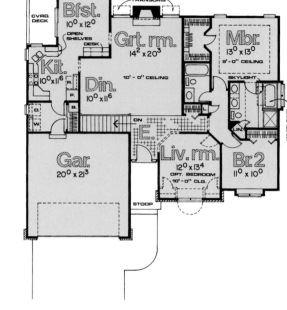

(#) HPK2300255

Style: Traditional

Square Footage: 1,561

Bedrooms: 2

Bathrooms: 2

Width: 50' - 0"

Depth: 50' - 0"

eplans.com

HOME PLAN

HPK2300256

Style: Traditional

Square Footage: 1,574

Bedrooms: 2

Bathrooms: 2

Width: 50' - 0"

Depth: 65' - 0"

eplans.com

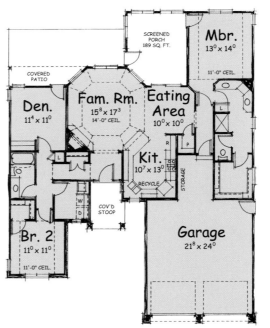

A WARM STUCCO-AND-STONE FACADE announces a wonderful floor plan with a fun, imaginative use of space. The entry leads to an octagonal family room with a 14-foot ceiling. From here, an eating area (make it as formal or casual as you like) opens to the kitchen, equipped with a recycling center. The master suite is located to the right with screened-porch access, a private bath and an enormous walk-in closet. A den—or make it a guest room—and secondary bedroom share the use of a full bath. Storage space in the garage is an added bonus.

A LOVELY FACADE OPENS THIS ONE-STORY HOME, with gable ends and dormer windows as decorative features. The interior features vaulted family and dining rooms—a fireplace in the family room offers warmth. Defined by columns, the formal dining experience is enhanced. The kitchen attaches to a bayed breakfast nook with a vaulted ceiling. A split floor plan has the family bedrooms on the right side and the master suite on the left. The master bedroom has a tray ceiling, vaulted bath, and walk-in closet.

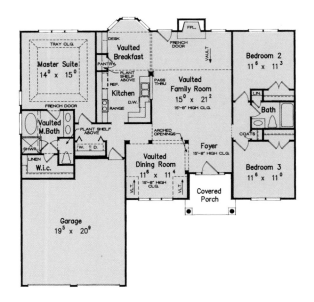

HPK2300257

HOME PLAN

Style: Traditional
Square Footage: 1,575
Bedrooms: 3
Bathrooms: 2
Width: 52' - 0"
Depth: 52' - 6"
Foundation: Crawlspace, Slab, Unfinished Walkout Basement

eplans.com

HPK2300258

Style: Country Cottage

Square Footage: 1,580

Bedrooms: 3

Bathrooms: 2 ½

Width: 50' - 0"

Depth: 48' - 0"

Foundation: Crawlspace

eplans.com

THIS CHARMING ONE-STORY PLAN FEATURES A FACADE THAT IS ACCENTED BY A STONE PEDIMENT and a shed-dormer window. Inside, elegant touches grace the efficient floor plan. Vaulted ceilings adorn the great room and master bedroom, and a 10-foot tray ceiling highlights the foyer. One of the front bedrooms makes a perfect den; another accesses a full hall bath with a linen closet. The great room, which opens to the porch, includes a fireplace and a media niche. The dining room offers outdoor access and built-ins for ultimate convenience.

HOME PLAN

HPK2300259

Style: Traditional
Square Footage: 1,583
Bedrooms: 3
Bathrooms: 2
Width: 34' - 0"
Depth: 77' - 2"

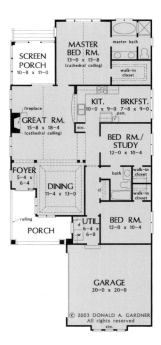

HOME PLAN

HPK2300260

Style: Traditional
Square Footage: 1,606
Bonus Space: 338 sq. ft.
Bedrooms: 3
Bathrooms: 2
Width: 50' - 0"
Depth: 54' - 0"

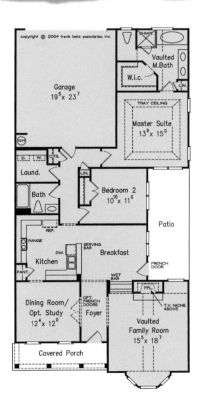

HOME PLAN

HPK2300261

Style: Country Cottage

Square Footage: 1,610

Bedrooms: 2

Bathrooms: 2

Width: 34' - 0"

Depth: 72' - 0"

Foundation: Crawlspace, Unfinished Walkout Basement

eplans.com

PERFECT FIT FOR A NARROW LOT, this home offers delicate details. A sweet front porch accents the country cottage facade and large gable roof. The foyer opens to optional French doors on the left for a grand dining room or study entry. Built-ins flank the fireplace and a stunning bumped-out bay adds character and beauty to the family room. A breakfast area connects to the spacious kitchen and a private side patio—a great spot for a garden. Two bedrooms sit to the rear; the master enjoys a private vaulted bath and walk-in closet.

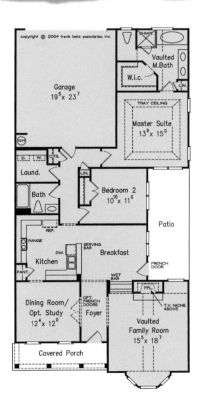

HOMES FOR EMPTY-NESTERS

Porch
19'7" x 6'10"

Master
Bedroom
13'2" x 15'9"

W.I.C.

Great Room
19'4" x 18'6"

Master

Bath

Kitchen
11'7" x 13'

Foyer

Laun.

Closet Closet

Lin.

Closet

Bedroom
12' x 12'

Closet

Dining Room
10'4 x 9'10"

Garage
20' x 23'6"

A BRICK-AND-STONE EXTERIOR WITH SHAKE SIDING decorates the front of this delightful home. The large great room enjoys an 11-foot ceiling, gas fireplace, and access to the rear porch. The master bedroom suite offers a luxury bath with a dual-bowl vanity, whirlpool tub, and large walk-in closet. Access to the rear porch from the master suite is an unexpected feature. This home, designed for a narrow lot, offers spaciousness and luxurious living.

HOME PLAN

HPK2300262

Style: European Cottage

Square Footage: 1,612

Bedrooms: 2

Bathrooms: 2

Width: 42' - 0"

Depth: 67' - 4"

Foundation: Slab, Unfinished Basement

eplans.com

HOME PLAN

HPK2300263

Style: Country

Square Footage: 1,632

Bedrooms: 3

Bathrooms: 2

Width: 62' - 4"

Depth: 55' - 2"

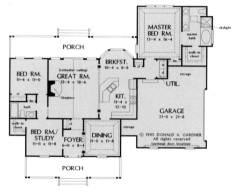

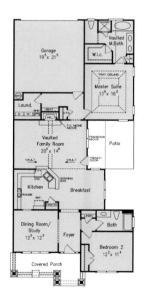

HOME PLAN

HPK2300264

Style: Craftsman

Square Footage: 1,670

Bedrooms: 2

Bathrooms: 2

Width: 34' - 0"

Depth: 77' - 0"

Foundation: Crawlspace, Unfinished Walkout Basement

HOMES FOR EMPTY-NESTERS

© 1999 Donald A. Gardner, Inc.

HOME PLAN #

HPK2300265

Style: Country
Square Footage: 1,671
Bonus Space: 348 sq. ft.
Bedrooms: 3
Bathrooms: 2
Width: 50' - 8"
Depth: 52' - 4"

HOME PLAN #

HPK2300266

Style: French
Square Footage: 1,684
Bedrooms: 3
Bathrooms: 2 ½
Width: 55' - 6"
Depth: 57' - 6"
Foundation: Walkout Basement

eplans.com

HPK2300267

Style: Traditional

Square Footage: 1,721

Bedrooms: 3

Bathrooms: 2

Width: 83' - 0"

Depth: 42' - 0"

Foundation: Unfinished Walkout Basement

HOME PLAN

THIS HOME OFFERS A BEAUTIFULLY TEXTURED FACADE.
Keystones and lintels highlight the beauty of the windows. The vaulted great room and dining room are immersed in light from the atrium window wall. The breakfast bay opens to the covered porch in the backyard. A curved counter connects the kitchen to the great room. Three bedrooms, including a deluxe master suite, share the right side of the plan. All enjoy large windows of their own. The garage is designed for two cars, plus space for a motorcycle or yard tractor.

HOMES FOR EMPTY-NESTERS

A NEW-AGE CONTEMPORARY TOUCH
graces the exterior of this impressive yet affordable home. The entry leads to the formal areas in the open dining room and vaulted living room. The kitchen overlooks a quaint morning room, which leads to a rear deck that's a perfect spot for outdoor activities. With a walk-in closet and private bath, homeowners will be pampered in the master suite. The second bedroom, the two-car garage, and a utility room complete the plan.

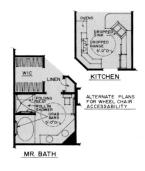

HOME PLAN # HPK2300268

Style: Bungalow

Square Footage: 1,723

Bedrooms: 2

Bathrooms: 2

Width: 45' - 0"

Depth: 62' - 6"

Foundation: Unfinished Basement

eplans.com

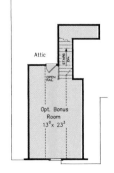

Attic

OPEN RAIL

Opt. Bonus
Room
13⁰ x 23³

HPK2300269

Style: Craftsman

Square Footage: 1,724

Bonus Space: 375 sq. ft.

Bedrooms: 3

Bathrooms: 2

Width: 53' - 6"

Depth: 58' - 6"

Foundation: Crawlspace, Unfinished Walkout Basement, Slab

eplans.com

THIS DOWN-HOME, ONE-STORY PLAN HAS ALL THE COMFORTS AND NECESSITIES for solid family living. The vaulted family room, along with the adjoining country-style kitchen and breakfast nook, is at the center of the plan. The extended hearth fireplace flanked by radius windows will make this a cozy focus for family get-togethers and entertaining visitors. A formal dining room is marked off by decorative columns. The resplendent master suite assumes the entire right wing, where it is separated from two bedrooms located on the other side of the home. Built-in plant shelves in the master bath create a garden-like environment. Additional space is available for building another bedroom or study.

HOME PLAN

HOMES FOR EMPTY-NESTERS

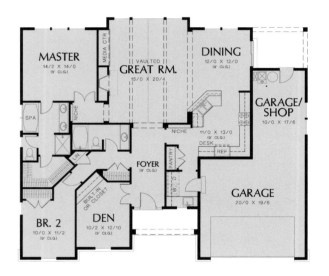

A CHARMING DORMER WINDOW ACCENTS THE FACADE of this cozy Craftsman home. To the left of the foyer, double doors open to a den; choose built-in shelves or a convenient wall closet for this room. The central great room boasts a vaulted ceiling, built-in media center, and fireplace, and is open to the dining room, which features sliding glass doors that open to a side porch. A built-in desk adds convenience to the kitchen. Bedrooms to the left of the plan include a master suite, with a private bath and walk-in closet, and one additional bedroom.

HOME PLAN

(#) HPK2300270

Style: Craftsman
Square Footage: 1,728
Bedrooms: 2
Bathrooms: 2
Width: 55' - 0"
Depth: 48' - 0"
Foundation: Crawlspace

eplans.com

HOME PLAN
HPK2300271

Style: Traditional

Square Footage: 1,758

Bedrooms: 2

Bathrooms: 2

Width: 48' - 0"

Depth: 63' - 0"

Foundation: Finished Basement

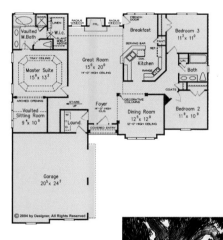

HOME PLAN
HPK2300272

Style: Georgian

Square Footage: 1,768

Bonus Space: 354 sq. ft.

Bedrooms: 3

Bathrooms: 2

Width: 54' - 0"

Depth: 59' - 6"

Foundation: Slab, Unfinished Walkout Basement, Crawlspace

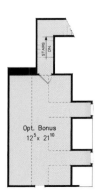

HOMES FOR EMPTY-NESTERS

HOME PLAN #

HPK2300273

Style: Contemporary

Square Footage: 1,797

Bedrooms: 3

Bathrooms: 2

Width: 45' - 0"

Depth: 45' - 2"

Foundation: Unfinished Walkout Basement

HOME PLAN #

HPK2300274

Style: Country

Square Footage: 1,828

Bonus Space: 352 sq. ft.

Bedrooms: 3

Bathrooms: 2

Width: 53' - 8"

Depth: 55' - 8"

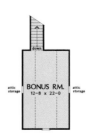

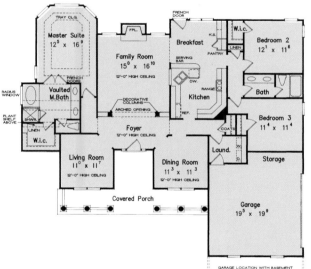

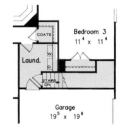

OPTIONAL LAYOUT

HOME PLAN

HPK2300275

Style: Greek Revival

Square Footage: 1,856

Bedrooms: 3

Bathrooms: 2

Width: 59' - 0"

Depth: 54' - 6"

Foundation: Crawlspace, Slab, Unfinished Walkout Basement

eplans.com

A COVERED PORCH WITH A RECESSED ENTRY IS CROWNED WITH THE ADDITION OF A FRONT GABLE. A symmetrical plan of living areas places the living and dining rooms to either side of the foyer, with the family room directly ahead. A graceful arched opening and a fireplace flanked by windows are complemented by extra-high ceilings in the foyer and family room. An efficiently designed kitchen features an abundance of counter and cabinet space along with a serving bar to the breakfast nook. The master suite is separated from the two family bedrooms for privacy.

© 1992 Donald A. Gardner Architects, Inc.

HOME PLAN

HPK2300276

Style: Traditional

Square Footage: 1,858

Bedrooms: 3

Bathrooms: 2

Width: 50' - 0"

Depth: 59' - 8"

HOME PLAN

HPK2300277

Style: Farmhouse

Square Footage: 1,864

Bedrooms: 3

Bathrooms: 2 ½

Width: 71' - 0"

Depth: 56' - 4"

A RUSTIC EXTERIOR OF SHINGLES, SIDING, AND STONE

provides a sweet country look. Inside, the foyer is flanked by a dining room and family bedrooms. Bedrooms 2 and 3 share a full hall bath. The master suite, located on the opposite side of the home for privacy, boasts a tray ceiling and a pampering bath with an oversized tub. The kitchen opens to a breakfast room that accesses the rear sun deck. The enormous living room is warmed by a central fireplace. The laundry room and double-car garage complete this plan.

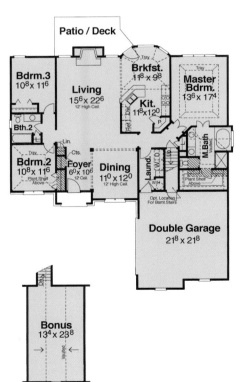

HPK2300278

Style: Traditional

Square Footage: 1,869

Bonus Space: 336 sq. ft.

Bedrooms: 3

Bathrooms: 2

Width: 54' - 0"

Depth: 60' - 6"

Foundation: Unfinished Walkout Basement, Crawlspace, Slab

HOME PLAN

eplans.com

(#) HPK2300279

Style: French

Square Footage: 1,891

Bedrooms: 2

Bathrooms: 2

Width: 49' - 0"

Depth: 64' - 0"

Foundation: Crawlspace, Slab

eplans.com

THE GATED COURTYARD ADDS PRIVACY and personality to this charming two-bedroom home. The open interior includes a sunken family room with a sloped ceiling, a gracious fireplace, built-ins, and access to a rear porch. A brilliantly sunny dining room sits opposite an open and cleverly angled kitchen—allowing for ease of service between the dining room and the morning room. The living room could be used as a third bedroom or a study. The master suite includes a dual-bowl vanity, a separate bath and shower, and a large walk-in closet.

HPK2300280

Style: Transitional

Square Footage: 1,911

Bedrooms: 3

Bathrooms: 2

Width: 45' - 0"

Depth: 78' - 5"

Foundation:
Crawlspace

HOME PLAN #

HPK2300281

Style: Country Cottage

Square Footage: 1,915

Bedrooms: 3

Bathrooms: 2

Width: 46' - 0"

Depth: 60' - 2"

Foundation:
Crawlspace

HOMES FOR EMPTY-NESTERS

A CRAFTSMAN COTTAGE WITH CAREFUL DETAILING,
this sweet country home is sure to please. From the covered porch, the foyer reveals an open floor plan. The dining room, defined by columns, leads into the vaulted family room. Here, a fireplace framed by windows makes this comfortable space feel cozy. The vaulted breakfast and keeping rooms are bathed in light; easy access to the gourmet kitchen includes a serving-bar island. The master suite features a vaulted spa bath with a radius window and a garden tub. Upstairs, two bedrooms share a full bath.

HPK2300282

HOME PLAN

Style: Cape Cod
First Floor: 1,506 sq. ft.
Second Floor: 426 sq. ft.
Total: 1,932 sq. ft.
Bedrooms: 3
Bathrooms: 2 ½
Width: 50' - 0"
Depth: 52' - 6"
Foundation: Crawlspace, Unfinished Walkout Basement

eplans.com

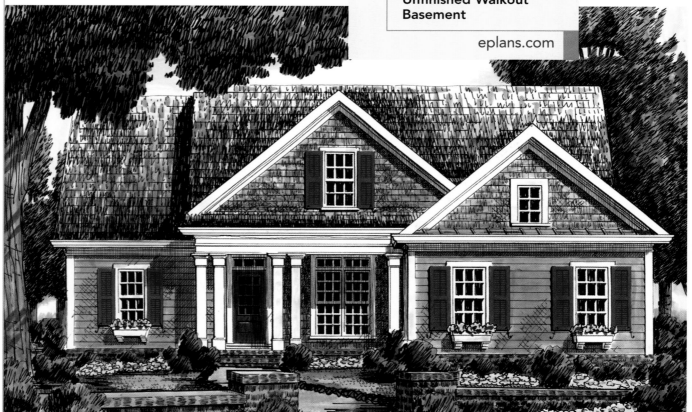

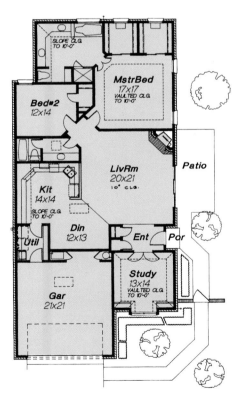

HPK2300283

Style: Traditional

Square Footage: 1,943

Bedrooms: 2

Bathrooms: 2

Width: 35' - 0"

Depth: 75' - 0"

Foundation: Slab

eplans.com

THIS TRADITIONAL-STYLE HOME BEGINS WITH A PRIVATE SIDE ENTRANCE and a covered entry porch. A large living room with a corner fireplace opens to the patio area. A laundry area is nestled between the garage, the U-shaped kitchen and the skylit dinette. Both the study and the master suite feature tray ceilings. The master suite also enjoys a double-sink vanity, a tub and separate shower, and two walk-in closets. A second bedroom features a walk-in closet and accesses a full hall bath.

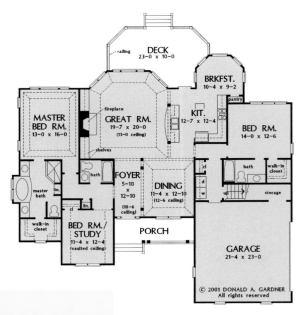

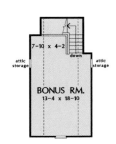

HOME PLAN

HPK2300284

Style: Traditional

Square Footage: 1,971

Bonus Space: 358 sq. ft.

Bedrooms: 3

Bathrooms: 3

Width: 62' - 6"

Depth: 57' - 2"

eplans.com

THIS CRAFTSMAN COTTAGE COMBINES STONE, SIDING, AND CEDAR SHAKE to create striking curb appeal. The interior features an open floor plan with high ceilings, columns, and bay windows to visually expand space. Built-in cabinetry, a fireplace, and a kitchen pass-through highlight and add convenience to the great room. The master suite features a tray ceiling in the bedroom and a bath with garden tub, separate shower, dual vanities, and a walk-in closet. On the opposite side of the home is another bedroom that could be used as a second master suite. Above the garage, a bonus room provides ample storage and space to grow.

GARAGE
20'-0" x 22'-0"

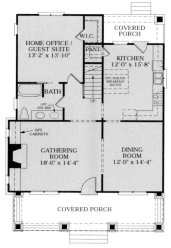

FIRST FLOOR

HOME OFFICE / GUEST SUITE
13'-2" x 13'-10"

W.I.C.

PANT.

COVERED PORCH

KITCHEN
12'-0" x 15'-8"

OPT. BUILT-IN BREAKFAST BOOTH

BATH

OPT. 2ND SINK

UP

OPT. CABINETS

GATHERING ROOM
18'-6" x 14'-4"

DINING ROOM
12'-0" x 14'-4"

COVERED PORCH

SECOND FLOOR

LIN.

MASTER BATH

DN

SUITE 2
12'-2" x 13'-4"

W.I.C.

LAUN.

BATH

ATTIC STOR.

MASTER SUITE
14'-0" x 15'-8"

W.I.C.

ATTIC STOR.

HOME PLAN

HPK2300285

Style: Craftsman

First Floor: 1,060 sq. ft.

Second Floor: 914 sq. ft.

Total: 1,974 sq. ft.

Bedrooms: 3

Bathrooms: 3

Width: 32' - 0"

Depth: 35' - 0"

Foundation: Crawlspace

eplans.com

THIS CHARMING CRAFTSMAN DESIGN offers a second-story master bedroom with four windows under the gabled dormer. The covered front porch displays column and pier supports. The hearth-warmed gathering room opens to the dining room on the right, where the adjoining kitchen offers enough space for an optional breakfast booth. A home office/guest suite is found in the rear. The second floor holds the lavish master suite and a second bedroom suite with its own private bath.

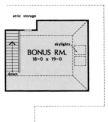

A TWO-STORY FOYER WITH A PALLADIAN WINDOW ABOVE sets the tone for this sunlit home. Columns mark the passage from the foyer to the great room, where a central fireplace and built-in cabinets are found. A screened porch with four skylights above and a wet bar provides a pleasant place to start the day or wind down after work. The kitchen is flanked by the formal dining room and the breakfast room. Hidden quietly at the rear, the master suite includes a bath with dual vanities and skylights. Two family bedrooms (one an optional study) share a bath that has twin sinks.

HPK2300286

Style: Traditional

Square Footage: 1,977

Bonus Space: 430 sq. ft.

Bedrooms: 3

Bathrooms: 2

Width: 69' - 8"

Depth: 59' - 6"

HOME PLAN

eplans.com

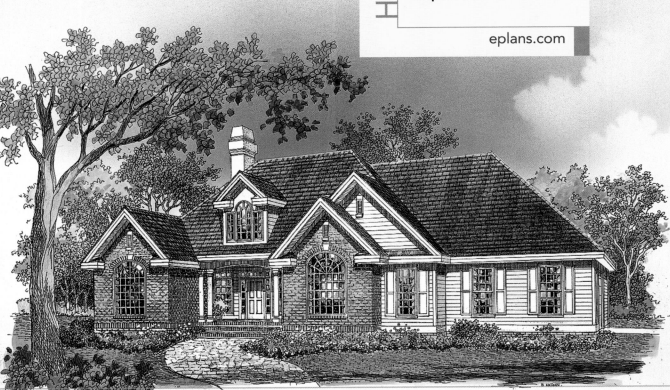

© 1994 Donald A. Gardner Architects, Inc.

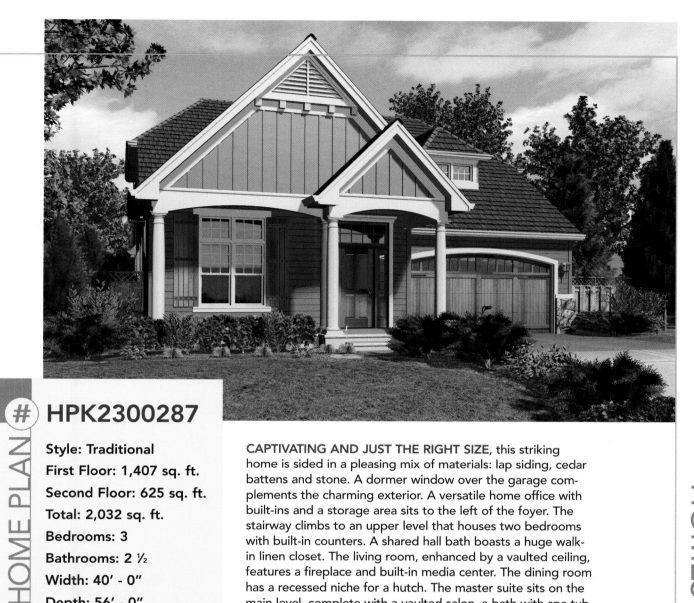

HOME PLAN

HPK2300287

Style: Traditional
First Floor: 1,407 sq. ft.
Second Floor: 625 sq. ft.
Total: 2,032 sq. ft.
Bedrooms: 3
Bathrooms: 2 ½
Width: 40' - 0"
Depth: 56' - 0"
Foundation: Crawlspace

eplans.com

CAPTIVATING AND JUST THE RIGHT SIZE, this striking home is sided in a pleasing mix of materials: lap siding, cedar battens and stone. A dormer window over the garage complements the charming exterior. A versatile home office with built-ins and a storage area sits to the left of the foyer. The stairway climbs to an upper level that houses two bedrooms with built-in counters. A shared hall bath boasts a huge walk-in linen closet. The living room, enhanced by a vaulted ceiling, features a fireplace and built-in media center. The dining room has a recessed niche for a hutch. The master suite sits on the main level, complete with a vaulted salon, a bath with spa tub and separate shower, and a massive walk-in closet. Look for a laundry room and half-bath nearby.

FIRST FLOOR

SECOND FLOOR

FIRST FLOOR

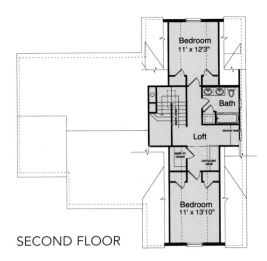

SECOND FLOOR

HPK2300288

Style: Country

First Floor: 1,399 sq. ft.

Second Floor: 671 sq. ft.

Total: 2,070 sq. ft.

Bedrooms: 3

Bathrooms: 2 ½

Width: 49' - 8"

Depth: 52' - 0"

Foundation: Unfinished Walkout Basement

eplans.com

AN OPEN AND CASUAL FLOOR PLAN combined with a first-floor master bedroom offers a relaxed lifestyle and stylish amenities for this exciting home. A sloped ceiling that expands through the great room and dining area adds volume. The warmth of the fireplace radiates throughout the living space, and a view from the kitchen allows this room to share in the cozy atmosphere. A first-floor master suite, secluded for privacy, is complemented by a whirlpool tub, double-bowl vanity, linen closet, compartmented shower and commode, and large walk-in closet. Split stairs lead to a second floor, which offers additional bedrooms and a computer loft.

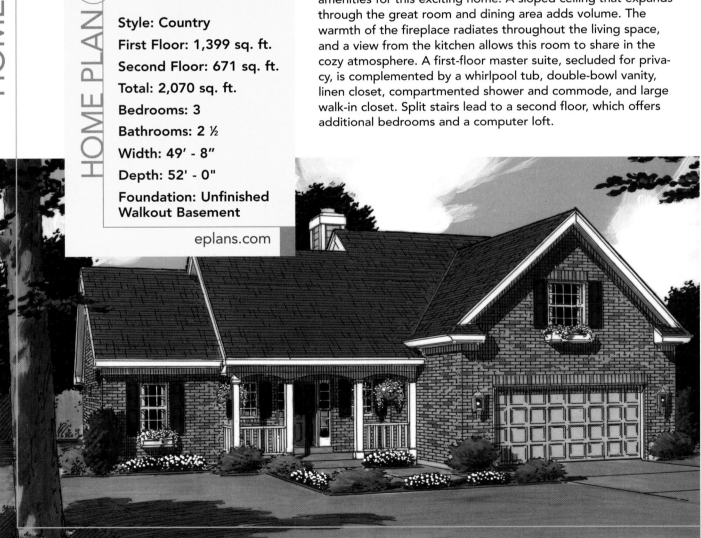

PORCH

MASTER BED RM.
15-0 x 14-0

BRKFST.
11-0 x 10-10

fireplace

walk-in closet

walk-in closet

KITCHEN
13-0 x 11-4

GREAT RM.
18-4 x 19-0
(cathedral ceiling)

lin.

UTIL.
7-0 x 6-0
d w

lin.

master bath

DINING
13-8 x 11-0

BED RM./ STUDY
12-8 x 11-0

cl

seat

sto.

(optional door)

FOYER
8-0 x 6-8

cl

bath

GARAGE
21-0 x 21-0

PORCH

cl

BED RM.
12-8 x 12-0
(vaulted ceiling)

HOME PLAN

HPK2300289

Style: Traditional

Square Footage: 2,070

Bedrooms: 3

Bathrooms: 2

Width: 46' - 3"

Depth: 67' - 7"

eplans.com

CLASSIC LINES WITH BRICK DETAIL AND A HIGH HIPPED ROOF make this narrow design an attractive addition to a fine neighborhood. Living spaces start at the foyer, which leads to an open dining room with column accents and to the great room featuring a cathedral ceiling and central fireplace. Two family bedrooms can be found to the right and share a full bath. The master suite is hidden at the rear for more privacy and boasts two walk-in closets, dual vanities, separate tub and shower and a compartmented toilet. The kitchen is a crown jewel of space. A work island affords even more room for special occasions and the breakfast area is perfect for company in the kitchen.

FIRST FLOOR

SECOND FLOOR

MASSIVE, MULTIPANED WINDOWS, DOUBLE GABLES, AND A CHARMING DORMER combine to create the appealing facade of this lovely two-story traditional home. The floor plan is classically devised, but also incorporates current design to make a layout that is timeless and convenient. A home office opens through double doors from a hallway to the left of the foyer. Optional built-ins in the office make the best use of space. The great room is sizeable, and has a 12-foot ceiling and gas fireplace. A bar counter separates the great room from the kitchen; a vaulted dining area with optional built-in hutch is nearby, and has access to a side porch and patio. A tray ceiling graces the master suite, further complemented by a walk-in closet, and bath with spa tub and separate shower. Two additional bedrooms are found on the upper level, and share the use of a full hall bath.

HOME PLAN # HPK2300290

Style: Traditional
First Floor: 1,601 sq. ft.
Second Floor: 479 sq. ft.
Total: 2,080 sq. ft.
Bedrooms: 3
Bathrooms: 2 ½
Width: 45' - 0"
Depth: 53' - 0"
Foundation: Crawlspace

eplans.com

FIRST FLOOR

GARAGE
20'-0" X 22'-0"

LAUNDRY

BREAKFAST
10'-4" X 10'-0"

GATHERING
ROOM
10'-0" X 14'-8"

KITCHEN
13'-0" X 15'-4"

OPT. CABINETS

PDR.

MASTER
BATH

W.I.C.   W.I.C.

PAN.

BTL'R
PAN.

DINING
ROOM
15'-0" X 12'-0"

MASTER
SUITE
14'-0" X 15'-8"

COVERED PORCH

SECOND FLOOR

SUITE 2
12'-8" X 13'-10"

BALCONY   LIN.

DN

BATH
OPT.
2ND SINK

SUITE 3
12'-8" X 15'-8"

HOME PLAN

(#) HPK2300291

Style: Cape Cod
First Floor: 1,466 sq. ft.
Second Floor: 629 sq. ft.
Total: 2,095 sq. ft.
Bedrooms: 3
Bathrooms: 2 ½
Width: 32' - 0"
Depth: 59' - 0"
Foundation: Crawlspace

eplans.com

DESIGNED FOR A NARROW LOT, this home's modest facade belies the functional, amenity-filled floor plan inside. You may enter through the front door to the dining area, but this casual home was meant to have family and friends come in through the back entrance. From here, the hearth-warmed gathering room opens to the sunny breakfast nook and angled serving-bar kitchen. A butler's pantry makes an elegant segue to the dining room. The master suite is located on this level and enjoys a splendid bath with dual amenities. Secondary bedrooms are upstairs and share a full bath with an optional twin sink. A two-car garage completes the plan, positioned at the rear to allow the home great curb appeal.

HOME PLAN

(#) HPK2300292

Style: French

Square Footage: 2,150

Bedrooms: 3

Bathrooms: 2 ½

Width: 64' - 0"

Depth: 60' - 4"

Foundation: Walkout Basement

eplans.com

THIS HOME DRAWS ITS INSPIRATION FROM BOTH FRENCH AND ENGLISH COUNTRY HOMES. The great room and dining room combine to form an impressive gathering space, with the dining area subtly defined by columns and a large triple window. The kitchen, with its work island, adjoins the breakfast area and keeping room with a fireplace. The home is completed by a master suite with a bay window and a garden tub. Space on the lower level can be developed later.

HPK2300293

Style: Country Cottage

First Floor: 1,390 sq. ft.

Second Floor: 764 sq. ft.

Total: 2,154 sq. ft.

Bonus Space: 282 sq. ft.

Bedrooms: 3

Bathrooms: 3 ½

Width: 42' - 0"

Depth: 57' - 4"

Foundation: Crawlspace, Unfinished Walkout Basement

eplans.com

HOME PLAN

DIVERSE ROOFLINES AND WINDOW STYLES BLEND TO PROJECT A SENSE OF SPLENDOR, which is continued throughout the interior of this Southern-style home. With a soaring two-story vault ceiling and an extended-hearth fireplace, the family room assumes center stage in this design. The island kitchen, located between the formal dining room and breakfast corner, is well suited to serve both. A fully furnished master suite, with French doors separating the bath from the sleeping area, occupies the entire left wing. Upstairs, a similar-size suite offers posh quarters for overnight guests. A third bedroom, and space for a fourth, also are on this floor. All the upstairs bedrooms share access to a balcony overlooking the family room.

FIRST FLOOR

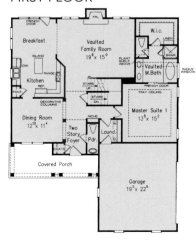

SECOND FLOOR

HOMES FOR EMPTY-NESTERS

FIRST FLOOR

SECOND FLOOR

ARCHED LINTELS AND A STONE PEDIMENT ADD EUROPEAN FLAIR to this design, while a wide porch support and matchstick detailing add a Craftsman flavor. The expansive great room, just to the left of the foyer, boasts a vaulted ceiling, a fireplace, and built-in bookshelves; elegant columns define the adjacent dining room. The kitchen showcases a central island cooktop and opens to a cozy porch. The master suite, conveniently close to the laundry area, also features a vaulted ceiling as well as a walk-in closet. On the second floor, two family bedrooms include walk-in closets and share a full bath.

HOME PLAN

#HPK2300294

Style: Tudor

First Floor: 1,608 sq. ft.

Second Floor: 581 sq. ft.

Total: 2,189 sq. ft.

Bedrooms: 3

Bathrooms: 2 ½

Width: 46' - 0"

Depth: 63' - 0"

eplans.com

FIRST FLOOR

SECOND FLOOR

HOME PLAN

HPK2300295

Style: Traditional

First Floor: 1,897 sq. ft.

Second Floor: 301 sq. ft.

Total: 2,198 sq. ft.

Bedrooms: 2

Bathrooms: 3

Width: 48' - 0"

Depth: 63' - 10"

Foundation: Unfinished Basement

eplans.com

DESIGNED FOR A NARROW LOT, this delightful home offers an open great room and dining area with views to the rear yard, a deluxe master bedroom suite, private library or optional second bedroom and cozy screened porch. Multiple closets help keep an orderly home and an open kitchen, defined by an island with seating, makes time spent preparing meals a pleasurable experience. This home makes a perfect vacation retreat or empty nester residence. A second floor bedroom with a private bath offers privacy for overnight guests or for additional family members.

FIRST FLOOR

SECOND FLOOR

HOME PLAN

HPK2300296

Style: Craftsman

First Floor: 1,675 sq. ft.

Second Floor: 614 sq. ft.

Total: 2,289 sq. ft.

Bedrooms: 3

Bathrooms: 2 ½

Width: 48' - 0"

Depth: 56' - 0"

Foundation: Crawlspace

eplans.com

WITH A NOD TO THE DETAILS OF THE ARTS AND CRAFTS MOVEMENT, this appealing bungalow has an eye-catching covered front porch, cedar-shingle accents, and light-catching windows. The main foyer separates a cozy den on the left from the formal dining room on the right. A butler's pantry connects the dining room and the convenient kitchen. An angled peninsula containing the cooktop joins the kitchen to a casual nook. There is patio access here for outdoor entertaining. A gas fireplace, skylights, and a built-in media center in the great room create a comfortable place in which to relax. Exquisite in design, the master suite includes a bath with a spa tub, dual lavatories, separate shower, walk-in closet and compartmented toilet. On the upper level is a hall bath with dual lavatories to serve the two family bedrooms on this floor.

HOME PLAN

HPK2300297

Style: French

Square Footage: 2,295

Bedrooms: 3

Bathrooms: 2

Width: 69' - 0"

Depth: 49' - 6"

Foundation: Walkout Basement

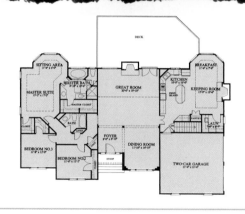

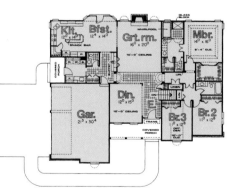

HOME PLAN

HPK2300298

Style: Traditional

Square Footage: 2,311

Bedrooms: 3

Bathrooms: 2 ½

Width: 64' - 0"

Depth: 57' - 2"

HOMES FOR EMPTY-NESTERS

HOME PLAN
HPK2300299

Style: Traditional
Square Footage: 2,452
Bedrooms: 3
Bathrooms: 2 ½
Width: 70' - 8"
Depth: 70' - 0"
Foundation: Unfinished Basement

HOME PLAN
HPK2300300

Style: Country Cottage
First Floor: 2,037 sq. ft.
Second Floor: 596 sq. ft.
Total: 2,633 sq. ft.
Bedrooms: 2
Bathrooms: 2
Width: 42' - 0"
Depth: 75' - 0"
Foundation: Unfinished Basement, Slab

SECOND FLOOR

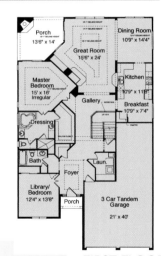

FIRST FLOOR

HOME PLAN

(#) HPK2300301

Style: European Cottage

First Floor: 1,763 sq. ft.

Second Floor: 947 sq. ft.

Total: 2,710 sq. ft.

Bedrooms: 3

Bathrooms: 2 ½

Width: 50' - 0"

Depth: 75' - 4"

Foundation: Walkout Basement

eplans.com

A SPECIAL FEATURE OF THIS CLASSY HOME IS THE SECOND-FLOOR MEDIA ROOM and adjoining exercise area. Convenient to two upstairs bedrooms and a full bath, the media room is a great place for family computers and a fax machine. On the main level, a gourmet kitchen provides a snack counter and a walk-in pantry. Double doors open to a gallery hall that leads to the formal dining room—an enchanting retreat for chandelier-lit evenings—that provides a breathtaking view of the front yard. A classic great room is warmed by a cozy fireplace and brightened by a wall of windows. The outdoor living area is spacious enough for grand events. The master suite is brightened by sweeping views of the backyard and a romantic fireplace just for two.

HOMES FOR EMPTY-NESTERS

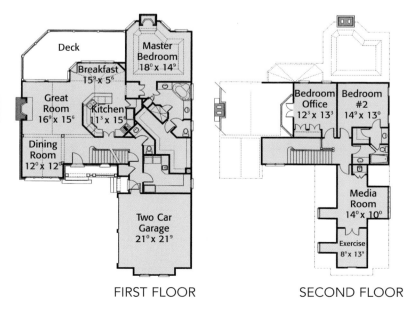

FIRST FLOOR   SECOND FLOOR

FIRST FLOOR

SECOND FLOOR

HOME PLAN

HPK2300302

Style: European Cottage

First Floor: 2,221 sq. ft.

Second Floor: 602 sq. ft.

Total: 2,823 sq. ft.

Bedrooms: 2

Bathrooms: 3

Width: 50' - 0"

Depth: 70' - 4"

Foundation: Unfinished Basement, Slab

HOME PLAN

HPK2300303

Style: European Cottage

First Floor: 2,230 sq. ft.

Second Floor: 601 sq. ft.

Total: 2,831 sq. ft.

Bedrooms: 2

Bathrooms: 3

Width: 50' - 0"

Depth: 70' - 4"

Foundation: Unfinished Basement, Slab

FIRST FLOOR

SECOND FLOOR

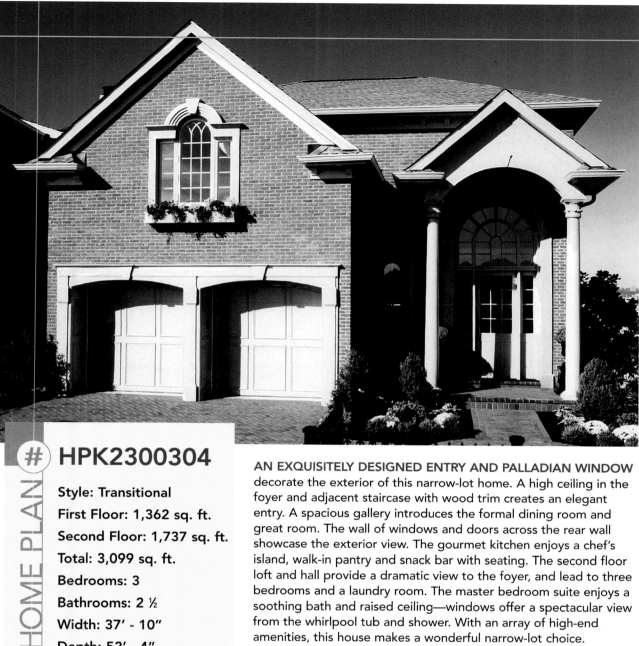

HOME PLAN

(#) HPK2300304

Style: Transitional

First Floor: 1,362 sq. ft.

Second Floor: 1,737 sq. ft.

Total: 3,099 sq. ft.

Bedrooms: 3

Bathrooms: 2 ½

Width: 37' - 10"

Depth: 52' - 4"

Foundation: Finished Walkout Basement

eplans.com

AN EXQUISITELY DESIGNED ENTRY AND PALLADIAN WINDOW decorate the exterior of this narrow-lot home. A high ceiling in the foyer and adjacent staircase with wood trim creates an elegant entry. A spacious gallery introduces the formal dining room and great room. The wall of windows and doors across the rear wall showcase the exterior view. The gourmet kitchen enjoys a chef's island, walk-in pantry and snack bar with seating. The second floor loft and hall provide a dramatic view to the foyer, and lead to three bedrooms and a laundry room. The master bedroom suite enjoys a soothing bath and raised ceiling—windows offer a spectacular view from the whirlpool tub and shower. With an array of high-end amenities, this house makes a wonderful narrow-lot choice.

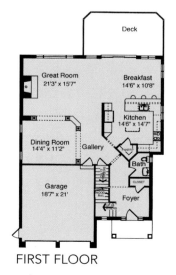

FIRST FLOOR

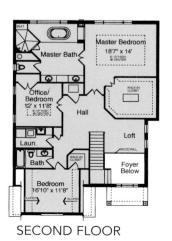

SECOND FLOOR

HOMES FOR EMPTY-NESTERS

Growing Trend—Landscapes and Projects Complete the Plan

A truly gratifying landscape design takes cues from the architecture of the home, your sense of style, and the natural properties of the land. You will also need to make a decision about the kind of landscape you desire. For instance, perennials and bulbs used throughout a design will establish a garden theme and provide cutting flowers for indoor bouquets. But remember that a garden will need a lot of care and constant attention. And a neglected garden will do nothing for a home's curb appeal. Similarly, edible gardens are very appropriate in a country-inspired design—but need to be protected from the elements. More shaded parts of the landscape call for sitting areas or outdoor structures, such as storage sheds or small barns.

The right landscaping design will effectively frame your home from the rest of the neighborhood. If your lot will not allow the placement of a tall fence or natural barrier between the home and the next-door neighbor, place "retreat" areas away from property lines. That is, resist the natural urge to place quiet areas in only the corners of the yard. With the right design, owners can create a relaxing getaway right in the middle of the plan.

The virtue of predrawn landscape and project plans is that you can enjoy the benefits of a professional design without paying for custom landscaping. Do-it-yourselfers can easily manage the tasks required to install a bed or build a gazebo. Your new landscape will improve your outdoor environment the day it's completed, and the initial investment will add greatly to the value of your home.

Getty Images; Ernest Braun

THIS AMBITIOUS DESIGN will take work to maintain. Of course, the results are spectacular.

Getty Images

EVENTUALLY, EVERY
LANDSCAPE DESIGN
matures into something
unique.

A RUSTIC SHED AND
NATURALISTIC GARDEN
DESIGN (below) look
surprisingly at home beside
a contemporary pool.

THIS PERGOLA (at left) is the kind
of simple addition to your landscape
that adds charm and function.

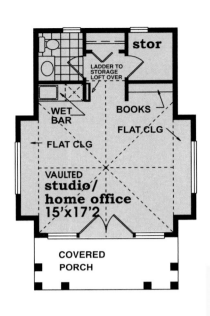

stor

LADDER TO
STORAGE
LOFT OVER

WET
BAR

BOOKS

FLAT CLG

FLAT CLG

VAULTED
**studio/
home office**
15'x17'2

COVERED
PORCH

HOME PLAN #

HPK2300305

Width: 20' - 0"

Depth: 30' - 0"

HOME PLAN #

HPK2300306

Width: 11' - 0"

Depth: 13' - 6"

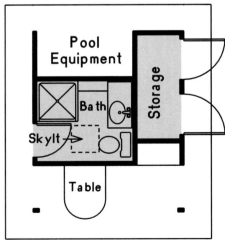

Pool
Equipment

Bath

Storage

Skylt

Table

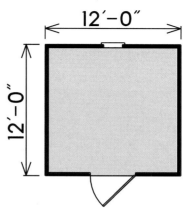

12'-0"

12'-0"

HOME PLAN

HPK2300307

Width: 12' - 0"

Depth: 12' - 0"

HOME PLAN

HPK2300308

Width: 16' - 0"

Depth: 12' - 0"

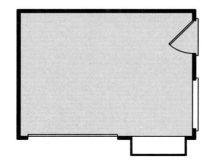

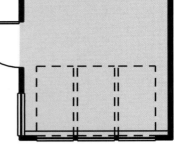

HOME PLAN
HPK2300309

Width: 10' - 0"
Depth: 10' - 0"

HOME PLAN
HPK2300310

Width: 17' - 0"
Depth: 11' - 8"

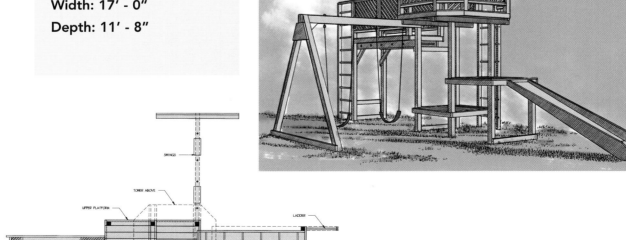

HOME PLAN #

HPK2300311

Width: 8' - 0"
Depth: 8' - 0"

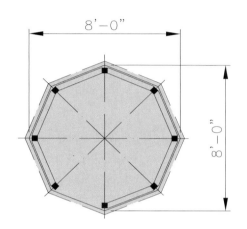

HOME PLAN #

HPK2300312

Width: 4' - 3"
Depth: 6' - 0"

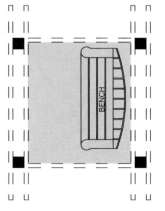

LANDSCAPES & OUTDOOR PROJECTS

HOME PLAN

HPK2300313

Square Footage: 12
Width: 3' - 0"
Depth: 4' - 0"

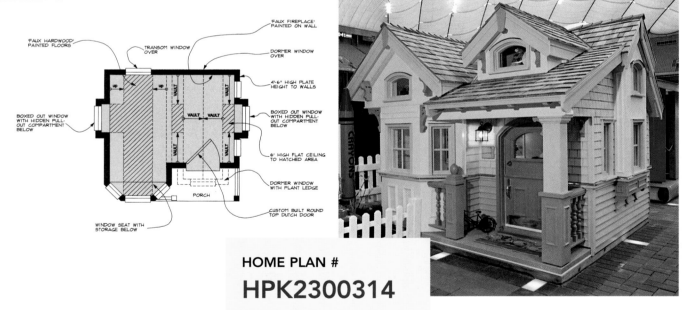

'FAUX HARDWOOD' PAINTED FLOORS

TRANSOM WINDOW OVER

'FAUX FIREPLACE' PAINTED ON WALL

DORMER WINDOW OVER

4'-6" HIGH PLATE HEIGHT TO WALLS

BOXED OUT WINDOW WITH HIDDEN PULL-OUT COMPARTMENT BELOW

BOXED OUT WINDOW WITH HIDDEN PULL-OUT COMPARTMENT BELOW

VAULT

6' HIGH FLAT CEILING TO HATCHED AREA

DORMER WINDOW WITH PLANT LEDGE

PORCH

CUSTOM BUILT ROUND TOP DUTCH DOOR

WINDOW SEAT WITH STORAGE BELOW

HOME PLAN

HPK2300314

Square Footage: 64
Width: 8' - 0"
Depth: 8' - 0"
Foundation: Slab

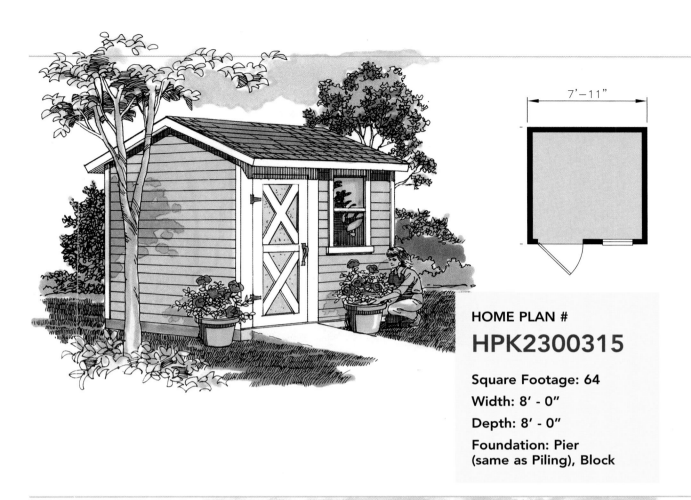

HOME PLAN

HPK2300315

Square Footage: 64

Width: 8' - 0"

Depth: 8' - 0"

**Foundation: Pier
(same as Piling), Block**

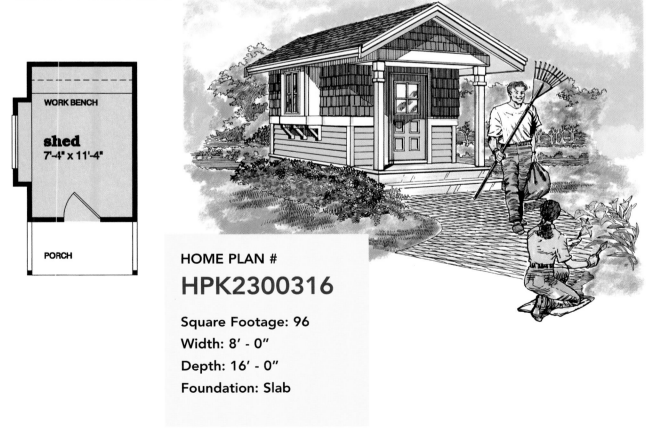

HOME PLAN

HPK2300316

Square Footage: 96

Width: 8' - 0"

Depth: 16' - 0"

Foundation: Slab

HOME PLAN

HPK2300317

Square Footage: 96
Width: 8' - 0"
Depth: 12' - 0"
Foundation: Slab

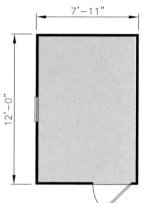

HOME PLAN

HPK2300318

Square Footage: 144
Width: 12' - 0"
Depth: 12' - 0"
Foundation: Slab

HOME PLAN

HPK2300319

Square Footage: 192
Width: 12' - 0"
Depth: 16' - 0"
Foundation: Slab

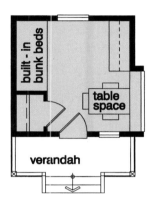

built - in bunk beds

table space

verandah

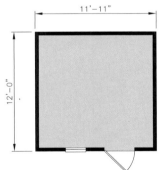

11' – 11"

12' - 0"

HOME PLAN

HPK2300320

Square Footage: 144
Width: 12' - 0"
Depth: 12' - 0"
Foundation: Slab

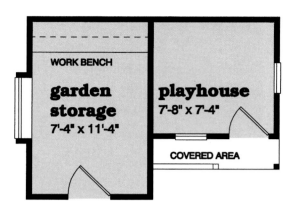

WORK BENCH

garden storage
7'-4" x 11'-4"

playhouse
7'-8" x 7'-4"

COVERED AREA

HOME PLAN

HPK2300321

Square Footage: 192

Width: 16' - 0"

Depth: 12' - 0"

Foundation: Slab

eplans.com

EFFICIENT FOR MOM AND DAD, WHILE MUNCHKIN-SIZED FOR YOUNGSTERS, this structure boasts practicality and playfulness. The exterior is dazzled in wood siding and cedar shingles—a pleasant display for any outdoor scenery. The garden storage area is separated from the playhouse by a wall and features a sufficient work bench and an illuminating side window. The playhouse resembles a petite version of a country cottage. A tiny covered porch with a wood railing and a window accent the outside and welcome young ones into the petite hideaway. Inside, another window graces the right wall and brightens the interior. There is room enough for a small table and chairs and, most importantly, plenty of toys.

THOUGH SIMPLE IN DESIGN, THIS SMALLER STUDIO/HOME OFFICE provides all the right stuff for your workspace. A covered entry shelters the double-French door access to a two-room area. The smaller space features a nine-foot flat ceiling and is separated from the main studio area by a columned arch. The main area seems larger than it is thanks to a vaulted ceiling and two bumped-out windows. Define your own work area with furniture, or modify this design to include handy built-ins.

HOME PLAN

 # HPK2300322

Square Footage: 288

Width: 20' - 0"

Depth: 16' - 0"

Foundation: Slab, Crawlspace

eplans.com

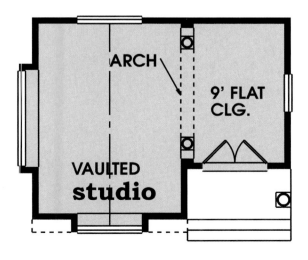

ARCH

9' FLAT CLG.

VAULTED
studio

THE LAYOUT OF THIS L-SHAPED HOME presents several landscaping challenges. The landscape design must provide cars with easy access to the two-car garage and enough turnaround space so they needn't back out of the driveway. The home's three front entrances need to be distinguished one from another, and plantings should counter the elongated look of the house.

(#) HPK2300323

PLAN

Season: Spring

Design by: Susan Roth

eplans.com

Inlaid cobblestones transform what could otherwise resemble a parking lot into an entry court that escorts visitors to the main entrance. A curving line of ornamental trees bordering the driveway leads the eye directly to the door. A low picket fence keeps this lovely garden even more private. A wide landing of bluestone paving further highlights the main entrance. The courtyard effect is reinforced by a border of ornamental trees, which can be enjoyed from a private garden encircled by a picket fence.

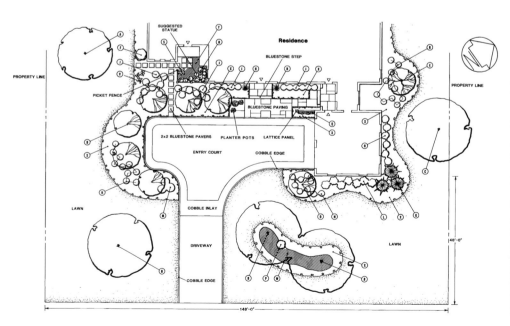

THE GRANDEUR OF A EUROPEAN PALACE OR ESTATE GARDEN comes alive in the formality and scale of this landscape design, which features a formal rose garden. In creating this mood, the designer makes the landscape completely symmetrical. Both sides of the garden are exact mirror images of each other, with extensive lawn areas on each side that can be used for relaxing or entertaining.

In the tradition of the formal rose garden, neat crisp evergreen hedges outline the rose plantings, providing interest and structure even during the off-season when the roses have been cut back to near the ground. The straight lines of the stepping-stone paths form a strong cross shape in the center of the garden. Each arm of the cross begins with a formal red rose and ends at the edge of the garden in a strong focal point. The sight line looking up the horizontal arms, which is emphasized by the overhead trellises and pergolas,

HPK2300324

Season: Summer
Design by: Jim Morgan

PLAN

eplans.com

terminates in groups of oval-shaped trees backed by lattice panels. Flowering vines adorn the trellises.

From the bluestone paving at the house, a sight line leads across the paving stones and culminates with a reflecting pool situated in a paved area at the far end. Note that, although the same paving material was used in the front and back areas, the pattern is formal near the house and more informal at the back. Within the strong geometrical space of the rose garden, an early-spring flowering perennial provides a blanket of color until the roses burst into their summer-long show.

The rose arbor and gate at each side of the house feature climbing roses, echoing the main theme of the garden.

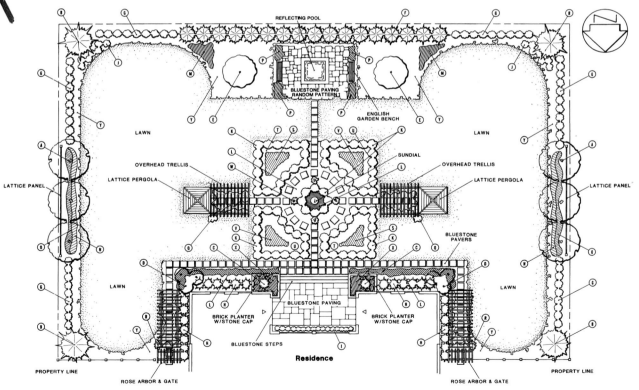

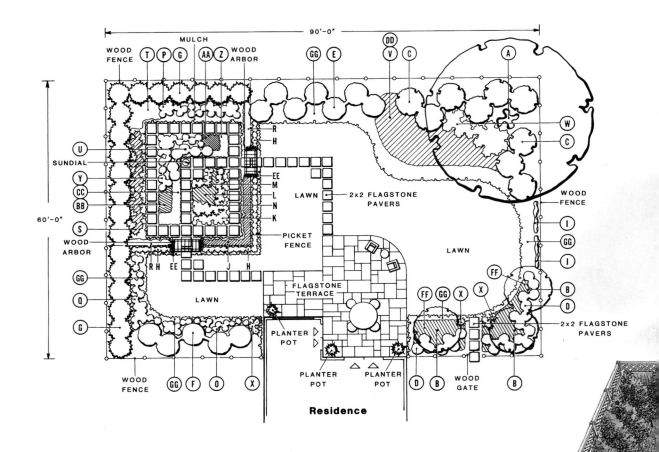

 # HPK2300325

Season: Summer
Design by: Damon Scott

eplans.com

YOU CAN HAVE YOUR GARDEN
FLOWERS AND CUT THEM TOO with
this charming backyard plan. The designer skillfully created a landscape that features a garden planted just to produce
flowers to cut for indoor arrangements,
yet still looks as pretty as a picture. Here
you'll find a serious gardening plot
attractively integrated into a landscape
of flowering trees, shrubs and groundcovers with plenty of patio and lawn for
the family.

Because you'll be removing most of the flowers as they
begin to open, a cut-flower garden has more in common
with a vegetable garden than a flower garden, so it's
best to camouflage the plants from direct view. The
designer chose a white picket fence to surround the
structure. Two gated arbors, draped with flowering
vines, provide easy access to the garden. The flowers
planted in front of the fence aren't meant for cutting but
for you to enjoy while relaxing on the patio.

Within the gated cut-flower garden itself, stepping-stone paths provide easy access for tending the flower beds. The designer devoted one section to perennial flowers, which return to grace the garden year after year. Another section contains annuals, which need replanting each year. The perennials include an assortment of spring-, summer-, and fall-blooming plants so you'll have months of different blossoms to cut, while the long-blooming annuals keep on producing more flowers after they're cut. All the flowers specified for this design make long-lasting arrangements.

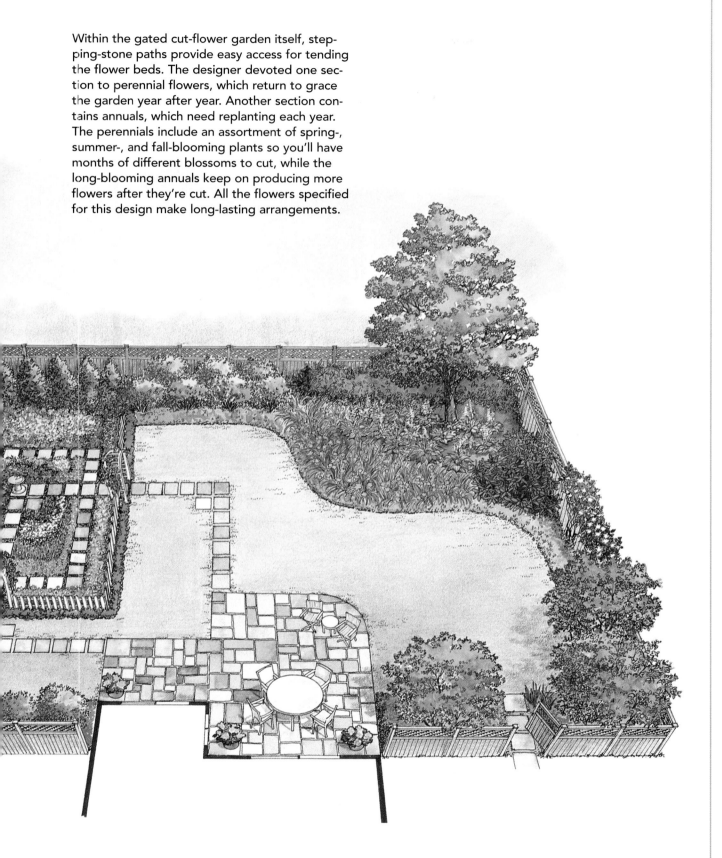

HPK2300326

Season: Summer

Design by: Salvatore A. Masullo

PLAN

eplans.com

DESIGNED IN THE STYLE OF OLD-FASHIONED DOORYARD GARDENS, this modern adaptation brings useful, edible plants within easy reach of your house. Site these beds and borders near the kitchen door so you'll have easy access to their bounty when cooking. Or move the entire garden to the center of a sunny lawn.

A herringbone-patterned brick walkway along one side of the garden guides you to one of the two entry gates. Mulched paths and irregular flagstones, interplanted with a scented, mat-forming groundcover, define the beds and borders. A picturesque wooden fence enclosing the entire garden provides a sense of structure, while its rectilinear form is echoed and softened by hedge plantings. If your space is limited, you might eliminate one or both of the hedges, the fence, or all of the hard- and softscape elements outside the garden beds.

The only maintenance tasks required involve harvesting, occasional cleanup and replacing the annual herbs each year. You'll also need to refresh the mulch each year to prevent weeds from sprouting and to keep the beds neat. An herb garden fenced in cottage-garden style and located just off the back door is both attractive and practical.

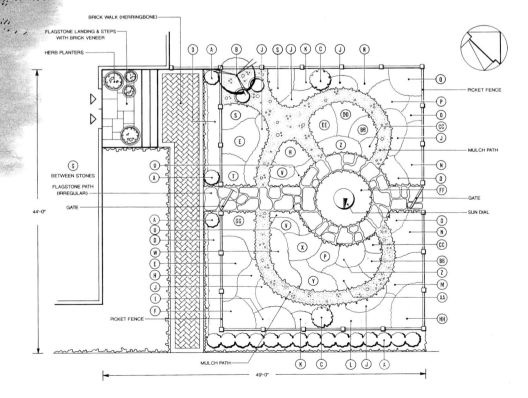

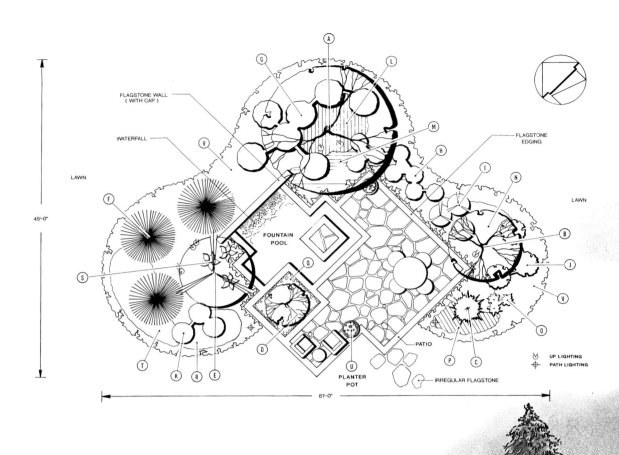

FLAGSTONE WALL
(WITH CAP)

WATERFALL

LAWN

45'-0"

FOUNTAIN
POOL

FLAGSTONE
EDGING

LAWN

PATIO

PLANTER
POT

IRREGULAR FLAGSTONE

UP LIGHTING
PATH LIGHTING

61'-0"

THIS PATIO GARDEN IS DESIGNED TO BE USED
DURING SUMMER EVENINGS when people are most
likely to sit or entertain guests outdoors. The designer chooses flowers in mostly white and pastel colors
that pop out of the shadows and glow in the moon-
light. Lamps are strategically placed to provide nighttime lighting; some lamps are used to cast reflections
on the formal pool or are directed upward to illumi-
nate the beautifully sculpted tree trunks.

A waterfall cascading as a sheet into the pool creates
soothing sound effects. The waterfall flows from a
free-standing stone wall
that creates a backdrop
for the pool. (The mech-
anism is available as a
kit from water garden
suppliers.) A stepping-
stone island near one
edge of the pool allows
you to move closer to
the waterfall and be
immersed in its sound.

HPK2300327

PLAN

Season: Summer
**Design by: Michael J.
Opisso**

eplans.com

This patio garden is designed to be sited in a lawn away from the house, but it can be easily modified to link directly with the house. You can do this by keeping the shape of the patio and extending the plantings and stepping-stones to the house's foundation.

You'll love entertaining outdoors if you install this design, which offers great garden views, musical sound effects and dramatic nighttime lighting.

IMAGINE BEING ENGULFED IN DELICATELY SCENTED AIR as you relax on your patio. You can enjoy such sensory pleasures everyday by installing this intricate design filled with fragrant plants. Be sure to provide plenty of seating around the patio so you'll have places to sit and enjoy the perfumed air.

This plan is as adaptable as it is beautiful. The designer includes a patio and combination fountain/planter, but you could plant the border around any existing patio. (NOTE: the fountain is not included in the landscape plans.) You might decide to add only a central planter or

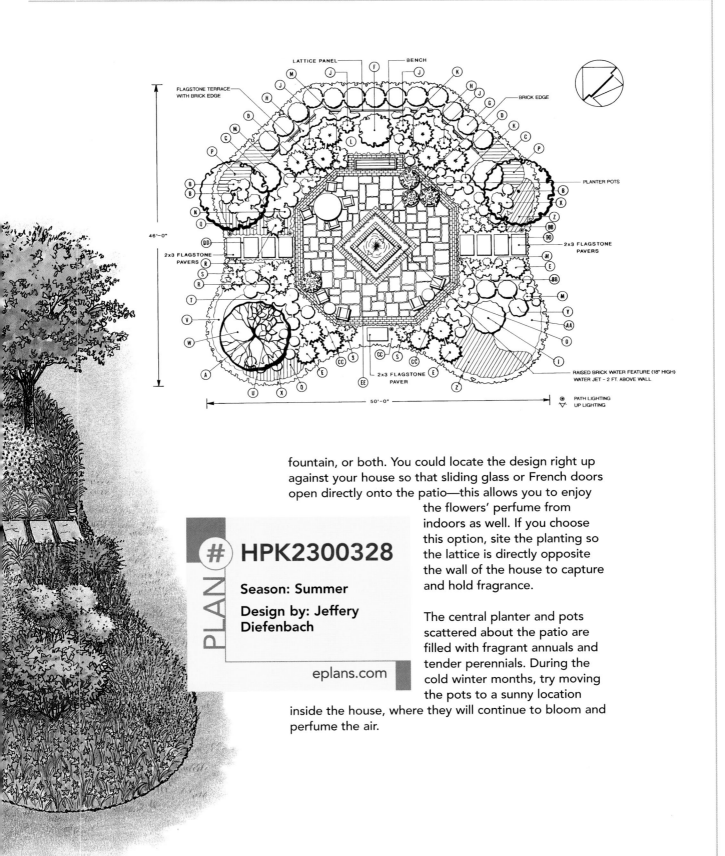

LATTICE PANEL — BENCH

FLAGSTONE TERRACE
WITH BRICK EDGE

BRICK EDGE

PLANTER POTS

46'-0"

2x3 FLAGSTONE
PAVERS

2x3 FLAGSTONE
PAVERS

2x3 FLAGSTONE
PAVER

RAISED BRICK WATER FEATURE (18" HIGH)
WATER JET – 2 FT. ABOVE WALL

50'-0"

⊕ PATH LIGHTING
▽ UP LIGHTING

fountain, or both. You could locate the design right up against your house so that sliding glass or French doors open directly onto the patio—this allows you to enjoy the flowers' perfume from indoors as well. If you choose this option, site the planting so the lattice is directly opposite the wall of the house to capture and hold fragrance.

The central planter and pots scattered about the patio are filled with fragrant annuals and tender perennials. During the cold winter months, try moving the pots to a sunny location inside the house, where they will continue to bloom and perfume the air.

PLAN

HPK2300328

Season: Summer

Design by: Jeffery Diefenbach

eplans.com

YOUR CARES MELT AWAY WHEN YOU ENTER THIS VERY PRIVATE AND TRANQUIL GARDEN through the vine-covered arbor. The designer sites an informal flagstone terrace with two seating areas in a sea of evergreen groundcover, entirely eliminating a lawn and making the garden about as carefree as it can be. Evergreens on the property border create privacy, while airy trees—selected because they cast light shade and are easy to clean up after—create a lacy overhead canopy. The overall effect is serene.

A half-circle rock wall, built of small moss-covered boulders, sets off the larger of the two seating areas and gives dimension to the area. (Five moss rocks on the opposite side of the patio echo and balance the wall.) Several types of perennials

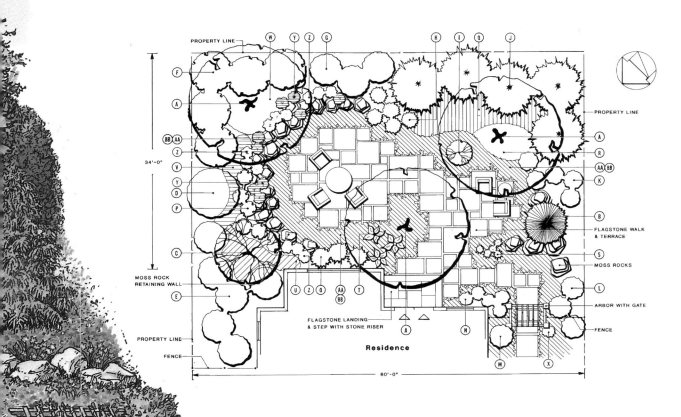

spill over the top and sprout from the crevices of the wall, decorating the area with their dainty flowers and foliage and creating a soft, natural look. Large drifts of spring bulbs and other perennials make lovely splashes of color where they grow through the groundcover.

Flowering shrubs—many of which also display evergreen leaves—give the garden year-round structure and interest while offering easy-care floral beauty. The lack of a lawn makes this garden especially easy to care for. The groundcover absorbs most of the leaves that drop from the deciduous trees in autumn, and the terrace can be quickly swept or blown free of leaves and debris, as needed. All you'll need to do is cut off the dead tops of the perennials once a year in late winter.

(#) HPK2300329

PLAN

Season: Summer

Design by: Michael J. Opisso

eplans.com

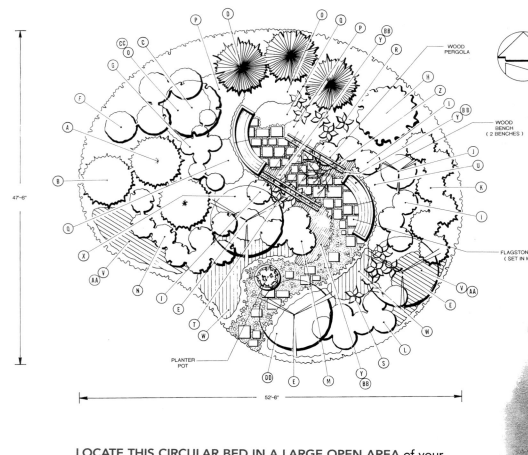

47'-6"

52'-6"

WOOD PERGOLA

WOOD BENCH (2 BENCHES)

FLAGSTONE PAVERS (SET IN MULCH)

PLANTER POT

LOCATE THIS CIRCULAR BED IN A LARGE OPEN AREA of your front- or backyard, where it will create a beautiful island of flowers and foliage. The garden becomes a focal point of the yard, and because it contains evergreens and small flowering trees and shrubs, it also provides privacy by blocking views into and out of the yard. Best of all, the planting is designed so you can stroll along a curving stepping-stone path into its center to discover a secluded sitting area within.

This private sitting area is formed from an open pocket in the center of the bed that features paving stones, two curved benches and an overhead structure. These elements furnish and define the pocket, creating the atmosphere of a garden room—a secluded outdoor retreat. There you can sit in quiet solitude, if you wish, but there's also room enough for the whole family.

The garden's year-round structure comes from its trees, shrubs, stones and pergola. During the growing season, an assortment of colorful flowering perennials and foliage plants fleshes out the scene, creating a changing show.

The surprise in this design is an open area situated within the center of the bed, where two dramatically curving benches and an overhead structure create an outdoor sitting room.

HPK2300330

Season: Spring

Design by: Timothy Barry and Paul Rodel

eplans.com

PLAN

HPK2300331

Season: Summer

Design by: Frank Esposito

eplans.com

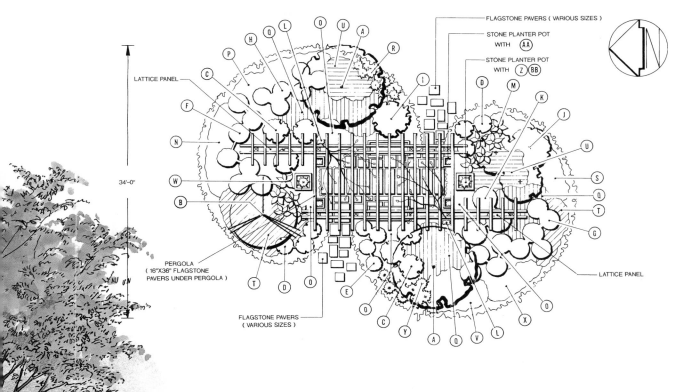

LATTICE PANEL

34'-0"

FLAGSTONE PAVERS (VARIOUS SIZES)

STONE PLANTER POT
WITH (AA)

STONE PLANTER POT
WITH (Z)(BB)

PERGOLA
(16"X36" FLAGSTONE
PAVERS UNDER PERGOLA)

FLAGSTONE PAVERS
(VARIOUS SIZES)

LATTICE PANEL

SITTING IN THE OPEN SHADE CAST BY THE PERGOLA

evokes the secure feeling of being in an outdoor room where you can fully enjoy the flowers in the surrounding garden. This plan's designer enhances the feeling of an outdoor room by adding lattice panels to the ends of the pergola, enclosing it further and providing the perfect place for a colorful cover of climbing vines.

Meant to be situated in an open area of the yard, this pergola planting creates a decorative centerpiece in the lawn—you can site it in either the front- or backyard. To prevent the pergola from looking too massive and dominant, the designer adds several tall trees to the bed, off-setting and balancing its size and shape and anchoring it to the surrounding landscape.

The flagstone patio under the pergola has two entrance paths from the lawn—one on each long side—so that you can walk through the garden. That way, the large island planting becomes a lovely destination rather than an obstacle in the middle of the lawn.

Site this beautiful pergola and its surrounding garden bed at a distance from the house, where it creates a dramatic focal point that draws visitors to come and explore.

A SIMPLE WOODEN BRIDGE crosses the pond to a stone seating area lined with tall prairie grasses and foliage.

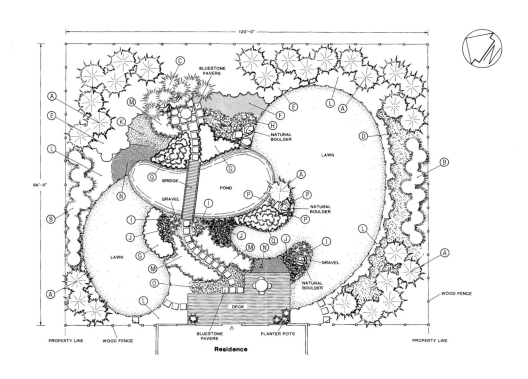

Plan diagram labels: 120'-0", BLUESTONE PAVERS, C, A, M, E, K, L, B, NATURAL BOULDER, E, H, F, L, A, D, B, LAWN, G, BRIDGE, Q, POND, P, A, GRAVEL, N, P, NATURAL BOULDER, P, 96'-0", I, I, J, L, J, M, N, Q, J, I, LAWN, G, GRAVEL, M, O, NATURAL BOULDER, A, A, L, DECK, PROPERTY LINE, WOOD FENCE, BLUESTONE PAVERS, PLANTER POTS, PROPERTY LINE, WOOD FENCE, **Residence**

HPK2300332

PLAN

Season: Summer
Design by: Damon Scott

eplans.com

MANY CULTURES SEEM TO HAVE AN IDENTIFIABLE GARDEN STYLE—there are formal Italian fountain gardens, French parterres, English perennial borders, and Japanese contemplation gardens. For many years, we didn't have an American-style garden. Now, a new trend has arisen which the originators have dubbed the "New American Garden." This style of landscaping is naturalistic and relies on sweeps of ornamental grasses to create the feel of the prairies that once dominated much of the American landscape.

The backyard garden presented here follows that theme. The grasses used vary from low-growing plants hugging the borders to tall plants reaching six feet or more. Some of the grasses are bold and upright; others arching and graceful. When the grasses flower, they produce plumes that dance in the wind and sparkle in the sun. Foliage colors include bright green, blue-green, variegated, and even blood-red. During autumn, foliage and flowers dry in place, forming a stunning scene of naturalistic hues in varying shades of straw, almond, brown, and rust. Most of the grasses remain interesting to look at all winter. In early spring, the dried foliage must be cut off and removed to make way for the new growth—but this is the only maintenance chore required by an established garden of ornamental grasses!

The design includes a large, realistic-looking pond (not included in the plan blueprints), which can be made from a vinyl-liner or concrete. At the end of the path leading from the bridge, a small seating area provides retreat.

LANDSCAPES & OUTDOOR PROJECTS

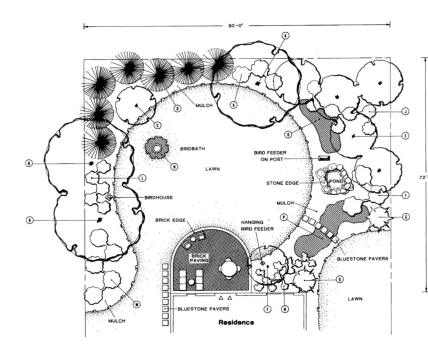

THERE IS NO BETTER WAY TO WAKE UP IN THE MORNING than to the sound of songbirds in the garden. Wherever you live, you will be surprised at the number and variety of birds you can attract by offering them a few basic necessities—water, shelter, nesting spots, and food. Birds need water for drinking and bathing. They need shrubs and trees, especially evergreens, for shelter and nesting.

Edge spaces—open areas with trees nearby for quick protection—provide ground feeders with foraging places, and plants with berries and nuts offer other natural sources of food. The garden presented here contains all the necessary elements to attract birds to the garden. The shrubs and trees are chosen especially to provide a mix of evergreen and deciduous species. All of these, together with the masses of flowering perennials, bear seeds, nuts, or berries that are known to appeal to birds. The berry show looks quite pretty, too, until the birds gobble them up! Planted densely enough for necessary shelter, the bird-attracting plants create a lovely private backyard that's enjoyable throughout the seasons. The birdbath is located in the lawn so it will be in the sun. A naturalistic pond provides water in a more protected setting.

The birdhouses and feeders aren't really necessary—though they may be the icing on the cake when it comes to luring the largest number of birds—because the landscape provides abundant natural food and shelter. Outside one of the main windows of the house, a birdfeeder hangs from a small flowering tree, providing an up-close view of your feathered friends.

HPK2300333

Season: Autumn
Design by: Michael J. Opisso

PLAN

eplans.com

NATURE LOVERS WILL DELIGHT IN THE ABUNDANT NUMBER OF BIRDS that will flock to this beautiful garden. An attractive collection of berried plants and evergreens offers food and shelter for the wildlife, while creating a handsome, pastoral setting.

HPK2300334

Season: Summer

Design by: Michael J. Opisso

eplans.com

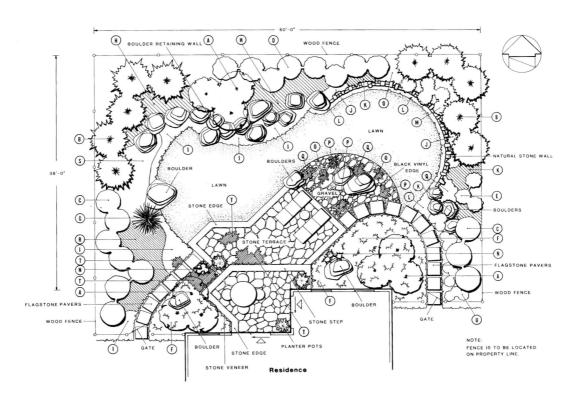

TAKE YOUR CUE FROM MOTHER NATURE: if you love the rocky outcroppings of the mountains or deserts, that may be the way to go in your garden. Boulders—single and sturdy, combined into groupings, or stacked for low walls—bring to a garden a solidity and substance that are impossible to create any other way. And rocky sites create an environment for a variety of special plants.

The designer raises the soil level of the yard slightly to create a curving contour at the back of the yard. The soil is retained by a wall of large boulders on one side and rough-chiseled natural stones forming a simple, low curvilinear dry wall on the other side. Underneath the trees and between the rocks and boulders, various creeping plants spread and spill their way toward the lawn. A combination of drought-tolerant deciduous and evergreen shrubs and trees provides softening foliage and flowers.

Flagstone pavers allow for circulation from the garden gates to the stone-paved terrace, which features two levels that have only a stair-step difference in height. Several types of creeping, fragrant paving plants mingle between the stones, releasing their scent when walked on. Rock garden plants mix in a chaos of color among the scattered boulders in the gravel-surfaced planting bed near the patio. The permanent structure provided by the plants, large boulders and paving stones creates a garden of year-round beauty.

For much of its visual excitement, this dynamic design relies on the contrast between the overlapping curves of the pathway, gravel bed and low rock wall on the right and the angles of the split-level stone terrace on the left. In arid areas, you may wish to substitute crushed granite or pea gravel for the lawn.

A SECOND-STORY DECK CAN BE THE ANSWER to many difficult landscaping problems. Sometimes this deck type is built with a mother-daughter house to provide a private deck for a second-story apartment. If a house is built on sloping property and cannot accommodate a ground-level deck, a raised deck is the answer. With split-level or raised-ranch houses, where the kitchen is often on the second level, a second-story deck right off the kitchen eliminates the need to carry food and dishes up and down stairs.

Even a high deck can have two levels and therefore two separate use areas, as the designer accomplishes with this deck. The upper area features a built-in barbecue, service cabinet and space for dining. The lower area invites family and guests to lounge and relax in the sun. Because the deck is high enough off the ground that an accidental fall could be dangerous, a railing and planters ensure safety. Filled with masses of annuals, the planters bring living color above ground.

Without screening, the underside of the deck would be an eyesore when viewed from the yard. The designer

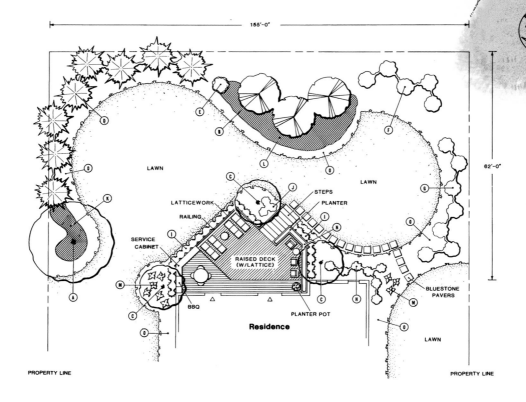

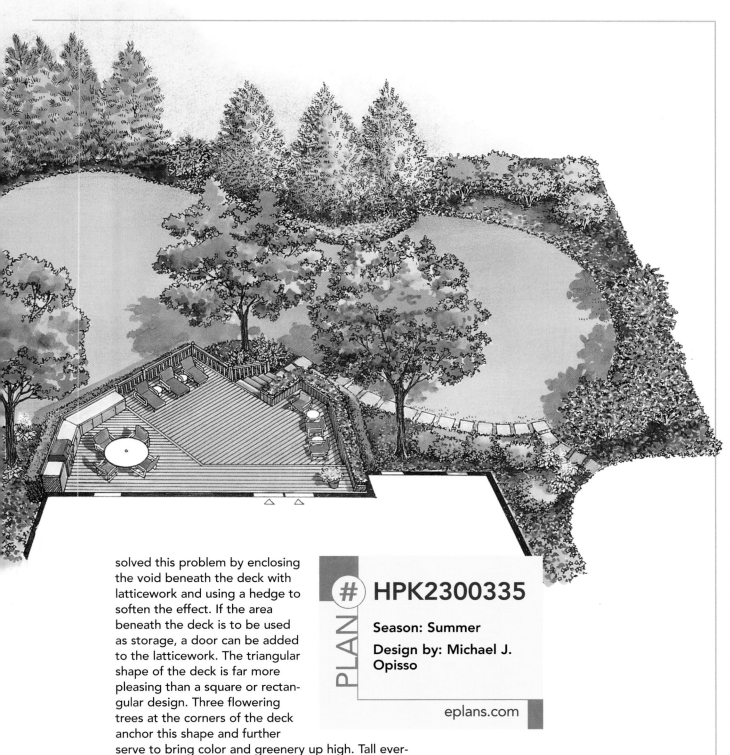

solved this problem by enclosing the void beneath the deck with latticework and using a hedge to soften the effect. If the area beneath the deck is to be used as storage, a door can be added to the latticework. The triangular shape of the deck is far more pleasing than a square or rectangular design. Three flowering trees at the corners of the deck anchor this shape and further serve to bring color and greenery up high. Tall evergreens help to screen the deck from the neighbors.

High above the rest of the garden, this second-story deck affords a beautiful view of the grounds.

PLAN

HPK2300335

Season: Summer

Design by: Michael J. Opisso

eplans.com

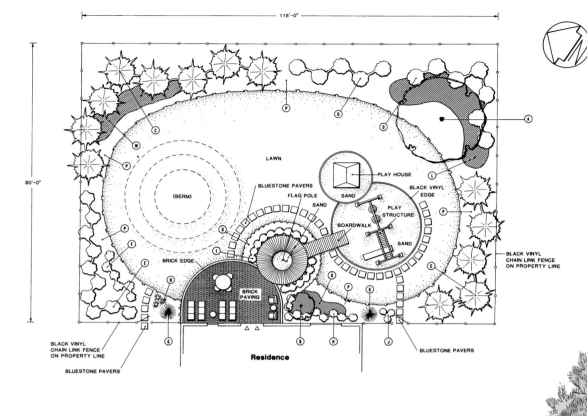

IF THERE'S ONE THING THAT CAN BE SAID ABOUT CHILDREN'S PLAY AREAS, it's that their function usually far outweighs their attractiveness. However, this backyard design presents an excellent solution to a functional children's play yard that is still pleasing to look at. The backyard includes all the fun elements a child would love. On one side of the yard are grouped a play structure for climbing and swinging, a playhouse, and a sandbox enclosed in a low boardwalk. A play mound, a perfect place for running, leaping and holding fort, rises from the lawn on the other side of the yard.

(#) **HPK2300336**

Season: Summer

Design by: Michael J. Opisso

eplans.com

These play areas are integrated into the landscape by their circular form, which is repeated in the sandbox, play mound, boardwalk, and the sand areas under the playhouse and play structure. The curved brick patio and planting border carry through the circular theme. The stepping stones leading to the play areas also follow a circular path a playful pattern that invites a child to "follow the yellow brick road."

From the house and patio, the views of both the garden and the play areas are unobstructed, affording constant adult supervision from both indoors and out.

The border surrounding the yard creates a private setting that offers a changing show of flowers from the masses of shrubs and perennials. Beyond the play structure, a large tree shades the area, providing landscape interest, and perhaps even a place for adventurous young feet to climb.

When the children are grown, this design can be adapted as a playground for older folk by removing the playhouse and play structure and planting lawn, or a flower or vegetable garden. Here is a special backyard designed for both children and adults. The yard offers youngsters their own place to escape into a world of imagination and discovery without compromising the attractiveness of a garden setting.

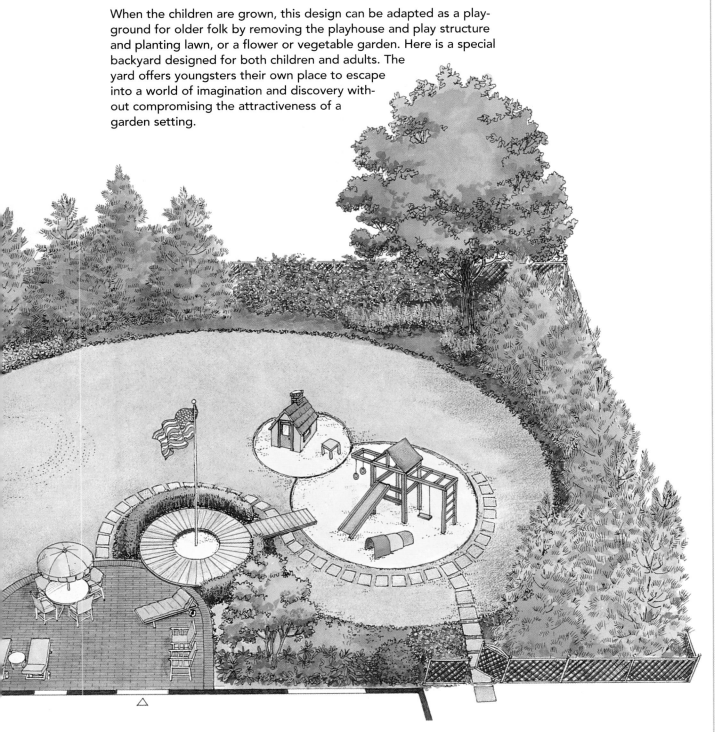

HERE'S A WONDERFUL PLAN FOR THE SERIOUS BACKYARD GARDENER and outdoor chef: a yard featuring a raised-bed vegetable garden and a spacious deck with an outdoor kitchen for serving and enjoying the homegrown bounty. And the plan doesn't neglect floral beauty for the sake of produce: large patches of easy-care, long-blooming perennials catch the eye, while flowering shrubs and evergreens provide privacy and beauty.

Vegetable gardens are difficult to live with in many suburban backyards because they look barren during the off-seasons. Once the spinach, lettuce and cabbages are harvested, it's back to bare dirt again. But this plan is designed with raised beds to provide visual structure and, at the same time, improve growing conditions by creating warmer, better-drained and more fertile soil.

The size of the beds in this garden permits easy tending because all the plants are within an arm's reach and grow closely together to discourage weeds. Wood chips cover the permanent pathways to reduce mud and improve the garden's appearance. The storage shed and compost area for recycling garden and kitchen waste are located conveniently close to the vegetable beds, but they're attractively screened by evergreens.

A spacious deck with an outdoor kitchen is effectively incorporated into this design for a medium-sized backyard. The large area devoted to vegetable gardening can produce more than enough vegetables for a family of four.

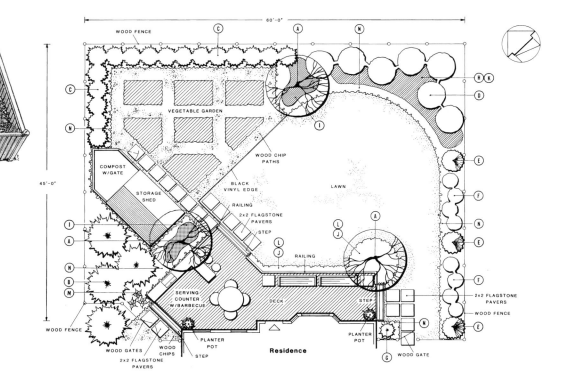

LANDSCAPES & OUTDOOR PROJECTS

A SHADE GARDEN NEED NOT DEPEND ON FLOWERS—which usually need some sun to perform well—for color. You can enliven a shady area with a border that relies on a rainbow of foliage color to provide subtle, yet engaging beauty. An assortment of plants with variegated or unusually tinted foliage, such as burgundy, blue-green, golden yellow, and chartreuse, thrives in shady conditions. This design contains an artful mix of foliage plants with colors and textures that range from understated to bold.

PLAN

HPK2300338

Season: Summer
Design by: Michael J. Opisso and Anne Rode

eplans.com

In this gently curving border, the designer combines a variety of deciduous and evergreen shrubs and trees with perennials to provide year-round foliage color. Many of the plants also add floral accents to the design. The simple green of some of the evergreen plants acts as a foil for variegated and colored leaves in the border and helps to create a harmonious scene. A semicircular flagstone path leads to a bench, enticing visitors to sit in the cool shade and enjoy the splendor of the leafy display.

Designed for a location where sunlight is insufficient to support most free-flowering plants, this showy border derives its color from an array of shade-loving shrubs and perennials featuring variegated, golden, or purplish-red leaves.

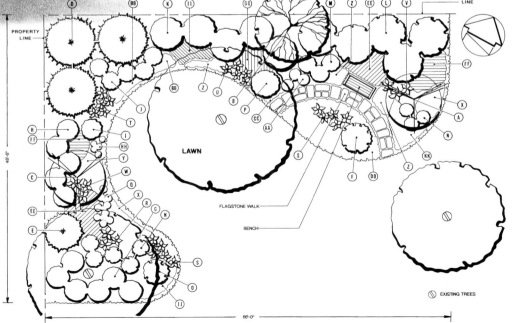

FLAGSTONE WALK

BENCH

LAWN

PROPERTY LINE

PROPERTY LINE

EXISTING TREES

IF YOU'RE THE KIND OF GARDENER whose nose is always buried in the nearest blossom and feels disappointed to find a gorgeous rose as scentless as it is beautiful, this landscape plan might be just the one for you. The designer makes every effort to choose the most fragrant plants available to fill this low-maintenance garden with sweet and spicy aromas from spring through fall.

Curving paths and romantic, secluded sitting areas invite you to stroll and rest among the scented plants. Sit under the arbor and enjoy the intensely fragrant flowering shrubs directly behind you in spring and the heady scent of climbing roses overhead in summer. In fall, the delicate perfume of the late bloomers will delight you. Even if you don't move from the patio, the sweet, pervasive perfume from the inconspicuous flowers of the surrounding shrubs will enhance warm July evenings for years to come.

You'll find the garden is as easy to care for as it is fragrant because the designer selects low-maintenance shrubs (including many dwarf types), trees and groundcovers, instead of labor-intensive annuals and perennials, to provide color and fragrance. The carefully arranged shrubs have plenty of room to grow without crowding each other or outgrowing their

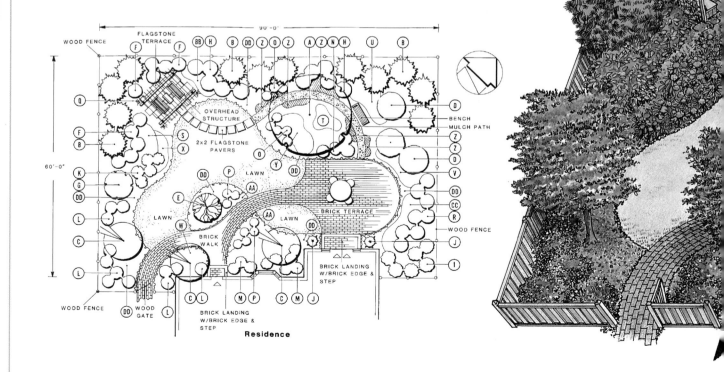

spaces, so you won't have to worry about extensive pruning chores. Much of the area that would be lawn in most yards is devoted here to the brick patio and shrub borders, allowing more kinds of plants to be included and minimizing lawn-care chores.

In this romantic garden devoted to especially sweet-smelling shrubs, you'll find special corners—an arbor, a patio and a wooden bench—pleasantly secluded. The repeated curves of the lawn, patio and paths create a harmonious and restful space, where family and friends can enjoy the delightful sights and scents permeating the air.

HPK2300339

Season: Spring
Design by: Tom Nordloh

eplans.com

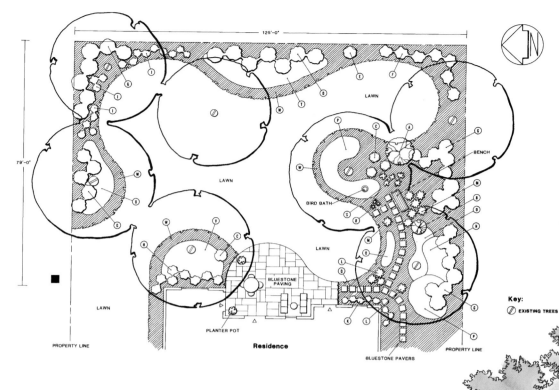

Key:
⊘ EXISTING TREES

WOE TO THE GARDENER WHO HAS TO DEAL WITH ESTABLISHED TALL TREES that cast a great deal of shade—a beautiful, colorful backyard is out of the question, right? Wrong! Nothing could be further from the truth, as demonstrated by this artfully designed shade garden.

The key to working with large existing trees is in using the shade as an asset, not as a liability, and in choosing shade-loving plants to grow beneath them. If the trees have a very dense canopy, branches can be selectively removed to thin the trees and create filtered shade below.

In this plan, the designer shapes the lawn and beds to respond to the locations of the trees. Note that all but one of the trees are situated in planting beds, not in open lawn.

Placing a single tree in the lawn helps to integrate the lawn and planting beds, creating a cohesive design. At the right, the deep planting area is enhanced by pavers, a bench and a birdbath, creating an inviting, shady retreat. Near the house, a small patio provides a lounging spot; its curving shape echoes the curving form of the planting beds.

HPK2300340

Season: Summer

Design by: Michael J. Opisso

PLAN #

eplans.com

Throughout the garden, perennials, woody plants and groundcovers are arranged in drifts to create a comfortable and serene space. The garden is in constant but ever-changing bloom from early spring through fall, as its special plants—chosen because they thrive in just such a shady setting in their native habitats—go in and out of bloom. Fall brings big splashes of foliage color to complete the year-long show. To provide the finishing carpet to this beautiful and cool shade garden, choose a grass-seed variety selected to tolerate shade.

SHADED YARDS NEED NOT BE DARK AND DULL, as this backyard design demonstrates. Here, beneath the shadows of seven mature trees, a colorful collection of shade-loving shrubs, perennials and groundcovers flourishes.

LANDSCAPES & OUTDOOR PROJECTS

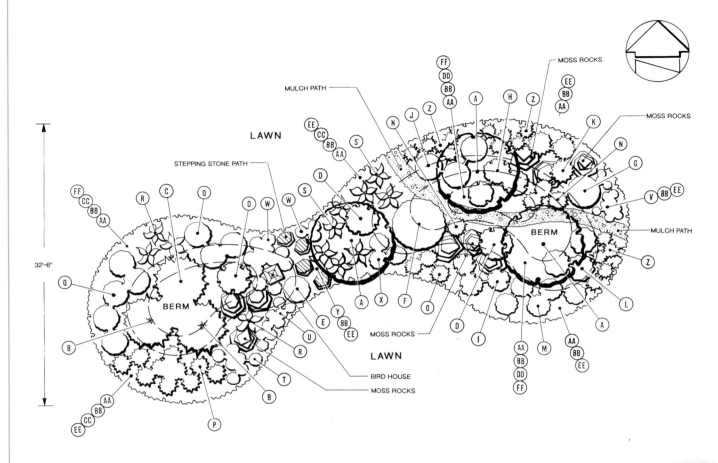

ONE OF THE GREAT JOYS OF A LOVELY LOW-MAINTE-NANCE GARDEN is having the time to really enjoy it. If you'd like a garden bed that is eye-catching as well as easy-care, this design is for you. This bow-tie-shaped bed contains a delightful variety of low-maintenance perennials, evergreens, deciduous trees and shrubs, and spring bulbs. Such a diverse blend of easy-care plants guarantees you'll have both year-round color and the time to take pleasure in every season's display.

The berms at each end of the bed create a small valley that is traversed by a natural stone path. Trees screen the peak of the higher berm, adding a bit of mystery and encouraging visitors to explore. Two pathways—one of mulch, the other of stepping stones—make it easy to enjoy the plantings up close and to perform maintenance tasks, such as occasional deadheading and weeding.

 # HPK2300341

Season: Summer

Design by: Jeffery Diefenbach

PLAN

eplans.com

MOSS ROCKS IN THREE AREAS of the garden and a birdhouse near the stepping-stone path provide pleasing structure and interest. Locate this easy-care bed in an open area of lawn in the front- or backyard to create a pretty view that can be enjoyed from indoors and out.

 # HPK2300342

Season: Summer

Design by: Salvatore A. Masullo

PLAN

eplans.com

A COLORFUL, EASY-CARE FLOWER BED LIKE THIS PAISLEY-SHAPED raised bed can be located almost anywhere on your property—it is perfectly suitable as an entry garden, or as a transition between different levels in a backyard. The bed's curving, organic shape echoes the sinuous stone wall that divides its upper and lower sections. Flagstone steps further divide the bed and lead visitors from the lower, more symmetrical area to the upper, more asymmetrical section of the garden.

The designer incorporates lovely low-growing flowering perennials to spill over the wall, creating a curtain of flowers. Twin flowering shrubs flank the entry steps, while a single specimen of the same

type marks the exit. The rest of the bed is planted with a profusion of easy-care perennials, bulbs, ornamental grasses and flowering shrubs.

This garden bed requires only a little of your precious time for routine maintenance. You'll need to remove spent blossoms, do a bit of cleanup in spring and fall and divide the perennials every few years.

A CURVING STONE RETAINING WALL and small flowering tree give this flower garden dimension and form, which keep it attractive throughout the year.

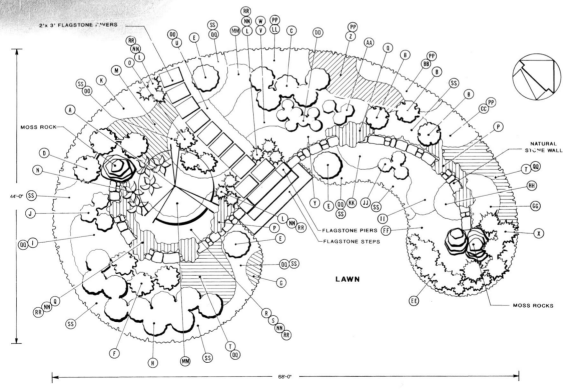

2'x 3' FLAGSTONE PAVERS

MOSS ROCK

NATURAL STONE WALL

FLAGSTONE PIERS
FLAGSTONE STEPS

LAWN

MOSS ROCKS

44'-0"

68'-0"

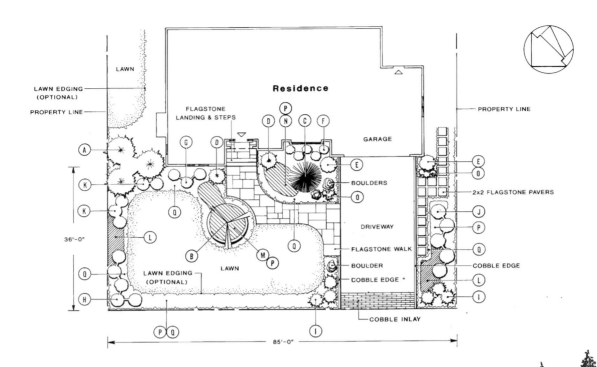

The landscape plan shows labeled areas including LAWN, LAWN EDGING (OPTIONAL), PROPERTY LINE, FLAGSTONE LANDING & STEPS, Residence, GARAGE, BOULDERS, DRIVEWAY, FLAGSTONE WALK, BOULDER, COBBLE EDGE, LAWN EDGING (OPTIONAL), COBBLE INLAY, 2x2 FLAGSTONE PAVERS, COBBLE EDGE. Dimensions: 36'-0" and 85'-0".

THE LANDSCAPE AROUND THIS RUSTIC STONE-FRONTED HOUSE is truly charming. The designer organizes the space into separate, easily maintained units that blend into a pleasing whole. The planting pockets—in front of the large window and the two areas bisected by pavers to the right of the drive—contain well-behaved plants that require little care to maintain their good looks. The small island of lawn can be quickly mowed, and maintenance is further reduced if lawn edging is installed, eliminating the need to edge by hand. A ribbon of small and moderate-sized shrubs, underplanted with a weed-smothering groundcover and spring bulbs, surrounds the lawn.

Shrubs in front of the windows were chosen for their low, unobtrusive growth habit. A dwarf conifer with pendulous branches forms the focus of the shrub grouping in front of the larger window. Although packed with interesting plants, this landscape is quite manageable for the easy-care gardener. Mowing the little island of lawn is a snap, and caring for the rest of the yard is just as easy, considering the shrubs don't need pruning and fall cleanup is minimal.

Paving is a strong unifying force in this design. The stone in the house facade is echoed in the walk that curves from the driveway up the steps to the landing and front door. Flagstone pavers border the other side of the drive and lead around the house. The cobblestone inlay at the foot of the drive not only breaks up the monotony of the asphalt, but also visually carries the lawn border across the entire width of the property. Also shown here is home plan HWEPL00588 by Home Planners. See more of this plan at eplans.com.

PLAN

 # HPK2300343

Season: Spring

Design by: Salvatore A. Masullo

eplans.com

A **SINGLE DECIDUOUS TREE**, set in a circle of bulbs and easy-care perennials that juts into the lawn, screens the entryway from street view and balances a triad of slow-growing, narrow conifers to the far left of the house.

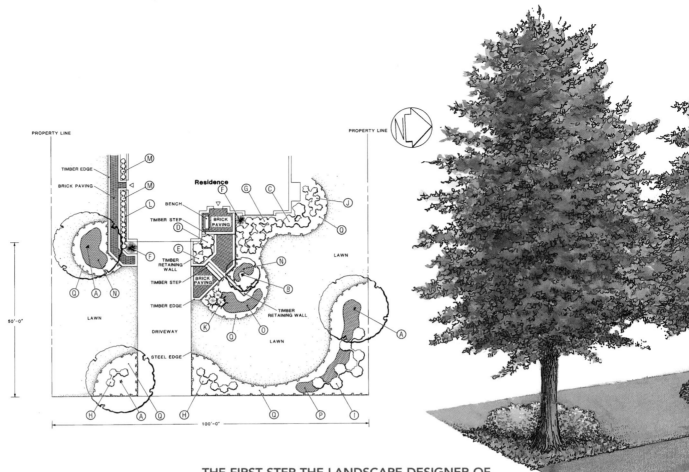

THE FIRST STEP THE LANDSCAPE DESIGNER OF
THIS TRADITIONAL SPLIT-LEVEL took was to make the
rolling grade of the property an asset rather than a liability.
The designer created a strong sense of entry with brick paving
that angles from the driveway to the front door. These angles do more
than add interest to the squareness of the house—they also present a pleasing sequence of entry, transition and arrival. This sequence is not only more visually appealing than a flat walkway coupled with a set of steps leading directly to
the door, but also makes maneuvering from the driveway to the front door easier.
The brick-and-timber combination for the walks and retaining walls offers a pleasing, informal quality that echoes the brick on the house.

Creating an entrance with various levels also allowed the designer to extend one
of the steps into a retaining wall, which defines a key planting area. The small
ornamental tree in this bed acts as a focal point and enhances the entry
by providing privacy and enclosure. The sweeping bed lines, together with the three large shade trees, serve to unify the changes in
height of both the house and the landscape. Also shown here
is home plan HEWEPL00395 by Home Planners, available at
eplans.com. A unique landscaping treatment can transform an
ordinary split-level home into a showplace that stands out
from its neighbors. Here, a multi-level entrance and a beautiful
combination of plants create a year-round garden-like setting
around the walkway.

PLAN

HPK2300344

Season: Spring
Design by: Michael J. Opisso

eplans.com

THE QUAINT CHARACTER OF THIS TRADITIONAL CAPE COD HOME calls for an intimate, comfortable landscape that reflects the formality of the house without being stiff or unfriendly. Notice how the repetition of curves throughout the landscape works to unite the design into a cohesive whole. The clean curving line of the large shrub border, which sweeps directly from the foundation planting toward the street, is repeated in the smaller curves of the planting borders along the street and in the shapes of the lawn areas. The stone walk and the driveway feature flowing curves. The front walk attractively leads to both the driveway and the street, where guests will probably park their cars.

Loose, informally-shaped trees soften the lines of the house and complement the curves of the landscape. By positioning these trees at the front edge of the property and in the center of the walkway, the

HPK2300345

Season: Spring

Design by: James Morgan

PLAN

eplans.com

BLUE-GRAY STONE complements this New England-style home's facade and forms a pathway to the front door framed by coniferous shrubs.

designer buffered the view of the house from the street, creating a sense of privacy while framing the home. Evergreen foundation shrubs used near the house match the traditional style of the architecture. Elsewhere, flowering shrubs provide seasonal color.

This landscape design works successfully because the gentle, repetitive lines and forms, which remain apparent even in the winter, unify the property, making it seem larger than it is. Also shown here is home plan HWEPL00512 by Home Planners, available at eplans.com.

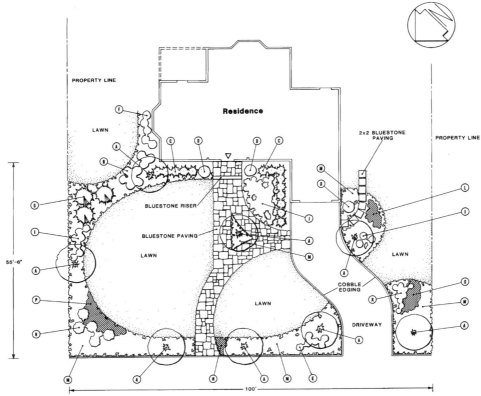

PROPERTY LINE

Residence

LAWN

2x2 BLUESTONE PAVING

PROPERTY LINE

BLUESTONE RISER

BLUESTONE PAVING

LAWN

LAWN

LAWN

COBBLE EDGING

DRIVEWAY

55'-6"

100'

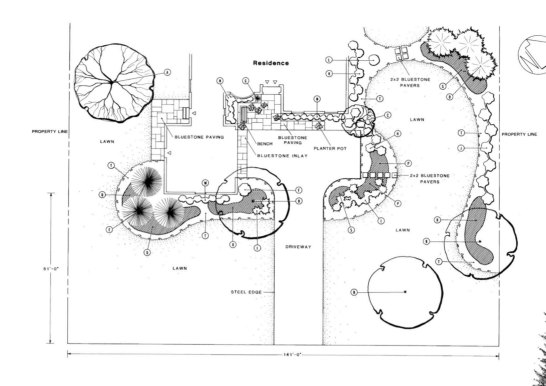

FOLLOW THE EXAMPLE SET BY THE DESIGNER OF THIS ENGLISH-STYLE COTTAGE landscape, and you will learn several tricks about how to make a small property appear larger. Space is limited, but a small entry court was created at the end of the driveway; the paving that extends across the front of the house and the garage harmonizes with the house and unites the entire area. The bench and planter pots overflowing with flowers lend an informal atmosphere and extend the living space into the garden. The lawn sweeps around the side of the house, with curved lines defined by planting beds filled with masses of flowering shrubs and perennials. Pavers leading through the planting bed welcome visitors into the yard to enjoy the flowers. Although more pavers provide access to the backyard, the two areas are clearly separated, leaving the impression of greater space and creating curiosity about what lies beyond.

HPK2300346

Season: Summer

Design by: Michael J. Opisso

PLAN

eplans.com

Narrow, upright evergreens placed at the corner of the garage balance and interplay with its low roofline and its strong horizontal lines. These are echoed and balanced by an evergreen screen on the right side of the property.

Tall shade trees, chosen for their pleasing shape and seasonal color, form a garden ceiling. The trees towering over the one-story house give a woodsy feeling to the scene, enhancing its cottage charm and matching the rustic character of the home's natural wood siding. Also shown here is home plan HWEPL00494 by Home Planners. See more of this plan at eplans.com.

THE TALL TREES SHADING THE PROPERTY contrast with the size of the cottage, emphasizing its cozy appearance. A well-defined entry court further enhances the friendly atmosphere created by the landscape design.

THE ABUNDANT FLOWERS IN THIS BACKYARD turn it into a paradise for butterflies as well as for garden lovers. Dozens of different kinds of nectar-rich plants, blooming from spring through fall, provide the necessary blossoms to lure the ephemeral beauties not only to stop and pay a visit, but perhaps to stay and set up a home.

COLORFUL BUTTERFLIES WILL FLOCK TO THIS FLORIFEROUS BACKYARD, which is planted with flowering shrubs and perennials irresistible to these welcome winged visitors. A butterfly's needs are simple: a sunny spot out of the wind to perch on, a puddle of water to drink from, nectar-rich flowers to sip from and food plants for the caterpillar phase to munch on. The designer incorporates all these needs into this landscape plan, while also providing for human visitors.

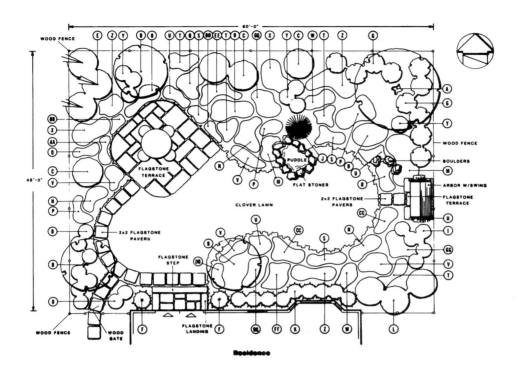

The flagstone patio, nestled among the flowers near the center of the yard, brings you away from the house right out where the butterflies congregate. This is a perfect place for a table and chairs, where you can sip coffee during a sunny spring morning or dine during a summer evening, all the while keeping an eye out for a visiting monarch, red admiral or swallowtail feeding on the nearby flowers or perching on the flat rocks near the puddle. The swing and arbor (not included in the plan) provide a cool spot to relax.

HPK2300347

PLAN

Season: Summer
Design by: Tom Nordloh

eplans.com

Instead of a pure grass lawn, the designer specified a lawn composed of mixed clover and grass. The clover provides nectar for the adult butterflies and forage for the caterpillars. Keep in mind that, as beautiful as they are, butterflies are insects. To enjoy the elusive winged stage, you'll have to tolerate a little feeding damage from the caterpillar stage. It's best to garden organically, steering clear of all insecticides—whether chemical or biological—in this garden, or you're likely to have few butterfly visitors.

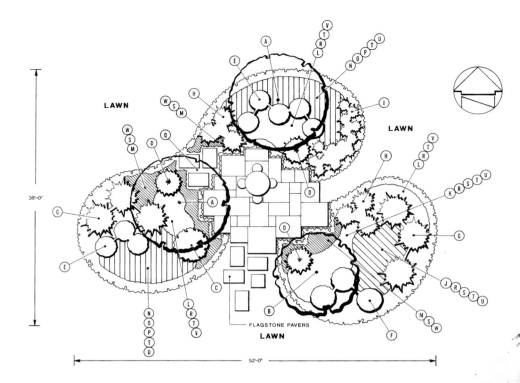

LAWN

LAWN

38'-0"

52'-0"

FLAGSTONE PAVERS

LAWN

DESIGNED WITH THE FLOWER-LOVER IN MIND, this oasis of flowers and grasses looks great all year. Bright flower colors during spring and summer are followed in fall by the pale, elegant flowers and seed heads of the ornamental grasses. The seed heads and foliage persist until the following spring, decorating the winter landscape with their delicate flower-like plumes and wheat-like fronds. Don't cut the dried grasses back to the ground until just before the new growing season begins, so you can enjoy them all winter.

The garden is formed from three connecting beds, with three paths leading into a central paved area between them. Flagstone pavers, which are interplanted with scented groundcover plants, lead into this central patio. A medium-sized deciduous tree in each bed shapes the flagstones and puts on a brilliant show before dropping leaves in fall. This allows you to add a table and chairs, so you can sit quietly and enjoy the trio of colorful garden beds. Be sure to site this lovely design so that the path is visible from a distance. That way, visitors will be tempted to come and enjoy the patio and surrounding plantings.

PLAN

(#) HPK2300348

Season: Summer
Design by: Damon Scott

eplans.com

YOU WON'T BE WORRYING
ABOUT YOUR GARDEN-
ING CHORES while sitting
on this pretty patio—the
flowers and ornamental
grasses used here thrive in
poor soil and low moisture.

IF YOU'D LIKE TO CREATE A PRIVATE HAVEN IN YOUR BACKYARD without putting up a fence, this plan is for you. This backyard border relies solely on massed plantings of evergreen and deciduous trees and shrubs to screen out neighboring properties and to buffer noise. The designer also includes a charming circular bench where you can sit and enjoy a peaceful yard under the shade of a tree. Edged with flowering groundcovers and bulbs, the circular bed and the main border fit together naturally like the pieces of a puzzle.

Starting with spring-flowering bulbs, this border design offers varied color and texture throughout the year. Broad-leaved and needle-leaved evergreens at the back of the border provide a permanent structure, effective screening and a pleasantly neutral color that sets off the vibrant perennials and bulbs planted in the front.

PLAN

HPK2300349

Season: Spring
Design by: Jim Morgan

eplans.com

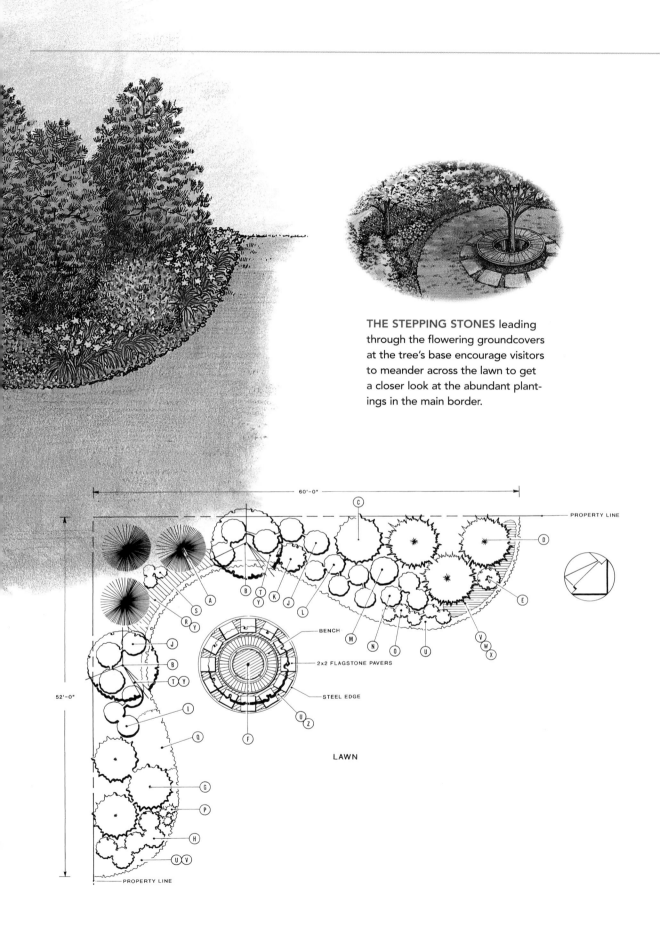

THE STEPPING STONES leading through the flowering groundcovers at the tree's base encourage visitors to meander across the lawn to get a closer look at the abundant plantings in the main border.

60'-0"

PROPERTY LINE

BENCH

2x2 FLAGSTONE PAVERS

STEEL EDGE

52'-0"

LAWN

PROPERTY LINE

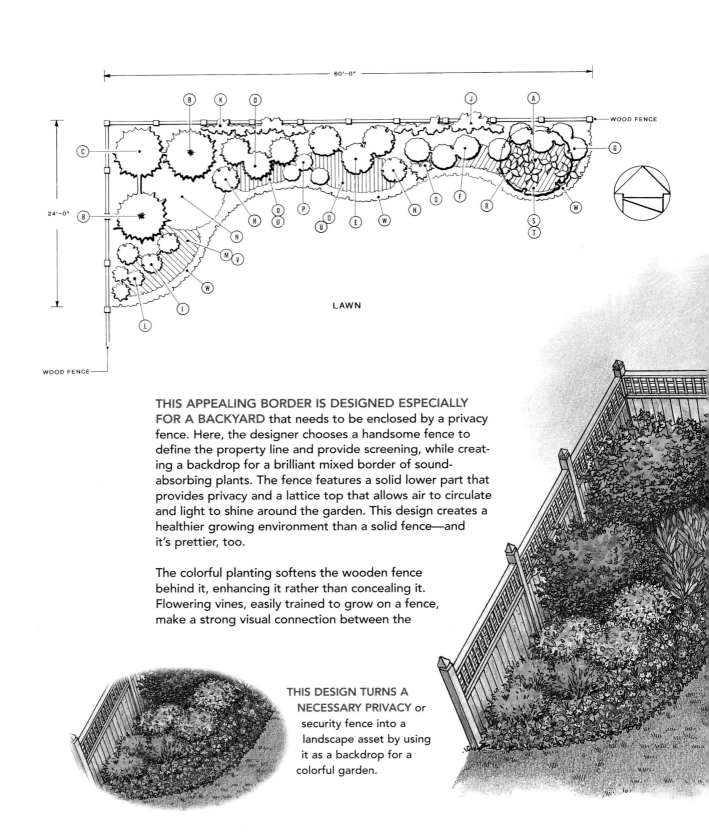

THIS APPEALING BORDER IS DESIGNED ESPECIALLY FOR A BACKYARD that needs to be enclosed by a privacy fence. Here, the designer chooses a handsome fence to define the property line and provide screening, while creating a backdrop for a brilliant mixed border of sound-absorbing plants. The fence features a solid lower part that provides privacy and a lattice top that allows air to circulate and light to shine around the garden. This design creates a healthier growing environment than a solid fence—and it's prettier, too.

The colorful planting softens the wooden fence behind it, enhancing it rather than concealing it. Flowering vines, easily trained to grow on a fence, make a strong visual connection between the

THIS DESIGN TURNS A NECESSARY PRIVACY or security fence into a landscape asset by using it as a backdrop for a colorful garden.

hardscape and softscape. Evergreens, perennials, bulbs, flowering shrubs and vines all contribute color and interest throughout the year, while the fence provides a comforting sense of enclosure and permanence. The strategically placed groups of evergreens also create additional privacy and help to anchor the design without obscuring the fence.

PLAN

 # HPK2300350

Season: Spring
Design by: Damon Scott

eplans.com

LANDSCAPES & OUTDOOR PROJECTS

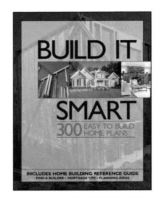
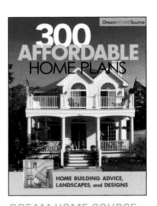

DREAM HOME SOURCE:
350 ONE-STORY HOME PLANS
$12.95
ISBN 1-931131-47-3
(384 PAGES)

200 BUDGET-SMART HOME PLANS
$8.95
ISBN 0-918894-97-2
(224 PAGES)

Finding the right new home to fit

▶ Your style
▶ Your budget
▶ Your life

...has never been easier.

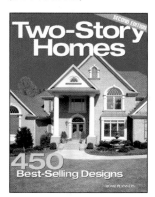

TWO-STORY HOMES, 2ND ED.
$9.95
ISBN 1-931131-15-5
(448 PAGES)

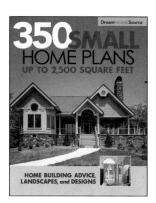

DREAM HOME SOURCE:
350 SMALL HOME PLANS
$12.95
ISBN 1-931131-42-2
(384 PAGES)

HANLEY WOOD
One Thomas Circle, NW, Suite 600, Washington, DC 20005

With more than 50 years of experience in the industry and millions of blueprints sold, Hanley Wood is a trusted source of high-quality, high-value pre-drawn home plans.

Using pre-drawn home plans is a **reliable, cost-effective way** to build your dream home, and our vast selection of plans is second-to-none. The nation's finest designers craft these plans that builders know they can trust. Meanwhile, our friendly, knowledgeable customer service representatives can help you every step of the way.

WHAT YOU'LL GET WITH YOUR ORDER

The contents of each designer's blueprint package is unique, but all contain detailed, high-quality working drawings. You can expect to find the following standard elements in most sets of plans:

1. FRONT PERSPECTIVE

This artist's sketch of the exterior of the house gives you an idea of how the house will look when built and landscaped.

2. FOUNDATION AND BASEMENT PLANS

This sheet shows the foundation layout including concrete walls, footings, pads, posts, beams, bearing walls, and foundation notes. If the home features a basement, the first-floor framing details may also be included on this plan. If your plan features slab construction rather than a basement, the plan shows footings and details for a monolithic slab. This page, or another in the set, may include a sample plot plan for locating your house on a building site. Additional sheets focus on foundation cross-sections and other details.

3. DETAILED FLOOR PLANS

These plans show the layout of each floor of the house. Rooms and interior spaces are carefully dimensioned, doors and windows located, and keys are given for cross-section details provided elsewhere in the plans.

4. HOUSE AND DETAIL CROSS-SECTIONS

Large-scale views show sections or cutaways of the foundation, interior walls, exterior walls, floors, stairways, and roof details. Additional cross-sections may show important changes in floor, ceiling, or roof heights, or the relationship of one level to another. These sections show exactly how the various parts of the house fit together and are extremely valuable during construction. Additional sheets may include enlarged wall, floor, and roof construction details.

5. FLOOR STRUCTURAL SUPPORTS

The floor framing plans provide detail for these crucial elements of your home. Each includes floor joist, ceiling joist, spacing, direction, span, and specifications. Beam and window headers, along with necessary details for framing connections, stairways, or dormers are also included.

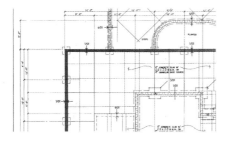

6. ELECTRICAL PLAN

The electrical plan offers suggested locations with notes for all lighting, outlets, switches, and circuits. A layout is provided for each level, as well as basements, garages, or other structures. This plan does not contain diagrams detailing how all wiring should be run, or how circuits should be engineered. These details should be designed by your electrician.

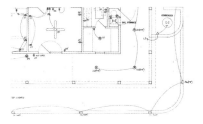

7. EXTERIOR ELEVATIONS

In addition to the front exterior, your blueprint set will include drawings of the rear and sides of your house as well. These drawings give notes on exterior materials and finishes. Particular attention is given to cornice detail, brick and stone accents, or other finish items that make your home unique.

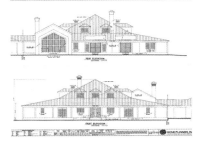

ROOF FRAMING PLANS — PLEASE READ

Some plans contain roof framing plans; however because of the wide variation in local requirements, many plans do not. If you buy a plan without a roof framing plan, you will need an engineer familiar with local building codes to create a plan to build your roof. Even if your plan does contain a roof framing plan, we recommend that a local engineer review the plan to verify that it will meet local codes.

BEFORE YOU CALL

You are making a terrific decision to use a pre-drawn house plan—it is one you can make with confidence, knowing that your blueprints are crafted by national-award-winning certified residential designers and architects, and trusted by builders.

Once you've selected the plan you want—or even if you have questions along the way—our experienced customer service representatives are available 24 hours a day, seven days a week to help you navigate the home-building process. To help them provide you with even better service, please consider the following questions before you call:

■ Have you chosen or purchased your lot?
If so, please review the building setback requirements of your local building authority before you call. You don't need to have a lot before ordering plans, but if you own land already, please have the width and depth dimensions handy when you call.

■ Have you chosen a builder?
Involving your builder in the plan selection and evaluation process may be beneficial. Luckily, builders know they can have confidence with pre-drawn plans because they've been designed for livability, functionality, and typically are builder-proven at successful home sites across the country.

■ Do you need a construction loan?
Construction loans are unique because they involve determining the value of something that is not yet constructed. Several lenders offer convenient contstruction-to-permanent loans. It is important to choose a good lending partner—one who will help guide you through the application and appraisal process. Most will even help you evaluate your contractor to ensure reliability and credit worthiness. Our partnership with IndyMac Bank, a nationwide leader in construction loans, can help you save on your loan, if needed.

■ How many sets of plans do you need?
Building a home can typically require a number of sets of blueprints—one for yourself, two or three for the builder and subcontractors, two for the local building department, and one or more for your lender. For this reason, we offer 5- and 8-set plan packages, but your best value is the Reproducible Plan Package. Reproducible plans are accompanied by a license to make modifications and typically up to 12 duplicates of the plan so you have enough copies of the plan for everyone involved in the financing and construction of your home.

■ Do you want to make any changes to the plan?
We understand that it is difficult to find blueprints for a home that will meet all of your needs. That is why Hanley Wood is glad to offer plan Customization Services. We will work with you to design the modifications you'd like to see and to adjust your blueprint plans accordingly—anything from changing the foundation; adding square footage, redesigning baths, kitchens, or bedrooms; or most other modifications. This simple, cost-effective service saves you from hiring an outside architect to make alterations. Modifications may only be made to Reproducible Plan Packages that include the license to modify.

■ Do you have to make any changes to meet local building codes?
While all of our plans are drawn to meet national building codes at the time they were created, many areas required that plans be stamped by a local engineer to certify that they meet local building codes. Building codes are updated frequently and can vary by state, county, city, or municipality. Contact your local building inspection department, office of planning and zoning, or department of permits to determine how your local codes will affect your construction project. The best way to assure that you can make changes to your plan, if necessary, is to purchase a Reproducible Plan Package.

■ Has everyone—from family members to contractors—been involved in selecting the plan?
Building a new home is an exciting process, and using pre-drawn plans is a great way to realize your dreams. Make sure that everyone involved has had an opportunity to review the plan you've selected. While Hanley Wood is the only plans provider with an exchange policy, it's best to be sure all parties agree on your selection before you buy.

CALL TOLL-FREE 1-800-521-6797

Source Key
HPK23

CUSTOMIZE YOUR PLAN –
HANLEY WOOD CUSTOMIZATION SERVICES

Creating custom home plans has never been easier and more directly accessible. Using state-of-the-art technology and top-performing architectural expertise, Hanley Wood delivers on a long-standing customer commitment to provide world-class home-plans and customization services. Our valued customers—professional home builders and individual home owners—appreciate the convenience and accessibility of this interactive, consultative service.

With the Hanley Wood Customization Service you can:

■ Save valuable time by avoiding drawn-out and frequently repetitive face-to-face design meetings

■ Communicate design and home-plan changes faster and more efficiently
■ Speed-up project turn-around time
■ Build on a budget without sacrificing quality
■ Transform master home plans to suit your design needs and unique personal style

All of our design options and prices are impressively affordable. A detailed quote is available for a $50 consultation fee. Plan modification is an interactive service. Our skilled team of designers will guide you through the customization process from start to finish making recommendations, offering ideas, and determining the feasibility of your changes. This level of service is offered to ensure the final modified plan meets your expectations. If you use our service the $50 fee will be applied to the cost of the modifications.

You may purchase the customization consultation before or after purchasing a plan. In either case, it is necessary to purchase the Reproducible Plan Package and complete the accompanying license to modify the plan before we can begin customization.

Customization Consultation **$50**

TOOLS TO WORK WITH YOUR BUILDER

Two Reverse Options For Your Convenience –
Mirror and Right-Reading Reverse (as available)

Mirror reverse plans simply flip the design 180 degrees—keep in mind, the text will also be flipped. For a minimal fee you can have one or all of your plans shipped mirror reverse, although we recommend having at least one regular set handy. Right-reading reverse plans show the design flipped 180 degrees but the text reads normally. When you choose this option, we ship each set of purchased blueprints in this format.

Mirror Reverse Fee (indicate the number of sets when ordering). . . . **$55**
Right Reading Reverse Fee (all sets are reversed). **$175**

A Shopping List Exclusively for Your Home – Materials List

A customized Materials List helps you plan and estimate the cost of your new home, outlining the quantity, type, and size of materials needed to build your house (with the exception of mechanical system items). Included are framing lumber, windows and doors, kitchen and bath cabinetry, rough and finished hardware, and much more.

Materials List. . . . . **$85 each**
Additional Materials Lists (at original time of purchase only). . **$20 each**

Plan Your Home-
Building Process – Specification Outline

Work with your builder on this step-by-step chronicle of 166 stages or items crucial to the building process. It provides a comprehensive review of the construction process and helps you choose materials.

Specification Outline. . . . . **$10 each**

Get Accurate Cost Estimates for Your Home –
Quote One® Cost Reports

The Summary Cost Report, the first element in the Quote One® package, breaks down the cost of your home into various categories based on building materials, labor, and installation, and includes three grades of construction: Budget, Standard, and Custom. Make even more informed decisions about your project with the second element of our package, the Material Cost Report. The material and installation cost is shown for each of more than 1,000 line items provided in the standard-grade Materials List, which is included with this tool. Additional space is included for estimates from contractors and subcontractors, such as for mechanical materials, which are not included in our packages.

Quote One® Summary Cost Report. **$35**
Quote One® Detailed Material Cost Report. **$140***
***Detailed material cost report includes the Materials List**

Learn the Basics of Building – Electrical, Plumbing, Mechanical, Construction Detail Sheets

If you want to know more about building techniques—and deal more confidently with your subcontractors—we offer four useful detail sheets. These sheets provide non-plan-specific general information, but are excellent tools that will add to your understanding of Plumbing Details, Electrical Details, Construction Details, and Mechanical Details.

Electrical Detail Sheet. **$14.95**
Plumbing Detail Sheet. **$14.95**
Mechanical Detail Sheet. **$14.95**
Construction Detail Sheet. **$14.95**

SUPER VALUE SETS:
Buy any 2: $26.95; Buy any 3: $34.95; Buy All 4: $39.95

Best Value

MAKE YOUR HOME TECH-READY — HOME AUTOMATION UPGRADE

Building a new home provides a unique opportunity to wire it with a plan for future needs. A Home Automation-Ready (HA-Ready) home contains the wiring substructure of tomorrow's connected home. It means that every room—from the front porch to the backyard, and from the attic to the basement—is wired for security, lighting, telecommunications, climate control, home computer networking, whole-house audio, home theater, shade control, video surveillance, entry access control, and yes, video gaming electronic solutions.

Along with the conveniences HA-Ready homes provide, they also have a higher resale value. The Consumer Electronics Association (CEA), in conjunction with the Custom Electronic Design and Installation Association (CEDIA), have developed a TechHome™ Rating system that quantifies the value of HA-Ready homes. The rating system is gaining widespread recognition in the real estate industry.

Developed by CEDIA-certified installers, our Home Automation Upgrade package includes everything you need to work with an installer during the construction of your home. It provides a short explanation of the various subsystems, a wiring floor plan for each level of your home, a detailed materials list with estimated costs, and a list of CEDIA-certified installers in your local area.

Home Automation Upgrade $250

GET YOUR HOME PLANS PAID FOR!

IndyMac Bank, in partnership with Hanley Wood, will reimburse you up to $600 toward the cost of your home plans simply by financing the construction of your new home with IndyMac Bank Home Construction Lending.

IndyMac's construction and permanent loan is a one-time close loan, meaning that one application—and one set of closing fees—provides all the financing you need.

Apply today at www.indymacbank.com, call toll free at 1-866-237-3478, or ask a Hanley Wood customer service representative for details.

DESIGN YOUR HOME — INTERIOR AND EXTERIOR FINISHING TOUCHES

Be Your Own Interior Designer! — Home Furniture Planner
Effectively plan the space in your home using our Hands-On Home Furniture Planner. It's fun and easy—no more moving heavy pieces of furniture to see how the room will go together. The kit includes reusable peel-and-stick furniture templates that fit on a 12"x18" laminated layout board—enough space to lay out every room in your house.
Home Furniture Planning Kit $15.95

Enjoy the Outdoors! — Deck Plans
Many of our homes have a corresponding deck plan, sold separately, which includes a Deck Plan Frontal Sheet, Deck Framing and Floor Plans, Deck Elevations, and a Deck Materials List. A Standard Deck Details Package, also available, provides all the how-to information necessary for building any deck. Get both the Deck Plan and the Standard Deck Details Package for one low price in our Complete Deck Building Package. See the price tier chart below and call for deck plan availability.
Deck Details (only) $14.95
Deck Building Package . . . . Plan price + $14.95

Create a Professionally Designed Landscape — Landscape Plans
Many of our homes have a front-yard Landscape Plan that is complementary in design to the house plan. These comprehensive Landscape Blueprint Packages include a Frontal Sheet, Plan View, Regionalized Plant & Materials List, a sheet on Planting and Maintaining Your Landscape, Zone Maps, and a Plant Size and Description Guide. Each set of blueprints is a full 18" x 24" with clear, complete instructions in easy-to-read type. Our Landscape Plans are available with a Plant & Materials List adapted by horticultural experts to eight regions of the country. Please specify your region when ordering your plan—see region map below. Call for more information about landscape plan availability and applicable regions.

LANDSCAPE & DECK PRICE SCHEDULE

PRICE TIERS	1-SET STUDY PACKAGE	5-SET BUILDING PACKAGE	8-SET BUILDING PACKAGE	1-SET REPRODUCIBLE*
P1	$25	$55	$95	$145
P2	$45	$75	$115	$165
P3	$75	$105	$145	$195
P4	$105	$135	$175	$225
P5	$145	$175	$215	$275
P6	$185	$215	$255	$315

PRICES SUBJECT TO CHANGE   * REQUIRES A FAX NUMBER

TERMS & CONDITIONS

OUR 90-DAY EXCHANGE POLICY

BUY WITH CONFIDENCE!

Hanley Wood is committed to ensuring your satisfaction with your blueprint order, which is why a we offer a 90-day exchange policy. With the exception of Reproducible Plan Package orders, we will exchange your entire first order for an equal or greater number of blueprints from our plan collection within 90 days of the original order. The entire content of your original order must be returned before an exchange will be processed. Please call our customer service department at 1-888-690-1116 for your return authorization number and shipping instructions. If the returned blueprints look used, redlined, or copied, we will not honor your exchange. Fees for exchanging your blueprints are as follows: 20% of the amount of the original order, plus the difference in cost if exchanging for a design in a higher price bracket or less the difference in cost if exchanging for a design in a lower price bracket. (Because they can be copied, Reproducible blueprints are not exchangeable or refundable.) Please call for current postage and handling prices. Shipping and handling charges are not refundable.

ARCHITECTURAL AND ENGINEERING SEALS

Some cities and states now require that a licensed architect or engineer review and "seal" a blueprint, or officially approve it, prior to construction. Prior to application for a building permit or the start of actual construction, we strongly advise that you consult your local building official who can tell you if such a review is required.

LOCAL BUILDING CODES AND ZONING REQUIREMENTS

Each plan was designed to meet or exceed the requirements of a nationally recognized model building code in effect at the time and place the plan was drawn. Typically plans designed after the year 2000 conform to the International Residential Building Code (IRC 2000 or 2003). The IRC is comprised of portions of the three major codes below. Plans drawn before 2000 conform to one of the three recognized building codes in effect at the time: Building Officials and Code Administrators (BOCA) International, Inc.; the Southern Building Code Congress International, (SBCCI) Inc.; the International Conference of Building Officials (ICBO); or the Council of American Building Officials (CABO).

Because of the great differences in geography and climate throughout the United States and Canada, each state, county, and municipality has its own building codes, zone requirements, ordinances, and building regulations. Your plan may need to be modified to comply with local requirements. In addition, you may need to obtain permits or inspections from local governments before and in the course of construction. We authorize the use of the blueprints on the express condition that you consult a local licensed architect or engineer of your choice prior to beginning construction and strictly comply with all local building codes, zoning requirements, and other applicable laws, regulations, ordinances, and requirements. Notice: Plans for homes to be built in Nevada must be redrawn by a Nevada-registered professional. Consult your local building official for more information on this subject.

TERMS AND CONDITIONS

These designs are protected under the terms of United States Copyright Law and may not be copied or reproduced in any way, by any means, unless you have purchased a Reproducible Plan Package and signed the accompanying license to modify and copy the plan, which clearly indicates your right to modify, copy, or reproduce. We authorize the use of your chosen design as an aid in the construction of ONE (1) single- or multifamily home only. You may not use this design to build a second dwelling or multiple dwellings without purchasing another blueprint or blueprints or paying additional design fees. Multi-use fees vary by designer—please call one of experienced sales representatives for a quote.

DISCLAIMER

The designers we work with have put substantial care and effort into the creation of their blueprints. However, because we cannot provide on-site consultation, supervision, and control over actual construction, and because of the great variance in local building requirements, building practices, and soil, seismic, weather, and other conditions, WE MAKE NO WARRANTY OF ANY KIND, EXPRESS OR IMPLIED, WITH RESPECT TO THE CONTENT OR USE OF THE BLUEPRINTS, INCLUDING BUT NOT LIMITED TO ANY WARRANTY OF MERCHANTABILITY OR OF FITNESS FOR A PARTICULAR PURPOSE. ITEMS, PRICES, TERMS, AND CONDITIONS ARE SUBJECT TO CHANGE WITHOUT NOTICE.

CALL TOLL-FREE 1-866-473-4052 OR VISIT EPLANS.COM

IMPORTANT COPYRIGHT NOTICE

From the Council of Publishing Home Designers

Blueprints for residential construction (or working drawings, as they are often called in the industry) are copyrighted intellectual property, protected under the terms of the United States Copyright Law and, therefore, cannot be copied legally for use in building. The following are some guidelines to help you get what you need to build your home, without violating copyright law:

1. HOME PLANS ARE COPYRIGHTED

Just like books, movies, and songs, home plans receive protection under the federal copyright laws. The copyright laws prevent anyone, other than the copyright owner, from reproducing, modifying, or reusing the plans or design without permission of the copyright owner.

2. DO NOT COPY DESIGNS OR FLOOR PLANS FROM ANY PUBLICATION, ELECTRONIC MEDIA, OR EXISTING HOME

It is illegal to copy, change, or redraw home designs found in a plan book, CDROM or on the Internet. The right to modify plans is one of the exclusive rights of copyright. It is also illegal to copy or redraw a constructed home that is protected by copyright, even if you have never seen the plans for the home. If you find a plan or home that you like, you must purchase a set of plans from an authorized source. The plans may not be lent, given away, or sold by the purchaser.

3. DO NOT USE PLANS TO BUILD MORE THAN ONE HOUSE

The original purchaser of house plans is typically licensed to build a single home from the plans. Building more than one home from the plans without permission is an infringement of the home designer's copyright. The purchase of a multiple-set package of plans is for the construction of a single home only. The purchase of additional sets of plans does not grant the right to construct more than one home.

4. HOUSE PLANS IN THE FORM OF BLUEPRINTS OR BLACKLINES CANNOT BE COPIED OR REPRODUCED

Plans, blueprints, or blacklines, unless they are reproducibles, cannot be copied or reproduced without prior written consent of the copyright owner. Copy shops and blueprinters are prohibited from making copies of these plans without the copyright release letter you receive with reproducible plans.

5. HOUSE PLANS IN THE FORM OF BLUEPRINTS OR BLACKLINES CANNOT BE REDRAWN

Plans cannot be modified or redrawn without first obtaining the copyright owner's permission. With your purchase of plans, you are licensed to make non-structural changes by "red-lining" the purchased plans. If you need to make structural changes or need to redraw the plans for any reason, you must purchase a reproducible set of plans (see topic 6) which includes a license to modify the plans. Blueprints do not come with a license to make structural changes or to redraw the plans. You may not reuse or sell the modified design.

6. REPRODUCIBILE HOME PLANS

Reproducible plans (for example sepias, mylars, CAD files, electronic files, and vellums) come with a license to make modifications to the plans. Once modified, the plans can be taken to a local copy shop or blueprinter to make up to 10 or 12 copies of the plans to use in the construction of a single home. Only one home can be constructed from any single purchased set of reproducible plans either in original form or as modified. The license to modify and copy must be completed and returned before the plan will be shipped.

7. MODIFIED DESIGNS CANNOT BE REUSED

Even if you are licensed to make modifica-tions to a copyrighted design, the modified design is not free from the original designer's copyright. The sale or reuse of the modified design is prohibited. Also, be aware that any modification to plans relieves the original designer from liability for design defects and voids all warranties expressed or implied.

8. WHO IS RESPONSIBLE FOR COPYRIGHT INFRINGEMENT?

Any party who participates in a copyright violation may be responsible including the purchaser, designers, architects, engineers, drafters, homeowners, builders, contractors, sub-contractors, copy shops, blueprinters, developers, and real estate agencies. It does not matter whether or not the individual knows that a violation is being committed. Ignorance of the law is not a valid defense.

9. PLEASE RESPECT HOME DESIGN COPYRIGHTS

In the event of any suspected violation of a copyright, or if there is any uncertainty about the plans purchased, the publisher, architect, designer, or the Council of Publishing Home Designers (www.cphd.org) should be contacted before proceeding. Awards are sometimes offered for information about home design copyright infringement.

10. PENALTIES FOR INFRINGEMENT

Penalties for violating a copyright may be severe. The responsible parties are required to pay actual damages caused by the infringement (which may be substantial), plus any profits made by the infringer commissions to include all profits from the sale of any home built from an infringing design. The copyright law also allows for the recovery of statutory damages, which may be as high as $150,000 for each infringement. Finally, the infringer may be required to pay legal fees which often exceed the damages.

BLUEPRINT PRICE SCHEDULE

PRICE TIERS	1-SET STUDY PACKAGE	5-SET BUILDING PACKAGE	8-SET BUILDING PACKAGE	1-SET REPRODUCIBLE*
A1	$465	$515	$570	$695
A2	$505	$560	$615	$755
A3	$555	$625	$685	$845
A4	$610	$680	$745	$920
C1	$660	$735	$800	$980
C2	$710	$785	$845	$1055
C3	$755	$835	$900	$1135
C4	$810	$885	$955	$1210
L1	$920	$1020	$1105	$1375
L2	$1000	$1095	$1185	$1500
L3	$1105	$1210	$1310	$1650
L4	$1220	$1335	$1425	$1830
SQ1				$0.40/SQ. FT.
SQ3				$0.55/SQ. FT.
SQ5				$0.80/SQ. FT.
SQ7				$1.00/SQ. FT.
SQ9				$1.25/SQ. FT.
SQ11				$1.50/SQ. FT.

PRICES SUBJECT TO CHANGE   * REQUIRES A FAX NUMBER

PLAN #	PRICE TIER	PAGE	MATERIALS LIST	QUOTE ONE®	DECK	DECK PRICE	LANDSCAPE	LANDSCAPE PRICE	REGIONS
HPK2300001	A3	6	Y						
HPK2300002	A3	10	Y						
HPK2300003	A4	16							
HPK2300004	C1	17							
HPK2300005	C1	18							
HPK2300006	C1	19	Y						
HPK2300007	A3	20							
HPK2300008	C1	21							
HPK2300009	C1	22	Y						
HPK2300010	C1	23							
HPK2300011	A3	24	Y		OLA001	P3	123568		
HPK2300012	C1	25	Y						
HPK2300013	A3	26	Y						
HPK2300014	C1	27	Y						
HPK2300015	C1	28	Y						
HPK2300016	C1	29	Y						
HPK2300017	C1	30							
HPK2300018	A3	31							
HPK2300019	C1	32	Y						
HPK2300020	C1	33	Y	Y					
HPK2300021	A4	34	Y						
HPK2300022	C1	35							
HPK2300023	C1	36	Y						
HPK2300024	C1	37	Y						
HPK2300025	A3	38	Y						
HPK2300026	A3	39							
HPK2300027	A3	40	Y						
HPK2300028	C1	41							
HPK2300029	C1	42	Y						
HPK2300030	A4	43	Y						
HPK2300031	A4	44	Y						
HPK2300032	C2	45	Y						
HPK2300033	C2	46	Y						
HPK2300034	C2	47	Y						
HPK2300035	C2	48	Y						
HPK2300036	C2	49	Y						
HPK2300037	C2	50	Y						
HPK2300038	C1	51	Y						
HPK2300039	C2	52	Y						
HPK2300040	A4	53							
HPK2300041	C2	54	Y						
HPK2300042	C2	55	Y						
HPK2300043	C2	56	Y	Y					
HPK2300044	A4	57	Y						
HPK2300045	C1	58	Y						
HPK2300046	C2	59	Y						
HPK2300047	C2	60	Y						
HPK2300048	C2	61	Y						
HPK2300049	C2	62	Y						
HPK2300050	C1	63	Y						
HPK2300051	C3	64	Y						
HPK2300052	C2	65							
HPK2300053	C2	66							
HPK2300054	C1	67	Y						
HPK2300055	C1	68	Y						
HPK2300056	C2	69	Y						
HPK2300057	C2	70							
HPK2300058	C2	71							
HPK2300059	C2	72	Y						
HPK2300060	A4	73							
HPK2300061	A4	74	Y						
HPK2300062	C1	75							
HPK2300063	C1	76	Y						
HPK2300064	C3	77	Y						
HPK2300065	C3	78	Y						
HPK2300066	C3	79							
HPK2300067	C3	80							
HPK2300068	C3	81							
HPK2300069	C3	82	Y						
HPK2300070	C3	83	Y						

PLAN #	PRICE TIER	PAGE	MATERIALS LIST	QUOTE ONE®	DECK	DECK PRICE	LANDSCAPE	LANDSCAPE PRICE	REGIONS
HPK2300071	C3	84							
HPK2300072	C3	85							
HPK2300073	C3	86							
HPK2300074	C1	87							
HPK2300075	C2	88							
HPK2300076	C2	89							
HPK2300077	A2	92	Y						
HPK2300078	A2	93	Y						
HPK2300079	A3	94	Y						
HPK2300080	A2	95							
HPK2300081	A2	96	Y						
HPK2300082	A2	97							
HPK2300083	A4	98							
HPK2300084	A2	99	Y						
HPK2300085	A4	100							
HPK2300086	A2	101	Y						
HPK2300087	A3	102	Y						
HPK2300088	A2	103	Y						
HPK2300089	A2	104	Y						
HPK2300090	A3	105							
HPK2300091	C1	106							
HPK2300092	A3	107	Y						
HPK2300093	A3	108							
HPK2300094	A4	109	Y						
HPK2300095	A3	110	Y						
HPK2300096	A3	111							
HPK2300097	A4	112	Y						
HPK2300098	A3	113	Y						
HPK2300099	A3	114	Y						
HPK2300100	A2	115							
HPK2300101	A4	116	Y	Y	ODA012	P3	OLA083	P3	12345678
HPK2300102	C1	117	Y						
HPK2300103	A3	118	Y						
HPK2300104	A3	119							
HPK2300105	C1	120	Y						
HPK2300106	A3	121	Y						
HPK2300107	A3	122							
HPK2300108	A3	123							
HPK2300109	A3	124							
HPK2300110	A3	125							
HPK2300111	A3	126	Y						
HPK2300112	A3	127	Y				OLA004	P3	123568
HPK2300113	A4	128	Y	Y					
HPK2300114	A3	129	Y						
HPK2300115	C1	130							
HPK2300116	A3	131							
HPK2300117	C1	132							
HPK2300118	A3	133							
HPK2300119	A3	134	Y						
HPK2300120	C1	135							
HPK2300121	C1	136							
HPK2300122	A3	137							
HPK2300123	C1	138	Y						
HPK2300124	A3	139	Y						
HPK2300125	C1	140	Y						
HPK2300126	A3	141	Y						
HPK2300127	C1	142							
HPK2300128	C2	143	Y						
HPK2300129	A3	144							
HPK2300130	A4	145							
HPK2300131	C2	146							
HPK2300132	C2	147							
HPK2300133	A4	148	Y						
HPK2300134	C2	149							
HPK2300135	C2	150							
HPK2300136	C2	151	Y	Y					
HPK2300137	C2	152							
HPK2300138	C2	153							
HPK2300139	C2	154							
HPK2300140	A4	155							

PLAN #	PRICE TIER	PAGE	MATERIALS LIST	QUOTE ONE®	DECK	DECK PRICE	LANDSCAPE	LANDSCAPE PRICE	REGIONS
HPK2300141	C2	156							
HPK2300142	A4	157	Y	Y					
HPK2300143	C1	158	Y						
HPK2300144	A4	159							
HPK2300145	A4	160	Y						
HPK2300146	A4	161							
HPK2300147	A4	162	Y						
HPK2300148	A4	163							
HPK2300149	A4	164							
HPK2300150	A4	165	Y						
HPK2300151	A4	166							
HPK2300152	C1	167							
HPK2300153	C1	168	Y						
HPK2300154	C1	169	Y						
HPK2300155	C3	170	Y	Y					
HPK2300156	C1	171							
HPK2300157	C1	172	Y						
HPK2300158	C2	173							
HPK2300159	C2	174							
HPK2300160	C2	175							
HPK2300161	A2	178							
HPK2300162	A2	179	Y						
HPK2300163	A2	180	Y						
HPK2300164	A2	181	Y						
HPK2300165	A2	182	Y						
HPK2300166	A3	183							
HPK2300167	C1	183	Y						
HPK2300168	C1	184							
HPK2300169	C1	185							
HPK2300170	A3	186	Y						
HPK2300171	A3	187							
HPK2300172	A4	188	Y						
HPK2300173	C1	189							
HPK2300174	A3	190	Y						
HPK2300175	C1	191	Y						
HPK2300176	C1	192							
HPK2300177	C1	193							
HPK2300178	A3	194	Y						
HPK2300179	C1	195	Y						
HPK2300180	C1	195	Y						
HPK2300181	A3	196							
HPK2300182	A3	197							
HPK2300183	C1	198							
HPK2300184	C1	199	Y	Y					
HPK2300185	C1	200							
HPK2300186	C1	200							
HPK2300187	A3	201							
HPK2300188	A3	202	Y						
HPK2300189	C1	203							
HPK2300190	C1	204	Y						
HPK2300191	A3	205	Y						
HPK2300192	C1	206							
HPK2300193	A3	207	Y						
HPK2300194	A3	208	Y						
HPK2300195	C1	209	Y						
HPK2300196	A3	210	Y						
HPK2300197	C1	211							
HPK2300198	C1	212	Y						
HPK2300199	C1	213							
HPK2300200	A3	214							
HPK2300201	C1	215							
HPK2300202	A3	216							
HPK2300203	A4	217	Y						
HPK2300204	A3	218	Y						
HPK2300205	C1	219							
HPK2300206	A4	220	Y						
HPK2300207	A3	221	Y						
HPK2300208	C2	222							
HPK2300209	A4	223	Y						
HPK2300210	C2	224							

PLAN #	PRICE TIER	PAGE	MATERIALS LIST	QUOTE ONE®	DECK	DECK PRICE	LANDSCAPE	LANDSCAPE PRICE	REGIONS
HPK2300211	A4	225	Y						
HPK2300212	C2	226							
HPK2300213	C1	227							
HPK2300214	A4	228	Y						
HPK2300215	A4	229	Y						
HPK2300216	C2	230							
HPK2300217	C2	231							
HPK2300218	C2	232	Y	Y					
HPK2300219	C1	233	Y	Y			OLA035	P3	1234567
HPK2300220	C2	234							
HPK2300221	C2	235	Y	Y	ODA012	P3	OLA003	P3	123568
HPK2300222	C2	236							
HPK2300223	A4	237	Y						
HPK2300224	C2	238							
HPK2300225	C1	239							
HPK2300226	C2	240							
HPK2300227	C2	241							
HPK2300228	C2	242							
HPK2300229	A4	243							
HPK2300230	C2	244							
HPK2300231	C2	244							
HPK2300232	A4	245	Y	Y			OLA001	P3	123568
HPK2300233	C2	246							
HPK2300234	C1	247	Y						
HPK2300235	A2	250	Y						
HPK2300236	A2	251							
HPK2300237	A3	252	Y						
HPK2300238	A2	253							
HPK2300239	A2	254	Y						
HPK2300240	A2	255							
HPK2300241	A2	256							
HPK2300242	A4	257							
HPK2300243	A4	257							
HPK2300244	A4	258							
HPK2300245	A2	258	Y				OLA001	P3	123568
HPK2300246	A2	259							
HPK2300247	A3	260							
HPK2300248	A4	261							
HPK2300249	A4	262							
HPK2300250	A4	263							
HPK2300251	C1	263							
HPK2300252	A3	264							
HPK2300253	C1	264							
HPK2300254	A3	265	Y						
HPK2300255	A3	266	Y						
HPK2300256	A3	267							
HPK2300257	C1	268							
HPK2300258	A3	269	Y						
HPK2300259	C1	270	Y						
HPK2300260	C1	270	Y						
HPK2300261	C1	271							
HPK2300262	A3	272	Y						
HPK2300263	C1	273	Y						
HPK2300264	C1	273							
HPK2300265	C1	274	Y						
HPK2300266	C1	274	Y	Y					
HPK2300267	A3	275	Y						
HPK2300268	A4	276							
HPK2300269	C1	277							
HPK2300270	A3	278	Y						
HPK2300271	C1	279							
HPK2300272	C1	279							
HPK2300273	A3	280							
HPK2300274	C1	280	Y						
HPK2300275	C1	281							
HPK2300276	C1	282	Y						
HPK2300277	C1	282	Y						
HPK2300278	A3	283							
HPK2300279	A3	284	Y						
HPK2300280	C1	285							
HPK2300281	A3	285							
HPK2300282	C1	286							
HPK2300283	A3	287							
HPK2300284	C1	288	Y						
HPK2300285	C1	289							
HPK2300286	C1	290	Y	Y					
HPK2300287	A4	291	Y						
HPK2300288	A4	292							
HPK2300289	C2	293	Y						
HPK2300290	A4	294	Y						
HPK2300291	C2	295							
HPK2300292	C2	296	Y	Y					
HPK2300293	C2	297							
HPK2300294	C2	298	Y						
HPK2300295	A4	299							
HPK2300296	A4	300	Y						
HPK2300297	C2	301	Y						
HPK2300298	A4	301	Y						
HPK2300299	C1	302	Y						
HPK2300300	C1	302	Y						
HPK2300301	C2	303							
HPK2300302	C1	304	Y						
HPK2300303	C1	304							
HPK2300304	C2	305							
HPK2300305	P4	308							
HPK2300306	P2	308							
HPK2300307	P4	309							
HPK2300308	P2	309							
HPK2300309	P2	310							
HPK2300310	P2	310							
HPK2300311	P2	311							
HPK2300312	P1	311							
HPK2300313	P1	312							
HPK2300314	P4	312	Y						
HPK2300315	P1	313							
HPK2300316	P1	313							
HPK2300317	P1	314							
HPK2300318	P1	314							
HPK2300319	P2	315							
HPK2300320	P2	315							
HPK2300321	P1	316							
HPK2300322	P4	317							
HPK2300323	P3	318							
HPK2300324	P4	320							
HPK2300325	P4	322							
HPK2300326	P3	324							
HPK2300327	P4	326							
HPK2300328	P3	328							
HPK2300329	P3	330							
HPK2300330	P3	332							
HPK2300331	P3	334							
HPK2300332	P4	336							
HPK2300333	P3	338							
HPK2300334	P3	340							
HPK2300335	P3	342							
HPK2300336	P3	344							
HPK2300337	P3	346							
HPK2300338	P3	348							
HPK2300339	P4	350							
HPK2300340	P3	352							
HPK2300341	P3	354							
HPK2300342	P3	356							
HPK2300343	P3	358							
HPK2300344	P3	360							
HPK2300345	P3	362							
HPK2300346	P3	364							
HPK2300347	P4	366							
HPK2300348	P3	368							
HPK2300349	P3	370							
HPK2300350	P2	372							